Political Tool Kit

Political Tool Kit

Secrets of Winning Campaigns

Ron Parsons

iUniverse, Inc.
Bloomington

Political Tool Kit
Secrets of Winning Campaigns

iUniverse books may be ordered through booksellers or by contacting:

iUniverse
1663 Liberty Drive
Bloomington, IN 47403
www.iuniverse.com
1-800-Authors (1-800-288-4677)

ISBN: 978-1-4759-7653-3 (sc)
ISBN: 978-1-4759-7654-0 (ebk)

Library of Congress Control Number: 2013902971

Printed in the United States of America

iUniverse rev. date: 04/16/2013

This book is dedicated to

Lance Corporal Thomas Wendell Goodrich, USMC
Cortland, New York,

and

Lance Corporal Willie B. Skrine, USMC
Mayfield, Georgia,

who perished in the DMZ with the 9th Marines on May 26, 1967, during Operation Hickory
in the Battle for Con Thien, Republic of Vietnam.

May the souls of the fallen rest in the living dream of America
we all carried into battle with our lives.
If failure is wrought from sacrifice, may it be at the hands of those who never served.

Wars are political!

CONTENTS

ACKNOWLEDGMENTS

▼

I want to thank Peter Firth, Esquire, Teresa Mercure, and Andrew Trombley, who edited my early drafts. Their suggestions helped me broaden and organize the manuscript.

Thanks are also due to Michael Grasso, Steven Rice, Kate Hogan, Mark Westcott, and Mary Maynard, author of *My Faraway Home*. Phil Casabona completed the Excel spreadsheets. My fantastic graphic designer is Robin Mac Rostie (www.choreographicdesign.com). My content editor was Nadine Battaglia, who spent many hours on the manuscript. Thanks, Nadine! I thank the staff and editing crew of iUniverse for their advice and for leading me down the publishing path. Special thanks to Dianne and Sarah.

The book's covers were designed by my daughter, Elizabeth Joyce Parsons (www.lizparsonsart. com). Nice job, Eliz! I would like to give an honorable mention to professor and retired New York City police detective John O'Kane.

Without mentioning anyone's name in particular, I want to acknowledge a group of people who influenced every page tremendously. They taught me what *not* to do. Many campaigns have gone south because of their influence, and every campaign has them. Unfortunately, the most assertive and vocal are often the least knowledgeable, but I have learned much from them.

Three authors helped to inspire the direction of this book—Ruby Payne, Peter Senge, and Paula Underwood. Paula was of the Seneca Turtle clan. I have included a holistic "vision quest" and a Native American blend with learning stories. *Who speaks for Wolf?* Paula does.

I thank the Marines who tried like hell to keep me alive to write this: John Kuhrt, Richard Daerr, Angi Manni, Xavier Lugo, Tony Rivera, Randolph Baker, Tommy Scheib, Troy Shirley, Doc. Galen Eugene Warren, and Rita Thomas Monahan of the northwestern tier. I served with heroes.

To my wife, Jane, a.k.a. Lefty, "the principal," my central and centrist protagonist.

Thank you!

Ron Parsons

SECTION 1

Foundation: Getting Started

☞ Organizational Flow Chart

☞ Introduction

☞ Foundation: Getting Started

ORGANIZATIONAL FLOW CHART

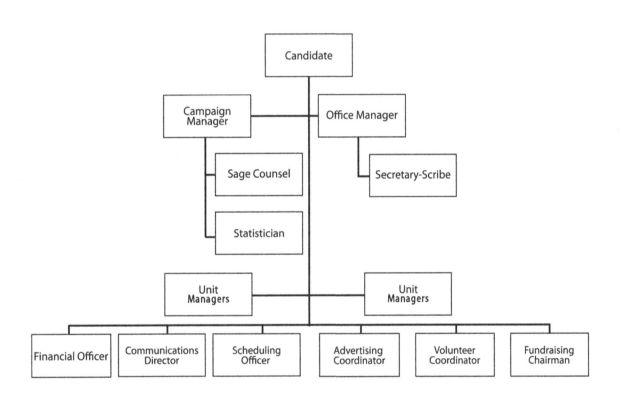

INTRODUCTION

▼

This work originated several years ago when a retired New York State police investigator, who was contemplating a run for county sheriff, phoned me one afternoon. He had been in law enforcement his entire life and was untarnished by political influence. I was serving as the district attorney's campaign treasurer at the time, and someone in law enforcement had given him my name.

Naturally, I was honored that he believed I had the required political knowledge and experience to offer credible input for his upcoming campaign. I felt I had the prerequisite qualifications after serving in multiple capacities in several congressional campaigns. I had been our county's Republican party treasurer for five years as well as our city committee's secretary for two and had served as county chairman for our election district's successful New York State senatorial race in 2002. Our new senator received almost 80 percent of the vote in that challenging race.

I immediately jotted down two pages of notes to take to my meeting with him the next day. In the course of a few weeks, I outlined a string of tasks and experiences. That string evolved into the initial chapters of a book, and every day I added to it. As I refined my notes, a web of political intrigue began to emerge and reveal itself. I became aware of how insular and esoteric the current political climate had become. Without insight into the hidden rules of the local political hierarchy, there was little or no hope of someone new gaining the support needed to win an election.

This book is intended as a guide for aspiring local and state politicians who wish to seek public service through the election process. It is designed for Americans who are interested in pursuing political candidacy and takes a business-oriented approach that includes delineated job functions and assignments.

Politics is an interactive, multitasking domain. *Political Tool Kit* quantifies a process that many view as subjective and experiential. The tool kit offers a step-by-step progressive model candidates can mold to fit their candidacies. It is up to candidates to make their campaigns unique by choosing the areas and tasks that are of the greatest interest and best fit for their philosophies and their campaigns' size and scope.

In America, each city, district, town, parish, ward, county, and state is a reasonably autonomous political entity. Many have grandfathered in their local laws, hidden rules, and layers of culture that govern the electoral process. If a person is to seek political office, those rules and laws must be known and followed to the letter. No single book can include every state's peculiar eccentricities or the culture embedded within each election district.

Candidates, their campaign managers, and their executive committees can use *Political Tool Kit* as a platform to build better campaigns and adopt techniques that are a good fit. This book can serve as an invaluable tool in establishing a winning campaign strategy. It introduces a comprehensive delineation of jobs and responsibilities by using functional managers as a resource base. It also maximizes a contributory system of unit managers (parish or county managers) who provide the professional integrity a larger campaign demands.

The election process consists of meeting a series of deadlines and milestones. Assign the right task to the appropriate qualified person, who should be highly motivated and loyal. In all cases, task deadlines must be identified and met; goals must be achieved. In many states, a considerable fine will be levied if the treasurer or financial officer does not file a financial disclosure statement on time (Grey 1999, 43).

Each campaign will accentuate and enhance its candidate's positive attributes through its knowledge of political tools. Having the qualifications to be the best manager is not necessarily the same as having the characteristics of a successful candidate. Similarly, a gifted intellectual may not possess the political skills required to win an election.

This book offers the training and tools to build a process that enables candidates to grow to their full potential. *Political Tool Kit* is a recruiting tool for good managers and promising leaders; it will sharpen political skills and help create great candidates.

A procedure or concept cannot be modeled or worked until it is clearly defined. Naming a task or process gives it definition and form. Such a structure may be one that is currently utilized in another discipline or be a completely new idea. Several new concepts are introduced in this book, including unlocking social structures with guides, political one-shot mentoring, *mokusatsu,* and the concept of valence voters.

The field of politics is an experiential trade, a learned craft that is team-oriented. If a candidate achieves party endorsement, that endorsement often includes a pledge for support with tasks, money, and volunteers. A political party is a team, and without that team's approval, or at least tacit compliance, there is little hope for a candidate's election.

After a successful election, even a candidate portrayed as a rebel usually is offered some degree of inclusion into the political system. The election of a maverick candidate may signal the emergence of new trends the leadership of an astute political party may wish to capture.

Candidacy is only the beginning of a career in public service. The winning ideals embedded within a campaign will follow candidates throughout their political careers and become foundational principles during their future community service and a building block if they seek higher office.

Never let anyone say that politics is not personal. It is. It takes an entire lifetime of experience for candidates to shape their platforms. Who they are as people is reflected in their candidacies.

A political life is not for the faint of heart because private matters can be placed under a public microscope (Grey 1999, 123). A candidate's ideals will be driven through the fire of debate and taken out of context—misquoted by the news media and denigrated by friend and foe alike. Some of the strongest people are crushed by inaccurate depictions of their lives and deeds by a media that frequently goes uncorrected (Woo 1980, 7).

As is the case with investment strategies, no process can guarantee absolute results. Success depends more upon trends, timing, and plain, old, ordinary luck. The more knowledge you have, the luckier you'll get.

Suggestions for tasks should never be misconstrued to imply that candidates, campaign staff, or volunteers should break any laws or moral standards. On the contrary, campaigns and candidates should be held to the highest standards. It is the candidate's responsibility to read and follow election and all laws. It is the responsibility of the campaign manager, treasurer, sage counsel, and mentor to guide the candidate along a path constructed on fact-based decision making.

The candidate alone must accept all responsibility for the formulation and implementation of the team that will determine the election results. No book or written document can be all inclusive. Laws and methods are continuously evolving.

This book offers you a "political tool kit" that may place you on the road to elected office. It will be the adventure of a lifetime.

Good luck!

FOUNDATION: GETTING STARTED

▼

Political candidacy requires a unique skill set and is a journey like no other. Candidates must realize where they are in life, where they wish to go, what tools and support they require, and who they will take on the adventure with them. They must set a preliminary strategy with specific goals they can accomplish through the offices they seek.

The problem with many political campaigns is that candidates are partially dependent on a process they don't fully understand, and they rely on an existing political infrastructure that may not fully or properly support their initiative. Their indebtedness to this structure can directly affect how reliant they are upon it. A candidate's political knowledge and acumen will foster a certain degree of autonomy. Candidates should represent their party's overall vision, but building alliances within a party is not the same as being dependent upon it. Dependence may lend itself to manipulation, and that may result in candidates failing to put their constituents first.

The political environment is composed of interdependent coalitions. The tasks below can be performed as individual functions at first, but at some point they must be aligned and integrated to form the continuum of a working campaign. Candidates should take the initiative to build a strong foundation by using the defined sequential tasks that are outlined in the following chapters. Campaign speeches, logos, themes, and strategies must project a continuous, flowing message of inspiration and leadership.

The people responsible for building their piece of the campaign puzzle must never lose sight of the overall picture and their place within it. The tasks outlined here may change over time as technologies and political climates evolve, but the basic concept will remain true. Hopefully, campaign managers, staff, and volunteers will find better ways of achieving higher standards by using *Political Tool Kit* as a framework.

Three Phases for Establishing and Activating Political Values and Beliefs

Phase I: Conduct research to determine the "lay of the land"
1. Which political party is best for the candidate's philosophy?
2. What office will be a "best résumé" fit?
3. Start political activism: work on other people's campaigns; volunteer.
4. Become a member of your local party's committee; contact the local chairman/woman.
5. Form a campaign organization at least nine to twelve months before the election.
6. Maintain a healthy lifestyle; exercise and diet.
7. Preserve a firm religious base; attend worship regularly.
8. Recruit a statistician; gather statistics—research demographics, population, and voter histories.

Phase II: Build coalitions and energize the campaign
1. Hone public-speaking skills; take courses and seek out organizations, if necessary.
2. Join influential social organizations, such as Kiwanis and Rotary Club.
3. Develop a rapport with political veterans, who are often party committee members.
4. Find a highly respected political mentor.
5. Select a campaign manager and treasurer.
6. Start a pledge list for seed money.
7. List projected expenses; develop a budget.
8. Announce candidacy; timing determined by executive committee (see appendix D).
9. Begin a registration drive; ensure that every possible supporter registers to vote.
10. Recruit party committee members for a possible endorsement.
11. Establish and maintain a rapport with local unions, professionals, and businesses.
12. Establish absentee-ballot list; consolidate board of election (BOE) and updated canvassing lists.

Phase III: Complete recruitment and activate message-delivery systems
1. Obtain a domain name, e.g., www.candidatesname.com.
2. Recruit sage counsel and functional managers.
3. Describe campaign positions to be filled; recruit remaining staff.
4. Create, collect, and analyze lists of voters and contributors.
5. Create a volunteer list and recruit.
6. Set goals and timetables for tasks; establish a schedule and event calendar.
7. Determine training for recruited staff; activate mentorship program.
8. Define campaign theme, including song or tune, mantra, logo, and slogan.
9. Outline topics for speeches, palm cards (handbills, door hangers), talking points.

10. Obtain endorsements; solidify previously established relationships with unions, civic and social organizations, news media, military veterans, seniors, and local corporations.
11. Select message-delivery systems (website, newspaper, direct mail, etc.), weighing each for effectiveness versus monetary expenditure.

Note: For more information on each subject, please refer to the index.

These three phases are designed to construct a powerful campaign with energy and vision by building a strong foundation with quantifiable data to clearly define sequential tasks. A quantifiable analysis is more trustworthy than historical perceptions (Green and Gerber 2004, 90). After analyzing the demographics and statistical research, the campaign team must brainstorm a message that will appeal to voters in the election district.

The message is the trunk of the tree, based on ideals and values, while the candidate's talking points are the branches (O'Day 2003, 25). The candidate's talking points will not only articulate the campaign's theme and message but how the candidate plans to achieve those central issues.

Phase I

First, it is essential to determine which elected office and which political party, if any, are the best fit. The prospective candidate must consider emerging trends and recent shifts in political power (see Voting Blocs/Under-vote Calculations). Being registered to vote and having a residence in a particular geographical area are essential as is voting in every election (Grey 1999, 21). A candidate's personal philosophy must be aligned with a political party's basic tenets. Changes in party affiliation can shadow people throughout their political careers. The electorate will value many personal qualities in a candidate, but one of the most salient is loyalty. If an aspiring candidate is going to change political affiliations, then the sooner the better.

Success in politics relies on organization and skill, but primarily depends upon *knowledge, timing, and following trends.*

Become politically active
Volunteering for other people's campaigns is an excellent way to become involved with the political process. Donating money is another avenue of involvement, but donating time is just as valuable for attaining party favor and loyalty. The view from inside the political system may be a defining moment. Place this experience in context; do not allow others to erode your foundational values and direction. Always be courteous, personable, and professional. Respect others.

A select group of people will work and volunteer for a political party and candidates in whom they believe. Work with them; develop and maintain a rapport with this group of dedicated volunteers (England 1992, 35). Cultivate and harvest future mentors from this group, as needed. When volunteering on a campaign, it may not be time to share with others that you wish to someday seek public office. To do so could be interpreted by some as a threatening gesture.

Maintain your health

Attractive and healthy candidates are an asset on the campaign trail. On the other hand, candidates who do not take care of themselves with proper exercise and diet are a harder sell. Canvassing door-to-door for three to four hours every evening and on weekends may be one of the benefits of seeking elected office. If candidates are not in good physical shape when they begin, they soon will be.

Maintain religious base

Maintaining a firm religious base is a fundamental principle of candidacy. Many people who are atheists or who do not attend a place of worship regularly are elected to public office, but they are the exception rather than the rule. A candidate should attend worship regularly and develop a rapport with others. Voters are often tolerant of candidates who do not hold their own personal religious convictions, realizing that religious faith is a guaranteed personal freedom and should never be used as a campaign issue (Key 1966, 118). However, faith is often a critical factor in how segments of the electorate vote (Bai 2007, 52; Joslyn 1984, 26).

Candidates should not open doors through which they do not wish to enter. Campaign topics should focus on the issues most relevant to their qualifications for elected office.

Obtain statistical analysis

An aspiring candidate must seek quantifiable statistic and demographic data from within the election district. The model formed by the gathered data will reveal the composition and flavor of the campaign tasks ahead. The basis of the campaign's statistical analysis will be built upon the data obtained from the state BOE or a national political party after endorsement. The statistician is among the first key team members the candidate must select.

Research will identify demographics, size, and composition within the election district. That determination will help the candidate craft a message, target specific populations, and identify the delivery systems most advantageous for the campaign's optimal effect (see appendices I and H).

Phase II

Develop public-speaking skills
Many organizations (e.g., Toastmasters, Dale Carnegie), seminars, and college courses can help potential candidates hone their public-speaking skills (Shaw 2000, 226; England 1992, 26). Did you ever wonder why there are so many lawyers in politics? One of the many reasons is that most lawyers are comfortable speaking before groups of people (see Communications Director).

Join influential social organizations
A political election is often a popularity contest in disguise. A winning candidate is usually active in several civic organizations. Candidates must extend their social reach, as substantive activity in civic organizations is often an important step toward election. However, membership without activity is a disingenuous façade, and other members may openly discuss a candidate's lack of participation during the election process.

Obtain political-veteran and party endorsement
Role models, mentors, and guides are the basis from which a political campaign gains much of its strategic focus. This group of people offers a campaign a well of knowledge and experience. Political veterans are often committee people who work in a party year after year because their own personal values and beliefs are aligned with party doctrine. The focus of the ground campaign will rely on unity with this faction of stalwart volunteers.

Political veterans will also have a group of loyal followers who usually sign the veterans' nominating petitions and rely on their judgment for guidance in selecting a candidate. Veterans often convey candidates' personal attributes or transgressions to voters within their spheres of influence as they are the party's foot soldiers. Candidates and campaign managers must develop a personal rapport with this group of volunteers. They must be convinced to carry candidates' nominating petitions and guide the electorate to believe in their campaign initiatives (see Mentoring).

Set action agenda
The core thesis of the campaign is the theme, the candidate's central message to the voters. It can be smaller government, more efficient government, lower taxes, quality education, reduced crime and stricter laws, or greater services (potable water, better sewers, highway improvements). Whatever the theme, it cannot be an issue that can be addressed and solved during the election cycle by an incumbent or opponent—such as a new bridge on Route 66, new sidewalks on Elm Street, or the repaving of Route 24 (see Going Negative).

Once invoked, the candidate's main issues cannot be abandoned because they are the focus of the entire campaign. In the foundation-building days of the campaign, it is important for candidates to have a firm grasp of issues affecting the electorate in the district where they are seeking office. Feedback from constituents and factual data must form perceptions.

Fundraising
When all the ducks are in a row, start the campaign by asking relatives and friends to volunteer. Money is important, and starting a pledge list for seed money is vital. Establish a timetable for raising funds, and adhere to its deadlines.

How much did previous successful candidates spend on their elections? Obtain financial disclosure statements (usually available online from the BOE; see appendix H) from every candidate in the last two elections for the office in question. This will indicate the minimum amount of money the campaign must raise. Disclosure statements from past elections will also help target future donors. Start making lists of their names.

Establish pledge card list
A pledge for seed money must be explored as soon as candidacy is decided upon. The lists for seed money (Shaw 2000, 83) follow the same rules as those of volunteerism outlined in the volunteer coordinator's job function (see Volunteer Coordinator). Some candidates will use their holiday card and family reunion-picnic list as a basis for their first solicitation for campaign donations.

The spreadsheet format for lists must be uniform in design, or the lists cannot be merged or used to target specific purposes. It may be advantageous to use the volunteer card as a basic format for the fields required in a spreadsheet for both voter and fundraising lists. Having a computer specialist on the campaign team is a must (Grey 1999, 79; see appendices A, B, and C).

Phase III

Select a domain name
Many candidates select a domain name that reflects the office they seek (e.g., www.johndoeforjudge. com). Unfortunately, this nearly eliminates any congruency for future elections, and it is important to utilize the Internet's capabilities from one election to another. A domain name with just the candidate's name or one that has a generic flavor (www.friendsofcandidatename.com or www. candidatename.com) is best.

Website and blog designers are very knowledgeable in their own fields of expertise, but often do not have a complete picture of the tools and methods available for all forms of political advertising (see Fundraising Chair; Communications Director; Internet Precinct).

Assign jobs

Get a handle on needs by merging the list of campaign tasks and jobs with the people who will fill them. Now is the time to identify friends, relatives, and associates with jobs and tasks; assign the team trainers and mentors as soon as applicable. Identify and rely on key people.

Building a campaign is like building a house. Few people can or should build a house by themselves. The most successful builders subcontract tasks to experts in their fields. No house or campaign can be constructed without a solid foundation. Identify the areas; assign the experts. Excite them. Sell your candidacy! Offer people training and a job. Let them do it! Guide them. Instill a vision. Set goals. However, take it incrementally, or the task of candidacy will be overwhelming.

Create computer lists

Lists are the single most important aspect for voter turnout, fundraising, and advertising. There is an entire section in *Political Tool Kit* dedicated to this topic (see Computer Lists).

Set specific goals and a timetable

It is essential to set specific goals and timetables. Research and identify the election cycle, duties and job descriptions, office term, and year of election for the position being sought. Create a tentative schedule and events calendar (see Scheduling Officer).

Create a timeline, a tactile schedule, using construction paper. Heavy-duty, light-colored paper (for house roofing) can be obtained at any home-improvement store. Rolls of paper can also be obtained at craft stores or medical-device retailers.

Place dates on the paper in a linear fashion, listing all the events that will transpire in the campaign. It is also important for the timeline to be coupled with monetary acquisitions and expenditures, i.e., the budget.

Cycle time management
1. Build an infrastructure; recruit and train the team.
2. Get all hands on deck for the ultimate effort on the nominating petition drive.
3. Prepare for the primary election.
4. Conduct a slow but extremely methodical door-to-door canvassing project (summer aggregate).
5. Make a door-to-door push and synchronize the advertising initiative (fall advantage).
6. Map out get-out-the-vote (GOTV) steps to Election Day. Develop just-in-time advertising (JITA) to peak during the GOTV initiative.

Garner endorsements

Endorsement by a major party may eliminate many barriers. Organized city, county, or state parties (Democrat, Republican, Conservative, Independent) often help to distribute, bind, notarize, and deliver a candidate's nominating petitions to the proper authorities as well as supply committee members as volunteers. Political parties can also help with fundraising, in-kind donations, and monetary transfers (Grey 1999, 97; see Endorsements).

Set strategic goals

The campaign must be organized at least six to nine months in advance; however, a year is best if it is a first campaign or a primary and strong opposition is anticipated. The campaign announcement must come at the most opportune time. An early announcement could backfire and energize the opposition.

Candidates who announce too early will eliminate any type of free media splash or excitement. An announcement that is properly timed will deter prospective opposition while gaining the candidate optimal free media coverage and campaign momentum. A good strategy is to tantalize the voters and the media with the possibility of a candidacy. Timing is critical, especially if a primary is in the wind. A large monetary war chest may deter potential opponents like no other strategy (Faucheux and Herrnson 2001, 157). If there is a primary fight, then the approach will be less transparent. When there is fighting within a political party, strategy cards must be held very close to the vest. If extreme hatred or venal confrontation surfaces during the primary, it may dilute a candidate's electability during the general election as well as deplete funds.

Save all newspaper articles and audio and video clips on local issues and politicians or people who may someday be political adversaries or advocates. File them by category for future use by your communications director. Pay close attention to local issues and quotes of opponents in the press as they may come in handy later. If possible, scan documents into computer files, identifying the issue or name of the person, author, origin, and date of the article. If articles are placed in computer files, they may be searchable for keywords and subjects, thereby greatly enhancing organization capabilities.

These days, you can also save audio clips of radio interviews and video clips of TV interviews. At times future candidates and elected officials will be complacent and the field of politics completely stagnant. Then, all of a sudden, the entire political landscape will change. The people who surge ahead in times of crisis and metamorphic change are the ones who have a campaign in place waiting for activation. This book offers the tools for such a leap. Incumbents can usually reactivate their old campaign staff on a moment's notice, but a novice must always be prepared.

Vote! Candidates can present their voting records as an attribute, or their opponents will use it as a liability. Always vote. All of the candidate's family, friends, neighbors, and acquaintances must be registered to vote.

Summation

This book is a treatise on how to obtain elected office, and yet it is really a step-by-step procedure on how to help people. It may be a trite cliché, but a single elected official really can change the world. One only needs the proper tools, guidance, perseverance, and support. Political candidacy and public office touch nearly every aspect of American life. Future candidates must at times read between the lines in this book to perceive the full depth intended. If elected to office, they will be integral players in the lives of the communities they represent.

Political candidacy is dependent upon establishing loyal relationships and maintaining a strong support network of friends and political activists (Payne and Krabill 2002, 138). Candidates must create trusted relationships through mentors, role models, and political veterans. They must have the physical stamina (Pelosi 2007, 63) to carry on despite hardships as well as the mental acuity to process information, multitask, and come to rational, fact-based conclusions.

The acquisition and distribution of financial resources is often based on culture and class. Therefore, it is important to create a stable, knowledge-based financial platform. Manage money wisely.

Political candidacy requires the candidate to flourish in every class and social structure. The candidate must be aware of the unwritten rules that reside within every group and class in society (Payne 2002, 20). This can only be accomplished with a strong grassroots political support system and the adroit use of mentors and guides.

A formal education is important and often considered an asset in most districts, but experiential political knowledge is a basic requirement for candidacy. Develop political acuity by volunteering on other people's campaigns. Strategies for political survival and growth are born from the abilities of the candidate, campaign manager, and campaign team to develop an in-depth, knowledge-based, professional support network of people.

In essence, a winning political campaign must do the necessary research to target specific voters, craft an appealing message, and deliver it to those voters again and again and again (O'Day 2003, 6). A campaign's financial resources are finite. The candidate and campaign manager must determine and select the most cost-effective methods available.

Note: The Board of Elections (BOE) is often mentioned in this document as the sole supplier of campaign software, maps, voter histories, and absentee-ballot and voter-registration lists. However, a candidate or campaign manager may choose to acquire software or data from other sources, such as the state department, political consultants or vendors, city or county clerk, or their political party.

SECTION 2

Personnel

- Campaign Team
- Candidate
- Campaign Manager/Chair
- Sage Counsel
- Statistician/Researcher
- Financial Officer/Treasurer
- Communications Director
- Scheduling Officer/Scheduler
- Advertising Coordinator
- Volunteer Coordinator/Recruiter
- Fundraising Chair
- Office Manager
- Unit Manager

CAMPAIGN TEAM

▼

A political campaign team is a select group of people who share a common bond. They are aligned to endorse a single candidate for elected office. The team has a shared vision, usually inspired by charismatic leadership. The most successful teams display a diverse ethnic and social composition of participants whose political activism and belief in a particular candidate, party, or issue may be their only common thread.

The United States has a representative form of government. Since all elections are local and are won at the grassroots level, a strong team is the essence of every successful election (Grey 1999, 15). The candidate is but a means for the team and the electorate to achieve their shared vision. It is important for the candidate to grasp major issues in the founding days of the campaign. Rather than lofty political ideals, local elections are usually more concerned with what will touch a voter's life on a daily basis, such as schools, sidewalks, roads, security or crime, property taxes, potable water, sewers, parks, and playgrounds.

The candidate and campaign manager must encourage altruistic behavior within the team to instill vision and achieve the common goals required for success. Volunteers and staff will enter a political campaign as individuals but emerge on Election Day as a team. A fragmented team is a recipe for disaster.

The political team embodies vertical, horizontal, and organizational unions and partnerships to meet and exceed clearly stated campaign goals through continuous process improvement (Creech 1995, 202). The candidate's image is projected to the electorate by every team member. Candidates must offer sound leadership and cannot waver or vacillate on their core campaign issues, but the methods through which the four basic talking points (outlined below) are delivered to people will often require adjustment (Shaw 2000, 216; Senge 1990, 150).

Membership on a political team gives individuals the chance to witness history in the making and contribute to the creativity released by the combined talents of a group. Campaign team members have the opportunity to improve the lives of people in their community in way that life may never have afforded them before. The team will enhance existing and establish new social relationships on the journey to Election Day. Always remember to treat people with dignity, honor, and respect. A successful political campaign team should be embedded within the community in which it serves, not viewed as an "add on" (Senge 1994, 38).

The team's structure is centralized through vertical pillars of expertise that rely on the knowledge of functional managers who build a foundation of stability based on highly trained, self-directed cross-functional work teams (Senge 1994, 186). The thread that ties all the functions together is the campaign theme, which is energized by the candidate's vision of governance and leadership (Melum and Collett 1995, 8; Creech 1994, 57).

A political campaign is more like a series of short-term sprints than like one continuous marathon. Its guiding principle is a shared vision with long-term goals. Every short-term goal that is achieved will build a ladder of integrity for continuous improvement and strengthen the campaign team (Senge 1994, 447).

Executive Committee

The following are the members of the executive committee:

- Candidate
- Campaign Manager/Chair (CM)
  - Sage Counsel
  - Statistician/Researcher
- Functional Managers
  - Financial Officer/Treasurer
  - Communications Director
  - Advertising Manager
  - Scheduling Officer
  - Volunteer Coordinator/Recruiter
  - Fundraising Chair
- Unit Manager (county, city or ward/parish)*

The committee also has the following housekeeping functions:
- Office Manager
  - Secretary/Scribe
- Vice chairman/woman (fills in for absent campaign member or functional manager)

*The inclusion of the unit manager's position indicates a large campaign, which will incorporate several unit managers who are subordinate only to the CM and the candidate.

The number of functional managers in the "Parsons Campaign Model" can be altered to suit individual talents as well as the size and needs of the campaign. The Parsons model incorporates two areas of administration to optimize command and control by defining the organizational framework for large and small campaigns. In larger campaigns with unit managers, the focus of functional managers will shift from direct administration of their areas of responsibility to support of the unit managers. Under both models, functional managers answer directly to the campaign manager and candidate and are experts in their individual disciplines. The best campaign model is the leanest operation, which allows the candidate and the CM to present a clearly defined message to a targeted audience (see Organizational Flow Chart).

Vertical Integration

This campaign model takes advantage of the many positive attributes associated with vertical integration. The campaign team embraces top-down leadership centered around the candidate's vision and stated goals. It enhances bottom-up membership from the electorate at the grassroots level in every ward, parish, and district through personal interaction. This top-to-bottom movement will be guided by the candidate's team and is a form of "creative interaction" that will propel the campaign forward to victory (Melum and Collett 1995, 15).

The functional-manager system creates areas of professional expertise and stability, enabling a leaner organizational structure that is responsive to change. Even though each functional manager's team often delivers a different product, all team members have a shared vision and unity in purpose (Creech 1994, 158).

Daily contact with the electorate generates one of the campaign's most important interactive communications tools: direct voter feedback. Team members must take constituents' messages back to weekly executive committee meetings to share the voters' needs, ideas, and fears. Do not let campaign meetings degenerate into gripe sessions when feedback is explored. A ward or precinct volunteer representative should bring the "voice of the people" to executive committee meetings on a regular basis.

Volunteers who conduct door-to-door canvassing, especially during the nominating petition cycle, interact with the voters directly at the grassroots level and must have a voice with the top decision makers in the campaign (Pelosi 2007, 200). Their feedback should stress what the campaign needs to do right, not just what the folks are doing wrong. Voters see how they are affected by employment, taxes, education, or crime, but are often unaware of the political remediation process. Concerns that the voters share with campaign volunteers are usually symptoms of real problems that should be addressed at the political level. It is the campaign team's responsibility to translate those symptoms into a concrete policy. Leaders do not vacillate on key issues but adopt fact-based campaign policies that best represent their constituencies.

The CM must communicate to managers and other vital staff members how much their work is valued and where it fits into the overall campaign. The CM must talk to functional managers to ensure they are not using the resources needed by a less assertive manager. The candidate will have an optimal conclusion on Election Day only if all functional managers are successful. Functional managers and team members must play well with others by sharing knowledge and resources. Even professionals who intend to do a great job can sometimes have tunnel vision within their areas of responsibility. Each functional manager's role is one of professional interaction, as outlined by the CM, who must not allow areas of expertise to degenerate into egocentric fiefdoms of dysfunction.

Cross-functional Integration

A well-trained and harmonious team is exceptionally strong. A successful team will integrate partnerships within the community and organizational structure, allowing the campaign to move forward as a unit. To achieve this, conduct an open forum at weekly meetings during which participants can raise any problem or initiative without fear of punishment or retribution. Every single volunteer and team member must be in alignment with the vision of the campaign. Personal empowerment will grow within the team if volunteers are well trained, motivated, and offered the tools to perform specific tasks. Training offers empowerment, which means taking responsibility, which leads to accountability (Creech 1994, 99).

Cross-functional team interaction occurs through formal and informal training and mentoring. The campaign must adequately train the volunteer staff for every assigned campaign task. Training material should clearly define the basic legal points and guidelines regarding all grassroots-level campaign tasks and election-related materials, including door-to-door canvassing techniques, nominating petition legalities, absentee ballots, and voter registration. Time may very well be the campaign's greatest enemy. Volunteers should be trained as early as possible.

Tip: Volunteers might not perform assignments if they have not been properly trained.

A political campaign must encapsulate nearly every aspect of American life and embody the art of relating to wholes. Unconnected social pillars (religious, military veterans, ethnic, and seniors groups) are often insular and exist in a community much like the pieces of a puzzle. The campaign must build those complex relationships into a unified system. Identifying the relationship of each puzzle piece to the overall picture will allow the proper leverage to be applied at the right time.

The Rubric of Campaign Teams

To be successful, candidates must interweave many disciplines into their teams. Campaign teams must have a universal mantra and share the candidate's vision and theme. The candidate's vision must flow and glow to every area of the campaign, and ultimately the voter will be infected as well. Honesty, openness, and mutual respect are fundamental principles of a successful team. The CM must instill honor, loyalty, and trust with a network of support. There should be no fear of failure within the team (Creech 1994, 79).

The greatest gift a candidate and CM can offer is to foster a nurturing environment in which a team can grow. Therefore, the CM must select the proper person for each job. One way to accomplish this is to ask each person which job he or she is most qualified to do. People usually do well at what they like best. Create a list of open positions and distribute it at weekly executive committee meetings (see Campaign Manager).

All team members have the opportunity to operate at optimal performance if they are well trained and properly motivated. It is the CM's responsibility to help team members grow beyond their comfort levels. The treasury, communications, advertising, and volunteer functions depend on one another for support. The CM offers people a job and must help remove any barriers, so they can effectively perform their duties. An ounce of prevention is worth a pound of cure. The CM also must be a conduit for the successful resolution of grievances, while referring most internal team disharmony (if it should arise) to individual functional managers for resolution. An open dialogue between functions will defuse potential problems before they grow out of control. Follow-through is important. Training through mentorship programs for unseasoned team members helps to prevent these problems (see Mentoring). Well-trained people interact professionally.

Note: The candidate should not directly resolve internal conflicts unless the direction of the campaign is in jeopardy. Administration of the dispute resolution process and daily oversight among functional managers is the CM's job. And, except in rare instances, resolution of team grievances is the functional manager's responsibility.

Greater supervision may be necessary if people are not fully trained. Having large groups of untrained volunteers in the field representing a candidate may pose problems (Thomas 1999, 18). Self-directed work teams are highly trained and motivated. Highly trained, self-directed teams require leadership and direction, not direct supervision. Micromanaging a highly motivated, self-directed work team may destroy it. The campaign manager must be aware of which is which (Senge 1994, 465).

> *Tip:* The candidate and campaign manager must be aware of campaign contributions and allocations. They should receive a copy of all financial statements (for both candidate and opponent) from the treasurer at the weekly executive committee meetings.

Today, thanks to innovations in technology, teams can go into the field with mobile devices that provide cutting-edge communications—GPS and mapping capabilities, texting, e-mail, and web browsers. Technology greatly enhances efficiency and team interaction. Match door-to-door walking lists to computers, tablets, and smartphones for end-result poll watching on Election Day and get-out-the-vote (GOTV) efforts. Managers must select specific technologies and optimize the use of a few, not minimize the use of many.

Technological innovations, however, are only tools for enhancing personal contact with the voters. They are never a substitute for personal interaction, such as the door-to-door canvassing that enables direct voter contact with low monetary expense. The more technology driven the campaign, the more vulnerable it will be to malfunctions. In addition, technology is often costly. Employ an adequate system to back up digital files, and have contingency plans in place for electronic and technical failures and emergencies.

Voters and the opposition should never have the opportunity to see the technological advancement utilized by the campaign. Voters may consider an abundance of modern innovations as wasted money. If an elderly couple on a fixed income donates $10 to a political campaign, they want to know their money is being wisely spent. Practice frugality when spending other people's contributions (McNamara 2008, 77). The campaign may need every penny for GOTV efforts as Election Day nears.

In every state, the campaign team must meet legal requirements set by the BOE. Most states only require legal documentation for the candidate and treasurer, but cities, towns, and counties may have additional laws (see appendix H).

Humor

Humor makes nearly every situation better, especially during the most hectic times. No matter how bad things are, there is always a funny side, and wit should be cultivated in a campaign team. Humor will boost morale and increase productivity.

Political veterans usually have a few anecdotal stories to share, which may be embellishments of the truth. Those colorful stories, true or not, are grist for good times and moments of levity in a campaign. A campaign is hard work, but it should also be fun.

It does not matter if people are laughing with or at something, even if it is themselves. One of the characteristics of a winning team's cohesiveness and intellect is its sense of humor. However, no member of the team or anyone else should ever be degraded or selected by others as a target using humor as a weapon.

Effective Teams

A winning team experience is not a haphazard coincidence. Members must be "team matched" for effectiveness, yet should also be diverse. An effective team shows diversity with a mix of genders, professionals and tradesmen, people with and without disabilities, retirees, and stay-at-home moms or dads. Teams should be a demographic mirror of the geographical areas they serve. Team composition is up to the candidate and the campaign manager. Do what works best.

Every team member has a job and will perform a needed function. Some team members will have more important functions—some will possess a higher degree of education or greater experience—but all team members must be valued at meetings. Knowledge, intellect, and success are always valuable personal attributes, but *honor, respect, and loyalty will make the strongest campaign team.*

Throughout the weeks and months of the campaign, the candidate's team will develop a personality and character all its own. With proper guidance and leadership, a sense of unity will develop, much like that of combat veterans during a military campaign. Shared vision and an external enemy are great unifiers. Team members will be like extended family, and the memory will be lifelong. Behind every winning candidate is a dynamic team that will contribute long hours of work for little to no compensation.

Years after the election, when all have returned to their own lives, they will remember the feeling of unity and the job they performed together. Many former members have been known to revisit their political team experience and reminisce over coffee from time to time. Great teams are the fabric of destiny and difficult to destroy, often outlasting a successful candidate's political longevity.

Nuts and Bolts

+ Unify and align the team with the candidate's shared vision.
+ Leverage existing vertical political structures: top-down and bottom-up.
+ Research demographics and statistics.
+ Fill positions with qualified people.
+ Create a training regimen with staff and volunteers.
+ Establish a feedback loop between team and electorate (Pelosi 2007, 121).
+ Reach out to groups in the community.
+ Grasp fundamental issues in the founding days.
+ Build team interaction through honor, respect, and loyalty.
+ Ensure that dialogue without fear of reprisal is the norm at weekly executive committee meetings.
+ Take full advantage of existing technology.
+ Remember that humor can boost morale and increase productivity.
+ Use a successful team experience for future mentor recruitment.

CANDIDATE

▼

Candidacy is the most difficult job to define because it is not a job. It is a mission. The candidate *is* the message. Being a successful candidate is dependent on so many factors, it is impossible to identify them all. There is no mold for a perfect candidate. What may be practical in New York City may not be a winning combination in Tyler, Texas.

Every elected office has a job description, quantifiable qualifications, hidden rules, powers, and predetermined formal and informal responsibilities. Articulating the job's duties and characteristics is the basis of candidacy (Shaw 2000, 206). The job's description may be found in a local repository, such as a public library, city or county clerk's office (state codes), or board of elections (Thomas 1999, 9). If documentation for the position does not exist, obtain a description from someone who has held the office in the past.

When a person contemplates a run for public office, certain foundational building blocks must be set in motion (see Foundation: Getting Started). Do not become overwhelmed. The experience of candidacy will be a fantastic adventure.

The aggressiveness and vision the candidate exudes will permeate all levels of their campaign and hopefully infect the opponent's campaign as well. From the candidate's perspective, there is only one way to run for elected office: to win and to stabilize and put forth a platform with vision and leadership from day one. Entering the race *not to lose* is a defensive posture with indecisive management. If the aspiring candidate wants to win an election, the next pages of this book will be of great interest.

Questions and Observations for the Candidate

1. Which is the right office for me?
2. What are the responsibilities of the office?
3. How much time will the office require?

4. What are the duties and job descriptions?
5. Is candidacy worth the effort?
6. A winning candidate has a strong team; identify team members.
7. Timeline nominating process: party endorsements, petitions, primary, general election.
8. It is important to identify basic campaign strategy and platform.
9. How much money will be needed?

Tasks must be segmented into bite-sized chunks to fit campaign needs, and preparation is essential for success. A frequent complaint of constituents is that government agencies do not work or communicate effectively with one another. If candidates seek a city office, they must attend meetings at the city council level and also attend county supervisor's and county manager's meetings. They or their campaign representatives should attend every public meeting that would directly influence the office being sought. Integrate and connect campaign activities at all levels.

If the meetings are televised, record and archive them. Minutes of some meetings may be available or may be posted on the Internet. File them electronically when possible. Candidates or their representatives must attend every public meeting or forum that will influence the office being sought, preferably in advance of their candidacy. They also must study and do their homework. They should read, record, and file all laws pertaining to the office, as well as city charters and future community, city, and county plans. They will need to draw from that knowledge base during media interviews and debates. Debates are often the best avenue for educating voters.

When it is time for the public announcement of candidacy, it is best to do so in front of the city hall or county building, if possible. A public park or bandstand is another good location. Invite the media and all the political supporters, campaign managers, and staff who support the candidate. The announcement should be a small but influential event.

> *Tip*: Some municipalities have strict laws regarding the political use of buildings or areas subsidized with tax dollars.

Send the media a printed announcement of candidacy, and after the event, send a list of notables who attended. Make sure the campaign's photographer is there. Send the print media good photographs that day by e-mail, direct mail, or hand delivery (see Advertising Coordinator and appendix D).

Name Recognition

There is a saying among veteran politicians, "It does not matter why a candidate is in the newspaper; it only matters that their name is in the paper and before the public." The theory is that people concentrate on their daily lives, and they only possess a ninety-day memory for external events. After ninety days, the only thing voters remember is the person's name, not a particular indiscretion or award. Although antiquated, this theory may have some validity. It does not presuppose the ignorance of voters, but does state that voters may have better things to do than follow the slightest nuance involved in each and every political drama.

Name recognition is one of the greatest assets and liabilities in politics (McNamara 2008, 5). The mere mention of their names brings Clint Eastwood, Ronald Reagan, the Kennedys, and the Rockefellers directly into the public's political eye. People with user-friendly names often happen to have truckloads of money too, but it is their political acumen, speaking ability, and leadership qualities that propel them into public office. Such names also offer the electorate a brand associated with government service and positive attributes (Grey 1999, 190). However, many multimillionaires have lost elections because they did not possess a winning candidate's attributes, failed to form a good campaign team, or did not realize the buy-in associated with fundraising (see Fundraising Chair). Name recognition is also a reason why negative campaigning provides a bounce to the opposition.

> *Tip:* Rarely address or mention an opponent by name. It offers him or her free advertising on your candidate's dime (see Going Negative).

Résumé

The candidate must prepare and maintain a concise, single-page résumé and may choose to supplement it with a biography, an in-depth, personal life chronology (Simpson 1972, 71). Offering any detailed information to the media is a judgment call. Providing too much data could become problematic, but striving for transparency is important. Obtain and keep all résumé-support documents: diplomas, birth certificate, marriage license, military discharge, etc. Ensure all the documents are completely accurate. In most instances, offer the media only the data they can obtain on their own, but no more, unless the circumstances are extreme.

> *Tip:* A résumé and support documents may be needed during a weekend or at a moment's notice.

Loyalty and Party Affiliation

Loyalty is a very endearing quality in politics. If the candidate, or anyone on the campaign staff, has volunteered to help other candidates during previous elections, now is the time to call in the favor and ask them for support. If any bargains are made for future support, do it before an election, not after.

Loyalty takes many forms. When people are elected as public officials, please remember that they are only part of a team. In many instances, the candidate's team is only a piece of the party's overall November effort. During off-years, when the elected official is not a candidate for office, team members should be available to others in their party running for office (see Voting Blocs/ Under-vote Calculations). In that way, they are strengthening the team and broadening their support for future elections. Note, however, it is often forbidden by law for some elected officials (usually judges and those in law enforcement) to be politically active outside of their designated campaign window.

A person's beliefs can change over time. If candidates' core values evolve and are no longer aligned with the party in which they are enrolled, they must register with the party that holds their heart and passion. Few candidates survive changing party affiliation unless it is early in their careers. Some do and survive unscathed. However, people do not like turncoats. To some, it is a clear signal that candidates were not able to bring about change within their original structures.

> *Tip:* When people change parties, there may be time restrictions as to how soon they can seek office under the new party's banner (see appendix H).

Candidate Attributes and Qualifications

+ Is ambitious, has inspirational drive and leadership, thrives on competition
+ Has stamina, is in for the long haul
+ Is an excellent speaker, articulate
+ Has strong leadership skills; is decisive, trustworthy, and dependable
+ Has good organizational skills
+ Is likeable, builds bridges rather than erects barriers
+ Is electable, personable
+ Is well educated, has college or experiential learning
+ Served in the military
+ Is socially active in the community
+ Is politically active, a committee member
+ Is successful in business, has a good job
+ Has a good family name, is honored and respected
+ Has residency in the voting district
+ Has an excellent personal voting record; votes in every election

Candidates should stress their personal strengths and realistically face their weaknesses, also identify reoccurring patterns of failure and how the campaign will overcome them. Many very successful candidates will lack some items on the above list, such as a formal education or military service. Such items are quantifiable (and to many, positive) attributes, but may not be highly valued by the electorate in some districts.

Issues

The local newspaper is an invaluable resource for information. Reporters do a great job in highlighting campaign issues of interest to voters. The issues that the candidate and campaign manager put forth as a platform must be substantive. Decide on four or five basic talking points for speeches and advertising (see Communications Director).

Mechanics

The candidate must assess how much time must be allocated for a successful campaign and to ensure an outstanding job performance after the election is won. Many political jobs are very demanding. In addition to the candidate's normal responsibilities of family and business commitments, there may be invitations to picnics, graduations, and a host of civic events. Never miss the funeral of a supporting constituent in the district; at the very least, send a card (Woo 1980, 5). There will be official and unofficial demands when in office. This is a key area candidates must discuss with their spouses or significant others, if they exist. Public service can be very demanding (Thomas 1999, 12).

Mentoring: Unofficial Methods for Functional Managers

This is one of the most critical areas of candidacy. Find people (usually in the same party) who have served in the office being sought or have worked close to it. They will be great mentors. Meet their friends and contacts.

Good mentors will have years of tried-and-true methods on their menu. They will possess a working knowledge of a campaign's internal characteristics from a historical best-practices perspective. A mentor must be free to discuss any political subject and will present a broader range of alternatives to the candidate and campaign manager.

Older political veterans may have the knowledge to critically address new untested methods or may have friends with the required expertise. Do not reinvent the wheel, but it is important to streamline proven techniques with new technology and methods (see Mentoring). Role models, candidate modeling (to replicate success), and mentoring are critical political components.

Names

The candidate's name can be important, not just in a social context but in a physical one. Married women may have an option of running with a maiden name or a hyphenated name, such as Barbara Smith-Jones. On the ballot, the name Jones may appear before Smith-Jones (Shaw 2000, 150). It depends upon how progressive the campaign district is and what the state law dictates. In some areas, a hyphenated name is the kiss of death. It may predispose the electorate to judge a candidate's values. Ask the BOE and sage counsel about legal procedure if the candidate desires a ballot name change.

Fundraisers and Events

Research the culture of the event and the form of attire in advance. It is always better to be slightly overdressed and professionally attired than to be underdressed. Attire for men is more rigid than for women, and yet it is more fluid. A man can remove his sports jacket and tie during a casual event (see Scheduling Officer and Fundraising Events).

> *Tip:* Remember names. There are books written on this topic. Read one. It is very important.

> *Tip:* At campaign appearances, candidates should drink beverages with their left hands. Right hands must be available to shake hands without being hot, cold, or wet. Candidates and campaign staff should never have a picture taken with drinks in their hands, even if the drinks are water, coffee, cranberry, or apple juice.

Physical

Candidates' journeys down the campaign trail will require a complete redirection of their personal schedule. The campaign will progressively demand more time, with breakfast gatherings, meet-and-greet events, fundraisers, interviews, speeches, and various other appearances. There will be hours of walking door-to-door in the district in addition to candidates' obligations to their families and businesses.

Campaigning activities are physically demanding. In addition, opponents will nearly always suggest that candidates suffer some form of physical or psychological malady that will influence decision making. Candidates should have a medical checkup before venturing out on the campaign trail. This will dispel any questions concerning their ability to fulfill the physical requirements of the elected office. However, never release personal medical information to anyone.

Logbook

Every good captain has a logbook for recording events and noting reminders. The logbook should have permanent pages that cannot be removed. Make sure it does not fall into enemy—i.e., the opponent's—hands. Do not enter anything in the logbook that anyone could deem inappropriate. It is an organizational book, not a diary nor personal journal. Electronic notebooks or other communications tools can be used for this purpose.

The log is a permanent record of events and transactions. Collect business cards, and start a reference list archive. If a constituent wants to register to vote, volunteer, contribute money, or obtain an absentee ballot, enter it in the logbook and give that information to the proper staff at the next weekly meeting (or electronically if that's the chosen method). Occasionally, touch base directly with voters to verify that the campaign staff is following up. Note: The candidate may also wish to start a scrap book with newspaper clippings, etc.

Incumbency

One of the greatest advantages in politics is a candidate's incumbency; yet few candidates take full advantage of it. Incumbents are often perceived to have an extensive knowledge of the issues, but that perception may not be valid in every case. Elected officials should always keep a log as a reminder of their past accomplishments. During their terms, they may have removed barriers and helped eliminate bureaucratic red tape for many constituents. Perhaps only a piece of curb or sidewalk in front of their houses was replaced, but constituents will remember it at voting time—if they are reminded. Many times, entire roadways are resurfaced or a sewer project is completed, helping a vast number of residents during an incumbent's political tenure.

In addition, elected officials may help others move forward in life. They are often called upon to write letters of reference for young people entering college, seeking employment, or applying to a military academy. All of these positive actions should be noted and mentioned during the election cycle. Door-to-door personal contact is an excellent time for the incumbent to highlight past achievements.

Elected officials should stay in contact with their constituents. Voters will appreciate office holders' efforts to communicate after the campaign is over. In addition, it is advisable to periodically remind constituents about major accomplishments. An incumbent often can tell voters about actions or proposed actions well before announcements are made to the opposition.

Sanctuary

The final autumn months of a campaign are often filled with turmoil. To ensure candidates' stability and psychological well-being, it is essential that they spend some time alone (Grey 1999, 124). It may be only twenty or thirty minutes walking the dog in the morning, yoga, or meditation. Whatever it is, candidates should set aside time to refill their energy reservoirs and reflect in a solitary environment. The time spent to rebuild the internal clock is vital to one's physical and psychological stability as well as one's overall well-being (Woo 1980, 12).

Nuts and Bolts

+ Build your campaign on a solid foundation (see Foundation: Getting Started).
+ Enter the race to win; that one statement says it all.
+ Find a mentor.
+ Create a résumé, and retain pertinent support documents.
+ Select people for key campaign positions; create a seed-money list.
+ Conduct interactive dialogue at all levels of the campaign.
+ Build a progressively improving rapport with the media.
+ Establish name recognition.
+ Never address an opponent by name.
+ List basic values, and create a shared vision.
+ Broaden your support for the future.
+ Research issues well and base decisions on fact.
+ Start and sustain a plan for diet and physical exercise.
+ Maintain a daily captain's logbook.
+ Have a plan A and a plan B.

CAMPAIGN MANAGER/CHAIR

▼

The selection of a campaign manager/chair (CM) is one of the candidate's most crucial decisions. Other than the candidate, the CM holds the most responsible leadership position. The CM will organize and direct the executive committee, who will in turn manage every operational phase of the campaign. The CM is responsible for the whole enchilada.

Candidates must choose someone with whom they have an excellent rapport and working relationship. They should interview several prospective managers before making a selection. The candidate and the CM ultimately must blend completely in thought and action. There can be no deep personal friction or animosity between the two.

The CM should be an articulate speaker and an exceptional leader who respects others and has the ability to work well in a multicultural environment. Volunteers and campaign staff must respect the CM on every level. Retaining oversight of the campaign without micromanaging is a unique ability. Campaign managers must be able to multitask and cannot be easily overwhelmed. They must be cool, resolute, and have clear focus and presence of mind under trying conditions. They should also maintain perspective and have the ability to step back from the campaign and see the candidate through the eyes of voters and the media. They must be well liked, accepted by the community, and be willing to donate vast amounts of time to the campaign.

The candidate and CM must touch base with every facet of the campaign, and all volunteers should believe they have access to both people. They must bond with volunteers and staff at every level in which the campaign functions. These relationships enable the grassroots volunteers to address their concerns to the executive committee in an open forum at weekly meetings.

The CM must maintain a professional approach at all times, offering firm leadership without appearing aloof. The CM must have the ability to listen as well as to talk, and definitely has to be able to keep a secret: "Those who know do not talk; those who talk do not know" (Pelosi 2007, 75). In a way, the CM will serve as a psychologist to everyone, especially to the candidate, has integrity, and does not gossip, unless it is an agreed-upon political tactic.

A few words about family: direct and strong family support is essential to the campaign. Relatives of the candidate usually are the hardest workers, but they are rarely the most impartial decision makers. For this reason, candidates' spouses or significant others should never fill the CM position or be involved in a forum demanding unbiased discourse (McNamara 2008, 19). They are, however, an invaluable source of strength, support, and positive public relations for the candidate.

A sibling with proper skills and personality may offer the campaign exceptional talent, but it is difficult to fire a close family member if things do not work out. Lastly, a word of caution: emotions often run high in families, and relatives may decide to use a candidate's vulnerability as a vehicle for addressing past issues that have no merit to the campaign. The CM also must be aware that bloodline relationships within the campaign often circumvent the normal chain of command. A child, spouse, or sibling may have direct access to the candidate or others in the executive committee and offer a disproportionate amount of influence, which is often more biased than professional.

For proper oversight, the CM must be aware of campaign barriers and deadlines. Debates, dinners, and other events have precise starting times. Nominating petitions must be certified, bound, and delivered to the proper authorities in a timely manner. Financial disclosures must be filed by a certain date, or a penalty may be assessed.

Essential Attributes of the Campaign Manager

+ Maintain loyalty, and be the candidate's number one advocate.
+ Listen to core staff's ideas on direction; set a path.
+ Question the candidate's direction and policy when necessary.
+ Act as a confidential sounding board for the candidate, staff, and volunteers.
+ Challenge the staff when making assignments; recognize talent.
+ Remain open to new and creative ideas and technological advances.
+ Be competent; develop a complex, interactive campaign strategy.
+ Maintain a good relationship with the candidate's friends and family.

The CM must be the candidate's number-one advocate, always placing the candidate's political well-being first. There should be no doubt about the winning outcome of the campaign. The CM should instill creative leadership, energy, and vision among the staff in a way that ultimately touches every voter.

The CM solicits the core staff members' ideas on direction and then sets a path. The candidate and CM may at times disagree, but the CM must realize that the candidate's name is the one on the ballot. The candidate has the final word after all the facts and opinions have been reviewed. If things do not go as planned, the CM cannot have an "I told you so" mentality. The campaign must learn from mistakes and move on as rapidly as possible.

To offer the campaign the necessary balance, it is the candidate's job to employ at least one person who will occasionally challenge the campaign's direction and policy. That unenviable job often belongs to the campaign manager. The CM can always play it safe, but leadership demands a degree of calculated risk in exploring new methods and emerging technology. People who do not have a history of team interaction may view the questioning of campaign policy as disloyalty rather than a timely infusion of team equilibrium. A team should have discipline, but feedback is essential for building quality into the campaign (Creech 1995, 98).

The campaign manager's primary attribute will be to intuitively assign jobs that fit best with staff members' and volunteers' talents and abilities. An exceptional manager identifies their talents, but also faults and deals with them realistically (Senge 1994, 17). When considering job assignments, the CM asks staff what their area of strength is, but always remembers that good people often limit themselves to known tasks. It is up to the CM to identify people's latent talents and challenge them to reach beyond their known abilities. Believe in them, and they will believe in themselves. A highly organized and developed training regimen is essential to staff development.

The CM sets the parameters in which all other teams will work. If the CM, the candidate, and volunteers clash too frequently, it will disrupt the team's cohesiveness. Internal bickering will limit or destroy the campaign's forward momentum. Disagreement with the core campaign strategy or tasks must be transparent and voiced at weekly meetings. However, there are issues that might require select executive committee members to meet in a closed session to resolve the problem.

Parameters That Must Be Addressed

+ Is the CM a volunteer or a paid position? Know the difference.
+ Will the candidate or CM hire the executive committee? (This is very important.)
+ The CM must be comfortable about giving *any* type of feedback or news to the candidate.
+ The CM will take the heat when bad things happen; define "bad things."

The Key Tasks of a Campaign Manager

+ Helps to write, review, and edit all major speeches.
+ Serves as liaison to the news media; helps to edit and clear all press releases.

- Organizes and facilitates all high-level meetings.
- Hosts fundraisers and serves as emcee; arranges for "star power" speakers.
- Attends events for the candidate when there are scheduling conflicts.
- Administers the crisis-resolution plan created with the communications director.
- Designs rules of contact (arbitration or mediation) between functional managers and staff.
- Assigns jobs that complement the staff's talents and abilities.
- Creates a training regimen for staff development, including mentoring.
- Utilizes a tiered system of staff rewards for outstanding performance.
- Delineates tasks within each functional manager's area of responsibility.
- Sets goals and timetables to keep functional managers on task.
- Requests a budget from each functional manager.
- Works with the treasurer on the overall budget.

The Question of Domain

In anticipation of any scheduling and personality conflicts, the campaign manager sets forth an internal and external set of rules of contact. With the advice of the candidate and executive committee, the CM establishes how rigid or fluid the chain of command will be among the teams and between staff and the executive committee.

At times, a functional manager will need to borrow another manager's volunteer, employee, or contractor. It is important for the CM and functional managers to discuss staff assignments at weekly meetings. Managers must know where their people are and who is assigned temporarily to special duty. Campaign managers also should tell functional managers to leave their egos at home and share resources as required. A functional manager should not hoard volunteers or other resources needed for the candidate's Election Day victory. The CM can shift the tasks within each functional manager's domain to accentuate an individual's expertise, realizing the size and needs of the campaign. If the job isn't a good fit, the person can move into something else that is. Emphasize possible movement and job restructuring when managers, staff, and volunteers are first brought on board.

Campaign managers set goals and timetables and are the people who ultimately determine which events the candidate will attend. They wear many hats—psychologist, statistician, diplomat, and leader (see Scheduling Officer). They assign tasks to functional managers, who assign tasks to staff and volunteers. The team will usually know most of what is happening in the district and will be aware of all the political gossip, but will not be the conduit for unfounded rumors. It is important for the CM to be the first person who is aware of problems.

Times and methods change. People change. If only tried-and-true policies were adopted, nothing in politics or business would ever change. Campaign direction and policy should always be fluid, ready to be challenged and revised. Similar to an automobile assembly line, high quality is built into each component throughout the process, not added by inspection at the end (Creech 1994, 47). The CM must introduce new ways to do old tasks while seeking out innovative technology. Even this book is only a foundational springboard; venture beyond it.

The CM makes sure the executive committee's functional managers realize that most of the people in their domains are volunteers, not employees. Make requests nicely; say please and thank you a lot (Pelosi 2007, 173). Praise should be administered to everyone and layered with a reward system. Use a tiered system of staff rewards (dinners, theater tickets, etc.) for outstanding performance. Praise those who do outstanding work. Remember, everyone feels they work hard.

> *Tip*: Rewarding staff and volunteers in an open forum may be detrimental to team cohesiveness. Exceptional praise in a confidential setting with a mention in an open forum may be best suited for political campaigns. Introduce a process that is the best fit for the team.

A Spy among Us

When the executive committee and its inner circle (Pelosi 2007, 59) of advisors has been formed, a phenomena that is not unique to politics may exist. Politicians usually have friends on both sides of the aisle. Those contacts can be of a business or social nature; sometimes they are relatives or close friends.

It is an extremely rare to have an intentional plant placed within the working committee by an opposing candidate's party or team (Hunt and Risch 2011, 124). It is more likely that a team member has talked to the wrong people, providing information he or she never thought would end up in the opposition's hands.

Check the party registrations of all active staff and volunteers to determine their degree of alignment with the candidate's core beliefs (Hunt and Risch 2011, 129). If a person is enrolled in the opposition party, that could be a red flag about their true allegiance. On the other hand, many people change their philosophical and political views over time, but never get around to changing their party affiliation. Inquire, if necessary.

Awareness of this phenomenon many be enough protection. Team members who are enrolled in an opposing political party should be encouraged to change their registration, but not required to do so. Loyalty is a highly sought after attribute. Loyalty to a particular candidate does not mandate registration in their party, but it should be encouraged.

Insurance Coverage

The candidate, CM, and treasurer must decide which insurance agent should cover the campaign, if it is deemed to be necessary (see Sage Counsel).

Subsidiary Tasks

The CM will consider many subsidiary tasks within a functional manager's job description as pool tasks or pool assignments. The volunteers in the phone bank, literature drops (leafleting), drivers, and intersection sign wave would be examples of pool tasks or cross-functional assignments, which will be assigned by several functional managers. The tasks assigned to each manager within this campaign model is only suggested. Campaign managers may reassign one or more tasks to form a more efficient model for their campaign.

One of the great things about a political campaign is that tasks are usually sequential; rarely will all volunteers be needed on-board at the same time. The only time all volunteers will have to be mobilized at once will be during the nominating petition drive and GOTV efforts as Election Day nears.

Nuts and Bolts

- Be the candidate's number-one advocate.
- Formulate campaign strategy; initiate proper feedback loops with voters and staff.
  - Listen to core staff's ideas on direction; set a path.
  - Question campaign direction and policy when required.
- Take certain personal risks; challenges the staff to "reach higher" in assignments.
- Facilitate all executive committee meetings.
  - Serve as a sounding board for the executive committee and volunteers.
- Set goals and timetables to keep functional managers on task.
- Harmonize relationships at all levels.
- Design rules of contact between functional managers and staff.
- Assign jobs that fit well with staff talents and abilities.
- Create a training regimen that includes mentoring for staff development.
- Utilize a tiered system of staff rewards for outstanding performance.

+ Delineate tasks within each functional manager's area of responsibility.
+ Serve as press liaison.
  o   Write or personally review all speeches and press releases.
+ Attend events for candidate when there are scheduling conflicts.
+ Serve as the master of ceremonies at fundraisers.
+ Invite "star" speakers to fundraisers.

SAGE COUNSEL

▼

The sage counsel is an executive committee position that answers directly to the candidate and campaign manager and advises them on legal matters concerning the campaign. This managerial-level position is usually held by an attorney. The sage counsel position is also a prime candidate for job sharing, depending on the attorney's social profile and expertise in subjects relevant to the campaign's legal needs.

The counsel is extremely important to the campaign and must legally guide it through many obstacles at crucial times. When a campaign runs smoothly, i.e., past every legal hurdle, it is invariably due to the sage counsel's abilities, attention, and interaction with the candidate and the CM. The counsel offers timely advice to circumvent any challenge the opposition may propose on a diversity of legal issues. Otherwise, the executive committee may spend untold hours trying to recover from unintended legal consequences. In addition, properly trained volunteers and staff will help avert potential legal indiscretions or missteps.

> *Tip:* Some candidates and campaign managers may unwisely place a highly respected member of a prominent law firm in an honorary position as sage counsel as an advertising ploy or attempt to intimidate the opposition. The sage counsel is a working position.

The sage counsel should establish a training seminar outlining the legal requirements for the following staff and volunteer positions:

- Financial disclosure statements (see Treasurer)
- Nominating petition's formal structure, circulator's duties, and filing procedures
- Poll watchers and voter fraud challenges on Election Day and during GOTV efforts
- Notary public licensing of campaign staff, if required
- Election law summaries, including those related to early voting, absentee ballots, and voter registration

There may be legal issues associated with compensation. For example, the campaign may reimburse volunteers for their expenses or use part-time or full-time paid employees; the tax requirements for each are different. Every campaign also will require several types of insurance coverage, as listed below:

- Travel/personal injury
- Libel/slander
- Property damage to facilities
- Workers' compensation
- Employment/unemployment insurance
- Bonding of the personnel who handle money

The sage counsel also advises campaign personnel on a myriad of other legal issues, including:

- Distribution/display permits and fees: lawn signs, bulletin boards, banners
- Public gathering permits: parades, corner blitz-intersection sign wave rallies
- Voter registration laws
- Absentee-ballot deadlines and legalities, especially where the military vote is concerned
- Post-Election Day absentee-ballot challenges and counting
  - o Early voting procedures, rules, and laws
- IRS: the candidate's personal taxes, paid staff deductions, EIN number (treasurer)
- The candidate's or the opponent's possible legal violations or infractions
- Hatch Act violations* (www.osc.gov)
- The candidate's financial disclosure statement and conflict-of-interest claims
- Finance: donation solicitation rules and campaign contribution limits
- Contractual agreements for services and leases (HQs, storefronts, events, bulletin boards)
- The FCC's broadcasting rules for campaigns

  * Basically, federal employees or certain civil servants paid through federal appropriations are restricted from partisan political activity or elections, as a candidate or using their office to intimidate voters. The Merit Systems Protections Board and the Office of Special Council enforce this law.

It is ultimately wiser for the sage counsel to be proactive and anticipate potential election law violations before they occur. Staff training and the presence of the sage counsel at weekly meetings will keep employees and volunteers informed of their duties and legal requirements. All areas of the campaign should synchronize their training periods.

Some states require notary publics to circulate certain types of nominating petitions. Some geographical areas or campaign districts may curtail campaign activities on Election Day, limiting GOTV initiatives. Early voting is allowed in a number of states. There are many campaign tasks that require a lawyer's advice.

The sage counsel is the appropriate person to handle problems related to voting practices. For instance, some voters may not be comfortable with newly introduced electronic voting machines. The sage counsel can alert the state and county boards of election about this issue. In response, the campaign may choose to initiate its own training regimen for its representatives at the polls and for the voters who support its candidate.

> *Tip:* The sage counsel should have a good rapport with the appropriate judicial authority
> in case there is need for a timely legal ruling on Election Day (Shadegg 1964, 184).

It is always a good idea to inform the candidate's supporters of their legal voting rights. More people will come out to vote on Election Day if they know their rights.

Voters' Rights

1. Can vote if they are in line when the polls close
2. Can cast a provisional ballot in case their right to vote is challenged
3. Can view a sample ballot before voting (Pelosi 2007, 218)
4. Can vote in a private area
5. Can receive instruction on how to cast a ballot
6. Can receive the proper implements (pen, ballot, cover folder) to aid voting

Nuts and Bolts

- Help remove legal barriers that surface concerning campaign or election laws.
- Offer timely proactive legal advice.
- Identify insurance obligations.
- Create a training seminar for volunteers concerning nominating petition legalities, early voting programs, absentee ballots, voter registration, and notary public licensing.
- Prepare for proactive intervention regarding Election Day issues or challenges.

STATISTICIAN/RESEARCHER

▼

The statistician reports directly to the candidate and campaign manager; attends meetings when requested; and provides data on demographics, polling, and voting characteristics (see appendix I). Their expertise also guides the campaign's strategic course by providing quantifiable insight into the district's population, industry, and employment history. The fact-based decision making required for debating, speaking, and formulating the campaign's theme and talking points is born from quantifiable statistical analysis. The statistician supplies the needed data.

Factual demographic and polling data are essential tools for both novice and seasoned candidates. It is important to know how many people reside in the voting district, how many are registered to vote, their voting frequency during targeted election years, and to which political party they belong. Statistics from state and local BOEs are central to any campaign effort. Data and computerized mailing lists may also be available from a political party that endorses a candidate.

The statistician will research voting histories and trends within the election district and will transfer demographics and polling data into a presentation-style format, often in a summary accompanied by charts and graphs. The CM will review and help analyze this information before it is disseminated to the candidate, designated staff, and volunteers to assist in formulating the campaign strategy. If requested, the statistician may present this information at select weekly executive committee meetings.

On occasion, the CM may ask the statistician to organize a sampling poll or to identify trends and pending lifestyle changes relevant to the district. Demographics are relatively static, and are measured once every ten years by the US Census Bureau. Population data also can be obtained from chambers of commerce, the Departments of State and Labor, libraries, or county and state election departments (Grey 1999, 49). New methods for capturing data will undoubtedly emerge through the Internet and other mediums. Take advantage of them. The data collected must be from verifiable professional and government resources.

When a campaign launches a highly aggressive effort to capture the maximum number of signatures on a nominating petition, the areas of high-density penetration will usually be mirrored on Election Day with voter support. After the nominating petition signature drive, the statistician will help analyze which geographical areas need more door-to-door coverage during the lax summer period and GOTV initiatives.

In addition, capturing postelection data is essential for the next election cycle. The statistician's creativity, intellect, knowledge, and ability will positively affect the types of data sets saved for future analysis.

Opposition Research

This book does not recommend conducting in-depth research on the opposition. But if it is done, here is a list of the information that may be collected (McNamara 2008, 35; Woo 1980, 49).

Personal
+ Arrest record
+ Employment record (business alliances)
+ Drug or alcohol addiction (if any)
+ Employment history
+ Civil liens or judgments
+ Orders of protection, for or against
+ Divorce: child support, alimony (whether in arrears)
+ Estimated net worth and financial obligations
+ Property owned or defaulted on
+ Current income; projected salary
+ Residency, renter or owner (for how long)
+ Relatives (children, parents) and friends or associates in low and high places
+ Hobbies and interests
+ Education: research, verify, and quantify claimed educational achievements, professional licenses (e.g., nurse, real estate, attorney)
+ Professional accolades or misconduct

Subjective
+ Possible conflicts of interest (e.g., nepotism, financial, moral)
+ Sexual indiscretions or affairs (evidence must be quantifiable)
+ Rumors about character (e.g., bad temper, intellect, reliability, honesty)

Political
+ Voting history and party enrollment (quantifiable evidence)
+ Campaign themes (current and past); a summary of ideals and values
+ Issues that separate candidates; project analysis
+ Residency in political district; how long and where?
+ Financial solvency and political campaign disclosures

Incumbents' concerns
+ Travel expenses (including possible misuse)
+ Pay increases (voted for themselves or others)
+ Attendance at required meetings
+ Previous candidate financial disclosure statements
+ Changes in policy
+ Hiring history: veterans, minorities, family, friends

If research into the opposition's campaign is pursued, a brief information summary should be placed in a "for your eyes only" folder and given only to the candidate and CM. This summary should critique the opposition's accomplishments and faults; and identify the political ideology and possible campaign strategy, highlighting weak areas and strengths. This research into the personality of the opposition will help to form opinions on how the other candidate will react to issues and questions, especially during a debate.

The greatest benefit to a candidate is to identify an opponent's differences on issues and ideology. Voters must be aware of how those differences will influence their lives. They also will help campaign staff present the candidate's platform in a positive light.

Very few candidates will admit that opposition research occurs. But everyone does it to a certain extent, even if it is a mere inquiry regarding a person's beverage preference (Shadegg 1964, 79). Direct intrusion into an opponent's life not only is tacky, it may be illegal. Exposing potentially damaging evidence about the opposition may reveal the candidate's and the campaign team's true character. Our political system is designed to protect the voter through factual discourse. The disclosure of accurate information is not a means of exercising a personal vendetta against the opposition, but an effort to seek political equilibrium through transparency.

> *Tip:* To avoid negative repercussions, properly dispose of the summary as soon as possible.

Resources for Gathering Statistics

Consult the US Census Bureau and city or business directories for information on geography (land area, water); population (ethnic composition, median age); education (schools and colleges); household demographics (median income, family sizes, house prices); county, state, national ranking; industry and employment data; transportation (air, rail, roads, car, bus, waterways).

Consult the BOE for election-related statistics, political party composition and population density, and voting preferences (see Voting Blocs).

Online Sources for Demographic and Statistical Research
   + http://factfinder.census.gov/
   + www.city-data.com
   + http://www.nased.org

Nuts and Bolts

   + Collect factual data on demographics, polling, and voting characteristics in the election district.
   + Analyze voting trends and lifestyle changes.
   + Analyze nominating petition signature geographical densities.*
   + Compile opposition research, if requested to do so by the candidate.
   + Archive relevant data for future use.

   * Some canvassers will work harder than others. Areas with low signature densities must be revisited.

FINANCIAL OFFICER/TREASURER

▼

Financial officers, or treasurers, are legally responsible for all campaign funds. They must comply with applicable federal, state, and local laws regarding their tasks and duties, including dates for filing campaign financial disclosure forms, guidance on legal contribution limits, and in-kind donations (Grey 1999, 75).

When starting a political campaign, the treasurer should establish a personal rapport with contacts at the IRS, BOE, and the campaign's financial institutions. The treasurer records all passwords, phone numbers, business, and e-mail addresses. This written record should be permanent and should be copied and placed in a secure location.

Foundational Tasks

+ Create a budget with the CM; each manager will submit projected budgets to the CM.
+ Establish a permanent legal mailing address (a PO box or street address).
+ Open a checking account or savings account; certificates of deposit and investments are appropriate as well. The following tasks are also included:
  o Online checking with passwords.
  o Balance and checking activity inquiry.
  o Automatic bill paying (paper check or online bill pay).
  o Online security and computer financial data back-up.
+ Find a mentor who is experienced in this field.
+ Create an online account with the state BOE.
+ Attend weekly executive committee meetings, as assigned.
  o Establish a working relationship with other staff members.
  o Present current financial information at meetings when requested.
+ Establish rules and policy for bill paying; e.g., no invoice, no check.
+ Determine the minimum amount that can be spent without clearance.

+ Obtain or create a working executive committee list, as requested.
+ Start a logbook to record contacts at the bank, BOE, vendors.
+ Advise the CM on investment strategy and cash management.

Items to Remember

+ Print and post campaign disclosure deadline dates.
+ Print and post contribution limits (personal, corporate, family).
+ Keep track of opponent's campaign expenditures (disclosure statements).
+ File end-of-year city, state, and federal tax forms as appropriate.
+ List and record all in-kind donations (see nos. 4 and 5 below).
+ Note fundraisers that are scheduled on or near financial statement cutoff dates.
+ Enter interest or income from investments in campaign financial statements.
+ Establish a separate housekeeping account (see no. 2 below).

1. Establish a Permanent Campaign Address

A post office box address and the address of the treasurer or candidate may be required to open a checking account, create an authorized campaign with the BOE, or to order supplies. Individuals associated with the campaign may come and go, but the PO box will be there, no matter who fills the treasurer's position. One PO box key is assigned to the candidate, and the others are assigned to the campaign manager and treasurer.

Once established, the PO box, headquarters, or other street address becomes the campaign's permanent mailing address and should not be changed. All checks and printed matter will be permanently linked to that address. Note: After Election Day, the candidate may want to continue to accept legal campaign contributions and choose to retain the PO box on a permanent basis.

Associated with permanent address
+ Letterhead and envelope return address
+ Vendor billing
+ Correspondence
+ Business cards for executive committee members
+ Donations; fundraising
+ Official bank, IRS, and BOE correspondence
+ Campaign promotional literature and advertising

Given today's continued challenges to privacy and that some people threaten those in the public eye, including candidates and elected officials, a PO box offers three distinct advantages:

a. A requirement for greater security with envelopes containing monetary contributions and other important documents.
b. An extra layer of insulation protecting the private lives of a candidate and treasurer from unwanted interference. This is particularly relevant if the candidate is a district attorney, sheriff, or judge who incarcerates or convicts criminals on a regular basis. All financial disclosures will contain the campaign's permanent address. Financial disclosures will be accessible to all citizens on request.
c. A stable address enhances the perception that the candidate is involved with an established and secure political campaign.

   Tip: The campaign's post office branch should be centrally located in case the assigned designee should become unavailable. Remember that post office branches (especially rural) do not have uniform hours of business and accessibility to postal lobbies is becoming more problematic.

Consolidation and downsizing of small post offices is on the horizon. If the campaign uses a storefront headquarters, that location will also influence which bank branch is used and where mail is received.

An active address—whether a post office box or a street address—lends permanency to the campaign and encourages donations throughout the year. Note: Some offices (law enforcement or judicial) may have a limited time when funds can be actively solicited. Accepting donations during times of "inactivity" may be legally restricted.

   Tip: Keep up with state laws and bank rules for they may change on a moment's notice. Maintaining a personal rapport and an e-mail relationship with critical personnel will make this task easier. There is a list of state election departments in appendix H. City or county elections departments are usually more user-friendly, but state offices are often more accurate.

2. Determine Banking Procedures

Suggested procedure for establishing a bank account for the campaign:

+ Establish a permanent campaign address (see above).
+ Obtain an Employer Identification Number (EIN) from the IRS.

- Obtain a notarized letter of authorization from the candidate, assigning the treasurer to act on the campaign's behalf.
  - o Many state BOEs have specific forms for banking/treasurer activation.
- Identify who is authorized to sign checks.
- Determine the campaign's legal name. For example:
  - o John Doe for City Council
  - o Committee to Elect Jane Doe
  - o Friends of John Doe
  - o Concerned Citizens for Jane Doe

Establish internal policies and rules for paying bills. Verbal orders are not acceptable. A check cannot be written for supplies or services without an invoice or funds reimbursed without a receipt. Never, under any circumstances, issue a check without the proper documentation in hand. This rule should be made clear at one of the first meetings and universally enforced upon all members of the campaign. Note: Some states do not require receipts when expenditures are under a certain amount. If appropriate, ink stamps may be used to sign checks from donations marked "for deposit only."

Several accounting and bookkeeping software programs are available. A mentor or past treasurer may be able to recommend one, if necessary. Many states have adequate online software for filing financial disclosures.

If state election laws permit, include a copy of each campaign contribution check in the financial disclosures report for the BOE. Record each check number and amount on the bank deposit slip. (Some banks have long business deposit slips with designated lines for individual check numbers and amounts. Use them if they are available.) Ask the bank teller to date stamp every deposit slip and transaction. Retain deposit slips and bank transactions in an orderly fashion. Some banks provide complimentary zippered deposit pouches when accounts are opened. Stationery stores also sell them at reasonable prices.

Many states allow housekeeping accounts, which are dedicated to specific campaign uses, such as paying certain office expenses. Their restrictions and donation limits can be different from those associated with a candidate's account, even though the housekeeping account is under the candidate's financial umbrella. Obtain information from the BOE.

3. Electronic/Online Banking

Choose a bank that has user-friendly Internet access. Place the checking account and financial assets on the bank's password-protected website. The campaign manager and candidate may request "read" capabilities to look at balances and expenditures. Only the treasurer should have "write" capabilities online.

Online accessibility may decrease the number of inquiries from the campaign manager and candidate regarding balances, deposits, and withdrawals. Retain a printed copy of balances for weekly meetings, if required. Change passwords periodically, as often as the bank recommends. The online bank may also offer the ability to print copies of cashed checks.

Having online access to the campaign's checking account is invaluable. To balance the checkbook, compare the online balance with that filed with the BOE. They should match. If not, the bank's copy is usually the one that is correct, but not always. During an active election cycle, the checkbook-balance comparison should be conducted at least once a week.

As Internet banking becomes more sophisticated, online-bill paying will become more accepted. It is instantaneous, eliminates the cost of snail-mail postage, and issues an immediate transaction receipt.

Tip: Obtain at least one set of paper checks as a backup, just in case technology fails.

The treasurer is responsible for the campaign's funds, even if the candidate or someone else has the authority to write checks. Always follow accepted accounting practices. Use a three-ring binder to store mail from the bank and other financial documents. The first page in the binder should be a copy of the codes, passwords, account numbers, and starting balances for all the accounts and software programs. Place a copy of access codes and passwords in a safe place and give one to the campaign manager (or someone trustworthy) in a sealed envelope for safekeeping.

Investment of campaign funds usually needs to be documented with the state BOE. Remember to claim all interest or income on certificates of deposit (CDs) and investments. If investments are made with campaign funds, the BOE usually requires written notification before they are made. Ask the BOE about its procedure.

4. Policy

The treasurer and the campaign manager must be aware of every financial transaction within the campaign. A host of financial business items will require direct communication with campaign members. These can be discussed during the weekly meetings.

The candidate or campaign manager will usually offer input about which bank and post office branch will best serve the campaign's needs. A bank with multiple branches throughout the district may be the best choice, enabling staff to deposit money immediately after a fundraiser, no matter where it is located.

Retain copies of every transaction. The counting of cash must be verified by at least two people in writing. The candidate and campaign manager should decide if one or two signatures will be required on checks. If two signatures are required—the treasurer's plus the candidate's or CM's—all must realize that there will be times when bills cannot be paid immediately. Because two signatures are cumbersome, using only one signature, that of the treasurer, is recommended. No matter which option is used, the treasurer will bear full financial responsibility.

The treasurer should keep a log of all contributions, update it on a daily basis during active periods, and send a copy of all donor and volunteer lists to the communications director. Send an acknowledgment of thanks to all contributors. The responsibility for sending thank-you notes will be assigned by the CM.

> *Tip*: Retain a spreadsheet of contributors for future campaigns, and adopt a universal spreadsheet format.

It is also the treasurer's duty to monitor the opponent's financial disclosure statements for irregularities and propose a course of action if any are discovered. This action should be addressed at the weekly executive committee meeting, documented, and entered into the minutes by the scribe.

A maximum allowable expenditure for bills must be determined. Make sure all disbursals over the set limits are discussed at weekly meetings and entered in the minutes by the secretary/scribe. The amount not requiring clearance is usually under $50–$100 per transaction. The decision is determined by campaign size, mutually agreed-upon internal policy, and state law where applicable. (If a $100-limit is decided on, that does not mean an item for $500 can be purchased without authorization using five checks.) State elections laws will help guide this decision.

The treasurer must maintain a good rapport with the other executive committee members. If a volunteer or functional manager receives an in-kind donation—for example, a computer, office equipment, or billboard space—it must be reported. Mention this at weekly executive committee meetings. Liquidation or transfer of in-kind donations must comply with state election laws. Retain all transaction records for the duration of the required reporting or filing period.

5. Board of Elections Filings

Many states have online or downloadable financial reports. New York State's program is called EFS (Electronic Filing Software) and is very user-friendly. It automatically adds and subtracts entered amounts from certain schedules. In New York and many progressive states, electronic filing is mandatory. Hard copies are accepted only rarely.

The required length of time for retaining documents is often five years, but it could be seven years or more depending on state election laws. A resignation does not absolve treasurers from liability during their periods of tenure. If someone questions a financial transaction, the treasurer must have all the support documents necessary to substantiate it, at least for the retention period.

The candidate, CM, treasurer, and sage counsel should post contribution limits and dates for filing deadlines conspicuously near the computer. Also place deadline reminders in any electronic devices or computers. The treasurer may wish to inform other functional managers of the financial filing dates and deadlines. It may not be in the treasurer's best interest to schedule a fundraising event on a filing cutoff date, although it's not always possible to avoid (Grey 1999, 98).

> *Tip*: There may be a fine if the treasurer files a late financial disclosure. A fine may be only a slight worry compared to the "bad press." A late filing may provoke the opposition candidate to issue a public accusation of malfeasance or possible fraud with illegal activity hidden in the lack of transparency (Thomas 1999, 21).

6. Computer Files

Many of the computer files and filing disclosure forms will need periodic backup. USB flash cards, memory sticks, or thumbnail drives are great for this purpose. They are inexpensive and highly portable. A copy of the campaign disclosure files can also be sent as an e-mail attachment to the candidate and campaign manager. When sending any files, please accentuate the importance of file backup to the recipient. Ultimately, the treasurer is responsible.

The treasurer may also want to make a hard-copy backup in case of computer failure. One of the first campaign expenditures should be for a large accordion file to retain support documents, bills, and receipts. Always print and retain a hard copy of receipts from online transactions. Even in the event of computer failure, the treasurer is still required to file a financial disclosure and tax statements with the state, and perhaps the city, county, and federal government as well.

Save e-mails from vendors, managers, and staff with instructions about which bills need to be paid. Always properly file and maintain receipts for paid bills. A bill can be scanned and attached to an e-mail, if it is legal in the state. Save both electronic and hard copies.

All in-kind donations, computers, and software purchases from campaign funds belong to the campaign, not to the treasurer or staff. If the campaign is liquidated after the election, disbursal of funds and donated items must comply with the state's election laws and be properly documented. Ask the sage counsel and BOE about how to proceed.

The treasurer must verify transactions and balance the checkbook on a weekly basis. It may help to print a hard copy of the disclosure and bank statement. Then compare it to the checkbook register and, if both match, write on the statement "balanced" with the date and your signature. Observe proper accounting practices. Place those documents in the three-ring binder, which should be stored in a safe place in the treasurer's residence. Treasurers should always retain copies of all transactions that occur during their tenures.

7. Mentoring

Ask the candidate, campaign manager, or party chair for an introduction to the party treasurer or campaign treasurer familiar with a similar elected office (see Mentoring).

8. Budget

Treasurers are the gatekeepers of the budget. They must compile the financial requests from each functional manager and present a unified budget to the candidate and CM for approval. It is the CM's and the treasurer's duty to instruct each manager on the need to develop a friendly yet professional rapport with vendors and to be frugal with purchases but search for the highest quality. Oversight of monetary expenditures is shared by the CM and treasurer.

The treasurer should not try to reinvent the wheel. Successful practices from previous campaigns can serve as a guide. The BOE has historical documents and financial statements from past and present campaigns. It may be advantageous for the treasurer to use past budgets as a framework to compile a budget for the office in question. The treasurer must scrutinize the opposition candidate's financial disclosure statements filed with the BOE (see Budget and appendix G).

Standards

In essence, the treasurer is held to the highest standard within the campaign. Cultures and trends change, as do laws. Applicable local, state, and federal election laws must be strictly followed. Note: Always keep in mind that the past indiscretions of previous treasurers or advice from a mentor does not excuse laxity or misappropriations. Treasurers are usually the only campaign staff members to take oaths of office (through their notarized signatures). They alone accept all responsibility for campaign finances.

Nuts and Bolts

+ Find a mentor.
+ Research and explore all campaign financial tasks.
+ Comply with federal, state, and county election laws.
+ Follow legal guidelines for contribution limits, whether individual, family, or corporate.
+ Take responsibility for all campaign finances: pay bills; deposit donations and loans.
+ Manage campaign bank savings and checking accounts and investments.
+ Establish a legal address for the campaign.
+ Maintain financial records, with computerized and hard-copy backup.
+ File accurate and timely financial statements with proper authorities.
+ Monitor and report on the opposition candidate's financial disclosure statements.
+ Archive records for future campaigns.
+ Keep up-to-date with online accessibility standards.
+ File federal, state, and local income tax forms as required.
+ Compile functional manager budget requests.
+ Create a campaign budget with the candidate and CM using previous campaigns as a guide.

COMMUNICATIONS DIRECTOR

▼

Communications directors connect the campaign to the media and voters through the use of available software programs and communications and marketing tools. They present the candidate's reputation and image to constituents.

This position also establishes and oversees the Internet precinct and campaign website, and uses it as a base for data mining within the candidate's district as well as for maintaining traditional methods of communication, such as debate talking points, press releases, and letters to the editor.

Communications Director's Responsibilities

+ Media: drafts and edits press releases.
    o Responds to reporter inquiries via the candidate or campaign manager.
+ Computers: performs the following duties:
    o Chooses an Internet service provider (ISP) and establishes a domain name.
    o Oversees voter and fundraising list acquisition, generation, and dissemination.
    o Handles the Internet precinct and weekly newscasts.
+ Oversees creation and maintains website—credit-card acceptance (e.g., Paypal).
+ Uses e-mail and texting as an advertising and communications tool.
+ Drafts speeches and talking points.
    o Arranges for and manages public-speaking opportunities.
+ Oversees the "letters to the editor" initiative on behalf of the candidate.
+ Manages the campaign's cell phones and phone banks.
+ Designs a thank-you note and campaign letterhead template for executive committee use.
+ Manages debates and similar events, e.g., evenings with the candidate.
+ Organizes and analyzes a voter feedback loop; Internet polling.
+ Creates and manages the crisis team (see Crisis Management).

Support Professionals

- ✦ Advertising agency/public relations representatives, political consultants (contractors)
- ✦ Computer specialist (contractor or staff)
- ✦ Graphic designer (contractor)
- ✦ Photographer (contractor or staff)
- ✦ Audiovisual specialist (contractor)

Corporations dealing exclusively with political advertising, communications, and public relations are a good investment if they can provide the campaign with talented people and strategic analysis on a contractual basis. However, their cost often ventures far beyond their effectiveness if they are left unsupervised. Obtain a recommendation from a previously successful candidate. Political consultants often lack objectivity and have a financial interest in corporations that market phone banks, direct mail, software, polling, or media advertising services (Green and Gerber 2004, 4).

Press Releases and Interviews

Many candidates are darlings of the press, and these positive relationships may follow them throughout their political careers. However, it would be disingenuous to present the media through rose-colored glasses and expect every candidate to be offered an equal degree of coverage and forgiveness (Faucheux and Herrnson 2001, 140). Because "political candidacy can be a full contact sport" (Shadegg 1964, 11), candidates and their executive committees should take the next few paragraphs to heart.

Reporters are ultimately rewarded for increasing readership or viewership. Therefore, they frequently seek stories with turmoil and confrontation because they generate greater public interest (Shaw 2000, 190). Any dealings with the press should be a strategic judgment call and merit discussion at the weekly executive committee meetings.

Journalists ultimately decide which candidate, events, and issues are noteworthy for coverage. A phenomenon known as "pack journalism" may unknowingly establish a theme that crushes or carries a candidate to victory (Joslyn 1984, 110; Morris 1999, 91). For example, the media falsely depicted President Gerald Ford as a "klutz" and "bumbler" who couldn't walk and chew gum at the same time (Kessler 2009, 52).

If the candidate is verbose, the media may slice and dice the communication and present it to the public in any way they desire—from out-of-context sound bites to downright inaccurate reports. In reality, the candidate has little recourse in correcting errant news articles. It may actually be more damaging to the candidate's image to revisit a divisive news article to seek corrective action. Once something is in print, it becomes reality to many voters. Even a retraction may only amplify the issue and perhaps ensure that the story reaches a completely new audience. However, that does not mean that conscious distortions by the media should go unaddressed. The campaign team should do everything possible to prevent negative stories from materializing in the first place.

The candidate must welcome reporters but should always be vigilant when they are nearby. Any verbal misstep, political gaffe, joke, or offhand remark may show up in an evening newscast, online video, or newspaper article.

It is an unfortunate reality that until a relationship of honor and trust is established with individual reporters, candidates should only offer brief talking points to the press. Yes, this is a defensive posture, but many very smart and adept politicians have been destroyed by media coverage that may or may not have been justified. Candidates and their staff should never speak to reporters off the record, since many people believe that no such attribute exists. In addition, a reporter might have established a professional or personal relationship with an opponent, especially if the opponent is an incumbent. Reporters are human, and some are more successful than others at distancing themselves from their own political ideals. This does not mean that reporters use their place in the public eye to generate media bias. However, some in the media may view the world through different eyes as they report what they see or hear (Pelosi 2007, 142).

In short, be very careful during any type of discourse with the press. A candidate might be a hardworking public servant whose campaign has made a Herculean effort for months. And thanks to the interpretation of one comment, it could all evaporate days before the election.

Press Kits

Kits are distributed to the media in a large envelope or folder. They should include:

- Candidate's résumé or biography
- Mission statement (a brief essay highlighting key issues) on campaign letterhead
- Three pictures:
    - Candidate frontal—shoulders up
    - Candidate with family
    - Candidate with voters
- Palm card, handbill
- Announcement of candidacy
- News releases

- Campaign media contact
  - o   Name, address, phone, e-mail
- Website address (e.g., www.johndoeformayor.com)
- Endorsements
- Logo and slogan

(Beaudry 1986, 126)

Database Specialists

It is mandatory to have at least one person on board the campaign who is computer savvy. Database specialists create spreadsheets and use them to sort the raw data and produce mailing labels for fundraising or voter mail merges. Volunteers can enter the data into spreadsheets (see Office Manager). An internal helpline can guide staff and volunteers through the labyrinth of lists and proper sorting of the data. Hold training sessions to help volunteers and staff complete mail merges and enter information in the database.

The Internet Precinct

The year 2008 was the first presidential election in which Washington, DC, truly discovered the Internet. It is one of the most powerful and useful tools in a campaign's arsenal, yet few capitalize on its full potential. The Internet precinct unites the existing political framework with modern technology to enhance communication and data collection. It is not a standalone electronic initiative but an embedded and technologically savvy platform that connects the campaign to voters.

The campaign's website is home base and should be multifunctional in scope, reaching out to constituents on a personal and professional basis and collecting their phone numbers, addresses, and e-mail addresses. The Internet precinct carries personal messages—taken from the candidate's speeches and talking points—to individual voters with issues tailored to their interests.

The website, e-mail, blogs, chat rooms, Myspace, Twitter, YouTube, LinkedIn, and Facebook are only a few of the social media networking tools that can be used in a campaign (Pelosi 2007, 40). They are invaluable sources of contributions and media exposure, and can inform the electorate about the candidate's platform and current political events. The list of innovative resources will soon incorporate many other ways of communicating with constituents. Proper oversight and adroit use of current technology is essential to the campaign's advertising program. Smaller campaigns may choose to focus only on one or two of these methods. Note: There is a growing concern among political insiders that the mainstream media, which has established a degree of professionalism, will be supplanted by Internet bloggers and aficionados who are gaining market share daily (Bai 2007, 232).

For the campaign to fully utilize the electorate's interest in the candidate, the website must be a valuable and accessible resource. While gathering demographic information, the statistician will access a great deal of data of likely interest to residents. For instance, a list of businesses in the election district might be of interest to job seekers; information on property tax exemptions may be valuable to homeowners.

The Internet precinct pools all the resources from each functional manager's discipline to enhance the physical presence of campaign personnel during door-to-door canvassing through GPS mapping, updated walking lists, voter registration, and absentee voter programs. Posting the candidate's biography, résumé, talking points, fundraising icons, and online video clips helps the campaign develop a rapport with the voters. Through the website, the campaign also can solicit input from constituents as well as donations and volunteers.

Updating voter registration rosters and obtaining e-mail addresses to keep voters in the campaign loop can be advantageous, but many people feel that phone calls and e-mail solicitations intrude on their privacy. Robo-calls (robotic-computerized phone calls) are often viewed very negatively by the electorate but are seen as positive by advertising agencies that profit from tools sold to candidates (Green and Gerber 2004, 5).

> *Tip:* Keep in mind that voters' telephone numbers and e-mail addresses may have been
> provided to the BOE during the voter registration process. Provide a mechanism online
> that allows people to (opt out) unsubscribe to mailings.

The Internet precinct mines data from established geopolitical areas, such as wards and precincts, to gather e-mail addresses from voters. This helps form an electronic link between the campaign and the electorate. In addition, voters should be informed by canvassers and campaign staff that the candidate's website is a valuable resource (see Internet Precinct).

The Blastcast

The blastcast is a weekly newsletter with the latest political news and events in the campaign and the election district. In both small campaigns (functional manager model) and large campaigns (unit manager model), the blastcast originates with the communications director. However, in the large campaign model, the communications director may send the newscast to unit managers, who then disseminate it with a message tailored to their areas of influence (voting districts).

Note: All weekly (re-mail) communications originating or modified by the unit managers, going to constituents in a given geopolitical area, must be edited for content and correctness by the communications director or a member of their staff.

> *Tip*: A style of e-mail software should be adopted that does not divulge the recipient's private e-mail address, but only shows one generic address from the campaign's address book.

The Website

The candidate and campaign manager select the domain name. The communications director determines the technical aspects of how to obtain the domain name and which company to use as an ISP or website hosting agent. The communications director also oversees the technical aspects of online credit card donations (e.g., Paypal). All discussions on obtaining contributions through the Internet must include the treasurer and fundraising chair. The website design, which should reflect the campaign theme, will be approved by the candidate and the executive committee.

List Creation

The communications director should save newspaper articles, video or audio clips, or online articles about possible adversaries and advocates, campaign issues, and topics of local interest. It is also a good policy to save the newspaper sections about those people in the voting district who are away in college or in the military; their names can be the beginning of an absentee-ballot list. Some newspapers publish "In the Military" and "Away to College" sections in their Sunday editions. If possible, obtain the electronic file, or scan the newspaper articles, filing them by topic and date to permit future keyword searching.

In this campaign model, the office manager is in charge of raw-data input and keyboarding. However, this can also be one of the "pool" tasks, as mentioned later. In a smaller campaign, one without an office manager or an official headquarters, the secretary/scribe will be responsible for this work. Assignment of tasks within job descriptions will be decided at executive committee meetings. Regardless, one person must be responsible for the input of the data. In larger campaigns, one person can be asked to create a list for a specific area (e.g., absentee ballots in ward 2). Ownership in the list will offer a person responsibility and inclusion in the campaign.

Without proper training, volunteers and staff will not know how to gather, enter, or sort raw data. A staff member must be designated to monitor work assignment progress, and the statistician should occasionally pattern match data between geographical areas. Voting districts with similar demographics should have relatively similar data. Dissimilar data may indicate the need for more volunteers to canvass areas to obtain nominating petition signatures, or to increase the number of registered voters or absentee ballots. Reward good work, but replace and reassign those who do not complete their assignments. Replicate success.

Updating voter and fundraising lists is an extremely important component of advertising, volunteerism, and fundraising. Accurate computerized lists will touch nearly every job function. This is why this book addresses lists as a separate entity (see Computer Lists).

Security

Computer security is an important issue in a campaign. The communications director should outline procedures for functional managers and staff to help secure confidential data. Many people have business e-mail accounts and their home computers might be accessed by their children or others. A staff member might lose a computer or have it stolen. A discarded or replaced computer could be sold at a garage sale, with the old files still intact and accessible.

Campaign personnel must act as though all e-mails have the potential to be accessed. E-mail correspondence is rarely 100-percent secure. Some businesses automatically include a security notification and agreement at the end of every sent e-mail to warn people about the lack of privacy. The campaign must consider several security techniques that do not hinder internal communication methods or the distribution of information.

Do not allow updated fundraising lists, voter lists, campaign schedules, or calendars to fall into the wrong hands. Every member should be well informed, but lists should be distributed on a need to know basis.

Speeches

The communications director should create four canned speeches on current issues. Suggestions include:

- ✦ Education
- ✦ Crime and punishment
- ✦ Environment
- ✦ Economic development: small business and job creation
- ✦ School, property, and sales taxes
- ✦ Consolidation of governmental services

- ◆ Health care, including Medicare and Medicaid
- ◆ Local infrastructure improvements: water, sewer, roads, sidewalks, and playgrounds

The content for these four basic speeches should be generated through brainstorming sessions in the executive committee, by utilizing the data from newspaper articles saved by the communications director and personal knowledge. The speeches and talking points can be refined through door-to-door polling and other feedback tools.

> *Tip:* Do not identify the campaign with any issue that can be resolved by an opposition incumbent or party during the election cycle.

Initially, candidates either memorize speeches verbatim or use an outline, whatever method works for them. Campaign managers or designated spokespeople have input too because they may fill in for candidates when scheduling conflicts arise. The candidate, campaign manager, and communications director will write and edit the candidate's speeches and press releases.

Once the campaign is in full swing, the speeches will be refined for style and honed to reflect current issues and voter feedback. The four talking points on speeches will be weighted and assigned value based on the audience's response. Rarely should a talking point be abandoned entirely; to do so may send a "waffling on the issues" message to voters, the media, and the opposition. Set a good course at the outset of the campaign by focusing on issues that will expand and resonate well in the community. Issues should be an extension of the campaign theme and the four talking points.

Voters work hard every day and are bombarded with information. Their exposure to a political campaign may be hit-and-miss newspaper articles, radio, or TV sound bites. Voters may become confused if the candidate focuses on more than four main issues. An elected official can focus on many issues, but a campaigning candidate is forced to address only key points during a limited time frame. When voters think of a political candidate, at least two positive issues must surface immediately.

> *Tip:* Voters cannot be in doubt with what the candidate is "all about."

Public Speaking

Candidates must hone their speaking abilities to a fine edge. The Dale Carnegie Course and Toastmasters are great training grounds for those who want to learn how to speak well in public. Local colleges usually offer courses too. Relaxed assuredness comes from speaking experience. Candidates should practice this skill by slowly increasing the size of their listening audiences.

There are a number of easy ways to improve one's speaking skills. Candidates can videotape their speeches (or use a webcam to do so) to help critique their technique. Publicists can also help to critique the video by offering professional suggestions. A webcam-recorded video message can be e-mailed to a publicist. In this case, a signed confidentiality agreement may be required.

Candidates should always speak slowly and be articulate, remain relaxed, and be knowledgeable on the subject matter. They should look the audience in the eye and glance from person to person, occasionally addressing someone by name. There are many effective ways to present issues, but this style of interaction is the best one when mastered properly. A selection of video clips showing the candidate's best speeches can be placed on the campaign website.

Letters to the Editor

This area of the campaign is extremely important and a philosophy unto itself (see Letters to the Editor).

Cell Phones and Phone Banks

Methods of communication can change very rapidly, and the campaign should utilize cutting-edge technologies, such as cell phones and handheld mobile devices. However, reliability, cost, cellular or Wi-Fi coverage, and ease of use are important features. When considering a contract for services, discuss this with telephone carriers (AT&T, Verizon, Sprint, etc.), campaign computer staff, and the executive committee members.

One thing to keep in mind is that any phone call made on behalf of the campaign will be viewed on the voter's caller ID. If phone banks are used in a location other than the headquarters, blocking the caller ID may be an issue. Phone banks using small groups of volunteers can be very effective, allowing managers, staff, and volunteers to reach out to neighbors, relatives, business associates, and friends during crucial phases of the campaign (see Volunteer Coordinator/Recruiter/Phone Banks).

Debates and Other Events with the Candidate

The strategy for debating is very involved and is not covered here in-depth. Candidates will soon realize that there are many issues that affect the entire district. Their remarks should be tailored to the audience and coincide with the campaign's theme and the four talking points. Interviewers and reporters may ask the same basic questions over and over throughout the election cycle.

No matter how trite or repetitive the questions become, candidates must respond with energy and enthusiasm every time. They should always remember to thank the person or organization hosting the debate. This should be done during the introductory statement as well as during the conclusion.

Maps and GPS Devices

Maps are available, usually at cost, from the BOE; county, city, or town engineering departments or clerks; or copied at the public library. Some Internet search engines, e.g., Google and Bing, have good map programs that are free of charge. Maps found on the Internet, however, may not include political or school district boundaries. If the candidate is endorsed by a political party, it may have electronic maps available for the campaign's use.

In the future, some search engines will provide a "3-D street view" to offer a photo of streets and houses on the ground level. Conceivably, computers at campaign headquarters or elsewhere could track and monitor the door-to-door progress of canvassers by using GPS tracking capability in real time (Grey 1999, 81).

The one advantage of the BOE-generated maps is that their political boundaries are clearly marked. However, sometimes the BOE maps are not as current as maps generated in other areas (such as the Internet). The campaign needs to have accurate maps that reflect political boundaries, party enrollment, and population densities to monitor canvassing progress.

Nuts and Bolts

- Press releases and interviews
- Press kits
- Internet precinct
  - Internet service provider
  - Website: advertising, contributions, blastcast, webcam video clips/YouTube, events roster, calendar of current events
  - E-mail address collection
  - Interactive team software compatibility
  - Blogs
  - Chat rooms
  - Social networking sites: MySpace, Facebook, Twitter, etc.

- Computer specialist and statistician
  - Mail merges: letters and envelopes
  - All lists: creation and maintenance:
    - Fundraising: contributors
    - Door-to-door walking lists
    - Demographics and statistics
    - Volunteers and staff
    - Targeted and bulk mailing lists
    - Nominating petitions
    - Lawn sign lists (who has, who wants)
    - Executive committee membership
    - Meeting minutes (from secretary/scribe)
  - Spreadsheets
  - Computer helpline
  - Computer security and firewalls
  - Domain name
- Speeches
- Maps and GPS devices
- Debates, interviews, and other events with the candidate
- Voter feedback loop
- Crisis-management team
- Letters to the editor
- Phone banks
  - Cell phones and phones at headquarters
- Volunteer media kit (see Volunteer Coordinator/Recruiter)

SCHEDULING OFFICER/SCHEDULER

▼

The scheduling officer's primary task is to maintain a calendar of events and ensure that the candidate, executive committee, and staff are properly notified about social events and campaign functions. The scheduler will guarantee that the candidate is transported to places on time, and events within the election district do not conflict with other activities on the campaign schedule.

The scheduling officer must maintain a good working relationship with the other functional managers and help them and the candidate resolve scheduling conflicts. This position requires a working familiarity with computers.

The planning of weekly executive committee meetings also falls within the scheduler's responsibilities. If necessary, the scheduler can help at events by arranging for the appropriate complement of volunteers and staff.

The scheduler also creates, manages, and staffs the transportation pool. Several vehicle drivers should be recruited and assigned to the candidate. The drivers must be familiar with the district and possess valid, conviction-free driver's licenses (Grey 1999, 120). Dates, times, and locations of events will be posted on a calendar and properly annotated in an associated linear schedule. A GPS and cell phone, with adequate coverage in the district, are always good traveling companions.

The overall goal is to remove as many menial tasks as possible from the candidate's plate. The candidate must be free to focus on interactions with people, which is difficult when they are trying to find a parking place.

The scheduler must be aware of polling results, demographics, voter enrollment, and voting patterns to properly assess the importance of why a candidate should attend a function in a specific geographical area. The candidate's personal needs and individual eccentricities must also be taken into account; he or she will need time to freshen up, go over a speech, go to the bathroom, and eat (Woo 1980, 111).

At the beginning of the campaign, a software program involving scheduling should be chosen jointly by the scheduling officer, campaign manager, computer specialist, and communications director. The program chosen must be applicable to and standardized for use throughout all areas of the campaign.

The foundation of the scheduler's organizational platform is the creation of a master spreadsheet for sorting and differentiating events and activities based on time, task, and district. The spreadsheet should include information gathered from all concerned sources (see appendices B and C). Unit managers can also enter local information on separate spreadsheets and send them via e-mail (or other method) to the scheduler. As technology advances, alternate methods for sharing information may become available. The communications director must incorporate these methods into the campaign model. Hard-copy forms for gathering information about events around the district can be given to those volunteers who may not have Internet access or be technically savvy. Do what is easiest and works best.

The scheduler should also add any information to the master spreadsheet that is only available at the central campaign level, such as personal or event data collected from the website. The scheduler will periodically inform the candidate, managers, and staff (via e-mail, reports at weekly meetings, or the US mail) about the data that have been collected.

There are state, county, and city offices, chambers of commerce, and independent advertising agencies that deal directly with tourism and civic and public events held within the election district. Such events include the Memorial Day parade, Founders Day activities, Independence Day picnics, and booths at the county fair, not to mention the senior citizens' quilting class. These offices can assist schedulers and unit managers in compiling the required data.

Foundational Tasks

+ Create a master spreadsheet that includes data about all campaign events.
+ Create two calendars and a linear schedule from the master spreadsheet.
   o Candidate's calendar: for rallies, speeches, and events
   o Linear schedule: outlining specific details from the candidate's calendar
      ▪ Unit managers will maintain separate calendars for their election districts (in unison with the master spreadsheet).
+ Schedule weekly executive committee meetings, at the same place, time, and day of the week, when possible.
+ Establish a transportation pool; serve as manager of transportation policy and driver recruitment.

- o Utilize driver pool for transport to the polls on Election Day and during GOTV efforts.
- • Set up a countdown calendar forty-five to thirty days prior to Election Day and GOTV efforts.
- • Ensure a seamless workflow by helping other managers with their projects when necessary.
  - o Provide material and literature at campaign events.
  - o Provide a sign-in clipboard at events to increase e-mail, fundraising, and volunteer lists.
  - o Send thank-you notes after events.
  - o Help to increase attendance at events, if requested (motivate and rally).

At first glance, the scheduler's duties seem sophisticated, but in fact they are not complex. A small campaign only needs a calendar for event compatibility and organization. In a larger campaign, with unit managers, the scheduler will create and use all the items listed above. The detail and complexity of the scheduler's duties depend upon the size of the campaign and the election district's population.

The master event spreadsheet consolidates every event in or near the campaign district. The candidate and managers can view, download, and print schedules using their mobile devices or computers. An Internet-based calendar will allow everyone to have equal access.

The candidate's calendar and linear schedule are outlined in the example below (see The Candidate's Calendar). Having a single-page, monthly calendar may be challenging if numerous events are scheduled. Instead, segment the calendar with one or two weeks on a page, as space allows. Leave vacant space in the calendars and linear schedule for the input of new events and impromptu invitations.

The linear schedule should accurately reflect contact names, phone numbers, addresses, event themes, times, and dress codes.

The unit manager's calendar is used in large campaigns. It includes all events, meetings, and functions held within the unit manager's geopolitical area (e.g., county, ward, or precinct).

Creation and maintenance of these calendars depends on what works best for the intended audience. The scheduler should create an easy-to-use framework that the unit and functional managers, staff, and volunteers can follow.

Software Framework

The computer team will design the master spreadsheet, using the examples in appendices B and C as a guide. This collaborative team will also determine which computer software program to use. This decision is purely an administrative one and should be discussed during a weekly executive committee meeting, with input from the computer specialist (see Communications Director). The style of calendar, coding of spreadsheet fields and the method employed to acquire and distribute the sorted event data will be a discussion for one of the first campaign meetings. If one style does not work, it can be scrapped and replaced with another. Use what works best for the campaign.

> *Tip*: Implement file backups at least weekly. Even a search engine like Google is not impervious to computer glitches, maintenance downtime, or computer hackers.

There are several types of calendars available online. One of the best, currently available free of charge, is produced by Google (see www.google.com/calendar). The calendar must have a clear and concise format. Create a hard-copy form that allows people to respond to and notify the campaign about events in their area; however, direct phone contact and e-mail follow-up is faster. With e-mail, there also is the ability to archive receipts. Contact the grassroots committee at the ward and precinct level to identify smaller neighborhood events that are normally off the campaign's radar. Keep in mind that the campaign staff may not have compatible software on their home computers or mobile devices. Thus, it might be a good idea to distribute an up-to-date hard copy at weekly meetings.

Once it is in place, the maintenance of the spreadsheet and associated calendars is in the domain of the scheduling officer. Inform the computer specialist about any technical glitches (see Communications Director).

The Candidate's Calendar

This calendar should list events in a plain and simple style without being complicated or cumbersome. One suggestion: code events by placing a number and letter after each one (see table on the next page). The linear schedule should include more information about the event: name, address, point-of-contact, phone numbers, e-mail addresses, and any other pertinent information. For example: *The contact person is your cousin Margie's hair stylist. Her name is Bridget Bar-Doughsky, phone 555-1234* (Woo 1980, 116).

Example: the candidate's calendar for August

21 Friday	22 Saturday	23 Sunday
5:00 p.m. Jones Theater 0821F5 7:00 p.m. Beauty contest 0821F7 8:30 p.m. Blues fest 0821F8:3	11:00 a.m. Elks picnic 0822SA11 2:00 p.m. VFW Atlanta 0822SA2 5:00 p.m. Open	8:00 a.m. Jeanie's Restaurant 23SU08 10:00 a.m. AL rodeo 23SU10 1:00 p.m. Open

The code for the linear schedule has the following format: Friday, August 21 (8/21) at 5:00 p.m. = 0821F5.

0821F5: 5:00 p.m. Jones Theater, 555-3333, 35 Maple Ave., Whatville, NY. Contact Jim Valero, 555-3312 (h), 555-3313 (w), 555-4112 (c); e-mail: Jim@blahjvc.com. Jim is a friend of the CM's. Dress code is semiformal.

0821F7: 7:00 p.m. Johnsville Beauty Contest, 13 Hair Dr., Johnsville, NY. Contact Liz Peupa, 555-2223 (h), 555-3312 (w), 555-4444 (c). She is the wife of Councilman John Peupa. Semiformal attire required (shirt, tie, jacket). Dinner will be served at 7:00 p.m. sharp.

> *Tip:* List physical addresses to aid GPS and map cross-referencing. It also may be advantageous to introduce a 24-hour military-style clock to the campaign. That would eliminate someone mistaking 8 a.m. for 8 p.m., but some people have trouble with military time. Determine what is best for the campaign at a weekly meeting.

> *Tip:* If generic names are used for spreadsheets, e.g., *candidatecalendar*, staff will not know whether the file they have is current. To avoid confusion, insert a date into the file name, e.g., *candidatecalendar0821F*. Internet-based calendars may not experience updating or software-compatibility problems.

Today, calendars and schedules can be accessed by smartphones or other mobile devices, or on the Internet. Every manager, volunteer, and staff member must be kept in the loop about and encouraged to attend all events. The candidate and campaign manager must be reminded of events by e-mail, phone, and at weekly meetings. Every manager should have access to a current list of executive committee members (see Treasurer).

All events must project an inclusive rather than an exclusive character. Introduce a feedback loop to allow staff and volunteers to suggest changes to policy and procedures.

Before any gathering or affair, the scheduler or a designee should place a clipboard and campaign literature at the entrance of the event. This could be one of the driver's duties. The clipboard should have a designated space for each attendee's name, address, zip code, phone and cell phone numbers, and e-mail address. The list's structure should be aligned with the volunteer card and master spreadsheet, so lists can be easily merged.

Place the attendee information in spreadsheets to data mine for possible volunteers, future fundraisers, and targeted direct mailings (Faucheux 2002, 144). Remove duplicates, and incorporate the lists into the core political mailing list. The scheduler must follow through with list creation from beginning to conclusion. The spreadsheet will also serve as a reference for sending thank-you notes, which are a crucial part of any campaign. They should be sent as soon as possible to all attendees at the culmination of every major event, especially where fundraising is concerned. Include a "volunteer" postcard, if that has been approved by the executive committee. Thank-you notes for attendance can be sent via e-mail (which also serves to verify e-mail addresses), but those for donations must be personalized and sent using first-class postage (see appendix A).

Thank-you notes should be signed by the candidate shortly after the event, while memories are fresh. That is one task that can be performed while the candidate is being driven to another event. If the candidate is idle, something is remiss. Efficiency is recognized by the electorate and the other members of the campaign team.

The thank-you notes and letterhead should be designed under the direction of the communications director at the beginning of the campaign. Templates should be available to every manager, offering a professional design with continuity of theme to all campaign correspondence.

Countdown Calendar

When the campaign enters its last days, develop a reverse calendar. Election Day is day zero, the day before Election Day is day one, etc. Businesses do a similar type of countdown calendar when Christmas nears. During the last thirty days, send regular e-mail reminders to all participants—executive committee members, volunteers, likely voters—about pending events and crucial milestones. The CM will determine when the countdown calendar will be activated, at ten, fifteen, thirty, forty-five, or sixty days. Do not spam constituents with too frequent e-mails.

Scheduling

Weekends and holidays are the most highly sought-after time slots for the candidate. Tight schedules are difficult to manage. Whenever possible, the scheduler should build in flexibility.

One good way to achieve this is to cushion the schedule with a less important event next to an important one.

Some candidates find it impossible to break away from talkative supporters at events. A campaign aide should be adept at the "breakaway" maneuver and diplomatically separate the candidate from their talkative supporters. No matter how tight the schedule, the candidate can never seem hurried or uptight. Offer business cards to supporters and invite them to contact the candidate at some point in the near future to continue the conversation.

> *Tip:* Campaign staff and volunteers should never allow the candidate to be manipulated into a time-consuming discussion with intrusive people. An opposition candidate's representative may bait a candidate into an argument and videotape the results for dissemination on the Internet. Campaign aides should be skilled in the polite, non-invasive "breakaway" maneuver.

The candidate must always seem cool, calm, and collected in every circumstance; to look otherwise may send an inaccurate message to their constituency. All the people the candidate meets must come away from the experience feeling enriched and believing that the candidate took time to listen to them and cared about what they had to say. It is a unique gift.

Many of the tasks listed below can be considered pool tasks, and the campaign manager (or executive committee) can reassign them to another functional manager, such as the volunteer coordinator, fundraising chair, or another manager with appropriate skills. The coordination of any event or meeting where donations will be solicited should include the treasurer and fundraising chair.

- Social events on a ward or precinct level (grassroots):
  - Meet and greet; host a home party
  - Pool party
  - Morning coffee
  - Afternoon lunch or tea
  - Rally or street dance
- Event sign-in sheet: design, clipboard responsibility
- Transportation/drivers

Meet and Greet (Hosting a Party)

Before and just after World War II, "meet and greet" events were among politicians' favorite tools. Neighborhood ladies would meet at least once a week for coffee and card games with their relatives, friends, and neighbors. They would love to invite local politicians or other influential community leaders to a morning coffee klatch. This style of gathering offered women political power and social standing at the local level.

Dual-income families are slowly eroding this method of social networking into near obsolescence. Still, the basic "host a party" method remains viable even though the audience has transitioned. Politicians came to realize that the average house party would take most of the evening or afternoon, and usually only ten to twenty people attended. The candidate could use the same time allocation more judiciously by walking door-to-door and meeting two or three times the number of people. However, an informal party ambiance gives voters a relaxed atmosphere in which to share their opinions and ideas.

This method stands out as an effective tool when a local person with influence in the neighborhood hosts the party. It can be a very effective fundraiser and introduce the candidate informally to a select group of voters to whom the campaign might not otherwise have exposure. Use creativity in presentation and good judgment about which functions the candidate attends.

Ensure that a photographer is present at functions where people of influence are in attendance. If money is being solicited, also include the fundraising chair and treasurer. The scheduler must obtain the signatures of influential people at the gathering for the letter of support, which will be printed in the newspaper during the closing days of the election. The volunteer card is another great way to unobtrusively obtain signatures for the letter of support (see appendices A and K).

For details on how to host a party, please refer to Fundraising Event. Hosting a party is similar to a mini-fundraising event, even though donations might not be solicited openly. Invitations can be postcards with follow-up phone calls to encourage attendance. Finger foods and other light refreshments are usually served.

The home party is an informal event whose core function is to distribute campaign literature and obtain pertinent contact information, such as e-mail addresses, from the guests. Ask the treasurer or sage counsel about election laws regarding in-kind donations to the sponsoring host, i.e., the expense for food, refreshments, decorations, etc. The scheduler should ensure the host has an adequate supply of lawn signs and campaign literature.

Do not confuse a "meet and greet" with a "coffee," which is used here to denote a breakfast or brunch get-together with selected voters. If candidates hold down day jobs, every minute of their spare time must be utilized to contact constituents. Pool parties are like meet-and-greet events, but of course they are at swimming pools.

Volunteer cards, the website, campaign headquarters, and sign-in sheets are only a few of the tools the campaign uses to actively recruit volunteers at events. The volunteer card will have a checkbox for those interested in hosting a party, and the scheduler should have regular access to the updated volunteer database. The scheduler also should keep track of all the people who want to host a party. Contact each volunteer to establish a tentative date for the party and the projected attendance and to resolve any conflicts, if necessary. The volunteers should be contacted within a week of their offer; they should feel energized by the scheduler and that they are now an integral part of the campaign team. Offer the hosts of the party a high degree of flexibility in designing their get-together. Party themes usually prove to be eclectic and fun.

Give hosts a list of event necessities to remind them of something they may have forgotten. The scheduler can offer a packet to hosts as a reminder, definitely not as a requirement (see Fundraising Events).

Coffee or Tea Event

The before-work breakfast, coffee, or brunch is friendly and casual. These are grassroots events that establish the candidate's rapport with voters. They are most effective if they take place at restaurants that cater to the breakfast in-crowd. A tea works best in the afternoon, between lunch and dinner.

The candidate must create an atmosphere of belonging. The people who eat at that restaurant every morning want to be members of that in-crowd. Make sure the coffee is inclusive; the campaign should never make anyone feel excluded. Ask the restaurant owner or manager to stop by the table. Project party unity by asking incumbents and party officials to stop by as well (England 1992, 81).

Candidates can informally introduce their agendas with brief talking points derived from their speeches. It is very important to maintain a casual ambiance and not be pushy at the coffee. Allow the restaurant patrons the opportunity to participate.

It is the scheduler's job to touch base with people by phone after a thank-you note has been sent. An inquiry can be made about lawn signs, donations, or volunteer work at that time. It is important not to pressure potential voters in any way, either at the coffee or later during the follow-up call. The focus should be on helping the candidate to tweak the message to voters. It is important to make potential voters feel valued, and their feedback is vital. Constituents need to have their concerns validated by the candidate.

Rally or Street Dance

This is also another holdover from a bygone era, but under certain circumstances it still may be a useful tool. At one time, a neighborhood's young people used to ask the city or town for permission to block off a whole street. The police or fire department would place barrier sawhorses at appropriate points. Then, they'd have a party or rally. There would be a DJ, some food, and Christmas lights in the trees. Festivities began at 6:00 or 7:00 p.m. and went till midnight.

If security is even remotely an issue, then don't use this method. Choose sponsors wisely for every event. Use good judgment. Unfortunately, this type of activity may only be viable in small, rural areas. The candidate, campaign manager, and sage counsel must decide what insurance agent should be consulted to ensure the campaign has proper liability coverage, if deemed necessary.

Conclusion

The fundraising manager, volunteer coordinator, and scheduler perform many similar tasks. Fundraising involves the solicitation of money from donors. The volunteer coordinator is concerned with recruitment and socialization. The scheduler resolves calendar conflicts and arranges small interactions with the candidate and constituents. Depending on the size of the campaign, the CM might consolidate some managerial tasks under one umbrella.

Employing a web-based calendar may decrease the need for cumbersome file transfers. Volunteers and staff may be more comfortable with Microsoft Word or Excel, but a web-based calendar means they do not have to have specific software or operating systems on their home computers. A web-based calendar will also be accessible by handheld mobile devices. Back up all calendars; have a plan A and a plan B.

If requested by the campaign manager, the scheduler can help direct others to supply appropriate support in the form of volunteers, literature, lawn signs, and other relevant materials needed for an event's success.

The election district may have a large population of disabled or elderly voters who do not have transportation to the polls on Election Day. The transportation pool of drivers can be used for this purpose.

Nuts and Bolts

- Create two calendars:
  - o A master calendar that lists all events in the election district.
  - o A linear calendar explaining those events and articulating event rules.
- Design the campaign and the candidate's schedule.
- Help to gather lists of the people who attend those events.
- Create a transportation pool for cars and drivers; recruit drivers.
- The CM will determine which functions and assignments are to be pool tasks.
- Schedule meet and greets with volunteer coordinator.
- Schedule coffees or teas.
- Organize street dance; neighborhood rally.
- GOTV efforts; arrange transportation to the polls on Election Day for the elderly and disabled.

ADVERTISING COORDINATOR

▼

The purpose of political advertising is to create positive name recognition for the candidate. A candidate is elected when a person enters the voting booth and recognizes the candidate's name, in an affirmative light, rather than someone else's. That's it!

The advertising coordinator researches the prices, order time, and setup costs and establishes procedures for purchasing all the advertising and associated items for the campaign. The advertising coordinator sets the stage for disseminating the candidate's vision and message to constituents. Feedback from that message—via the communications director, staff, and volunteers from door-to-door canvassing and phone banks—will help tweak future campaign messages and methods of dissemination. All press releases and interaction with the electorate through the media fall under the communications director's responsibility.

The advertising coordinator and the communications director work hand in glove with one another and must have an excellent rapport to produce a high-quality product. Many of their responsibilities are interchangeable and are assigned based on the size of the campaign and the individual's area of expertise. The two positions could be merged in a small campaign.

The level of assertiveness and tone of the campaign advertising must resonate with the electorate depending on the position the candidate is seeking.

- A district attorney may want to convey an unwavering and firm stance on crime and criminal prosecution.
- A judge may portray a mature tone with judicial acumen but tempered with a degree of compassion.
- A candidate for mayor, city council, or supervisor may choose to focus on current issues, capturing voters' interest before the fizz is gone.

Name recognition usually gives the incumbent an advantage. However, strategic advertising can bridge the gap between newcomer and incumbent. Here are some of the ways to achieve and maintain that advantage.

The Architecture of Campaign Advertising

Advertising materials
- Print advertising
  - Palm cards (handbills—door hangers)
  - Lawn signs and banners
  - Bumper stickers
  - Signs on bus-stop benches and buses
  - Buttons, pens, refrigerator magnets, nail files, etc.
- Preprinted envelopes and letterhead stationery
- Invitations and thank-you notes
- Billboards
- Literature drops (during door-to-door canvassing, rallies)

Delivery methods
- US mail (see Campaign Mailings)
  - Bulk
  - Targeted first-class (see appendix J)
  - Postcard bundling (see Volunteer Coordinator/Postcard Bundling)
- Internet (see Communications Director)
  - E-mail address acquisitions
  - Website
  - Blogs
  - Chat rooms
  - YouTube, Twitter, Facebook, Myspace, and online advertising
- Newspaper (daily and weekly)
  - Style, design, and placement of the advertisement
  - Letters to the editor (see Communications Director)
  - Letters of support (see appendix K)
- Radio
- Television

Support professionals
- Photographer
- Graphic designer

- Computer specialist: lists, e-mails, and file backup
- Advertising consultant for radio and television
- US mail consultant (there are bulk and first-class mail discounts depending on volume and address quality)

Cross-functional Manager Interaction
- Communications director
- Treasurer
- Office manager: sign and literature depot, mailing lists, and mail merges

Print Advertising

Palm cards (hand bills—door hangers), lawn signs, and business cards are campaign staples. They are mandatory items. If finances allow, secondary items are available, including buttons, pens, bumper stickers, refrigerator magnets, and nail files. Preprinted envelopes and letterhead are a classic touch for correspondence as are thank-you notes.

> *Tip:* Avoid purchasing useless trinkets the campaign may never use (McNamara 2008, 83).

The campaign's letterhead should include a list of all the functional managers and their positions as well as the website URL and e-mail addresses. Preprinted forms and blank letterhead should be available to every manager. To establish uniformity, the same style thank-you notes should be used by all managers who correspond with voters, vendors, and contributors. If candidates are endorsed by one or more parties, they may wish to convey that endorsement through advertising and on the letterhead.

Obtain estimates for advertising expenditures from a party member before asking a business owner, who might be associated with the opposition. National-brand stationery stores are usually less expensive. It is more politically astute to purchase locally when possible, keeping union shops and party loyalty in mind. To forgo printing costs, a template for the letterhead and thank-you notes can be created under the communications director's guidance and available to all functional managers for their personal computers (Grey 1999, 80).

Palm Card
Palm cards—handbills are among the best and least expensive forms of personalized advertising. They are the candidate's door-to-door introduction and usually are produced on 9- by 4-inch card stock—small enough to snugly fit inside a #10 envelope. They have bulleted lists with

several talking points and the candidate's picture and slogan. Because of the limited room, the text has to be both substantive and brief (see appendices E and F).

It is advantageous to design a card stock with hanging hook to enable the palm card to be secured to the doorknob when the resident is not home. In political parlance, this is called a "door hanger."

> *Tip:* It is against federal law to place anything but mail in a residential mailbox.

It is also a good idea to have some palm cards with the following note printed in cursive with blue ink: "Sorry I missed you. I'll try back again later" (Thomas 1999, 38). Before the word "sorry," the candidate or canvassing volunteer can write the first name of the absent resident (taken from the door-to-door walking lists), then leave the card at the person's front door. If it is not preprinted or written by the candidate, a campaign staffer can write it in a hand similar to the candidate's (see Door-to-Door Canvassing).

Place a minimal order for palm cards and lawn signs as soon as it is economically viable to do so. There is usually a greater cost for the setup during the first printing. The minimum initial order for palm cards should be a 10:1 ratio. If there are 50,000 registered voters in the affected district start with 5,000 palm cards. Use a 50:1 ratio for the initial lawn sign order unless there are extenuating circumstances, like a large geographical distance. If the distance between constituents is large, more signs may be required to fill the space. During a primary election, the number of palm cards and lawn signs ordered should correspond directly to those who can vote in it, particularly if budgets are tight.

Stay within the campaign's budget; be mindful of price breaks for quantities. Do not order too many initially unless the budget is not an issue. Develop a rapport with the supplier, and confirm delivery times. Write down and log the names and phone extensions of everyone with whom you speak. Be pleasant but professional.

> *Tip:* It is essential to keep tabs on the lead time for palm cards and lawn signs. During the last two months of the campaign, delivery times could double or triple due to increased demand. It would be a disaster to have the candidate or volunteers canvassing without literature, especially the palm card or lawn signs. Keep the treasurer in the loop.

Lawn and Yard Signs
Some cities and towns require a refundable deposit or nonrefundable permit fee before candidates can place lawn signs on private residences in their communities. In addition, some communities have zoning laws that prohibit signs completely or restrict their size, color, and time of placement.

It is usually the city, town, or county clerk (the building codes or zoning ordinance department) that handles this. Each municipality may have its own zoning laws (England 1992, 83).

> *Tip:* Know the zoning law restrictions throughout the election district before ordering signs.

Lawn signs are an integral part of the name-recognition process. Signs instantly deliver a message of endorsement and support. The candidate's last name must be prominent enough for the occupants in passing vehicles to notice at a glance.

Never place a sign on someone's property unless given explicit permission to do so. Voters, even relatives and close friends, can be very territorial, and placing signs on their lawns without permission may cause problems. It is important to have most lawn signs distributed to private homeowners instead of placing them on common highway areas, which many voters view as public land. In the last two weeks of the campaign, collect unused signs and redistribute them to areas where they will be displayed. Assign one person to be in charge of lawn signs—distribution, volunteers, zoning laws.

The optimal utilization of lawn signs is in direct relationship to local policy, culture, and laws. Some areas of the nation are very tolerant of "freedom of speech," and some are not. Sometimes the opposition party will use this as a tool to voice its outrage against a candidate or political party, citing its activism and interest in the welfare of the community against the candidate's placement of signs in public areas. Exuberant volunteers often find creative ways to place signs during GOTV initiatives, regardless of state and local laws or internal campaign rules.

To take advantage of quantity pricing, order signs in fixed batches from the distributor (Thomas 1999, 57). The production time from placing the order to delivery is critical. Be careful of tight scheduling near the campaign's conclusion. Obtain written zoning laws and rules, and send copies of sign ordinances and permits to the sage counsel for legal interpretation.

All campaign literature—palm cards, lawn signs, and bumper stickers—should have the same design and color scheme (Grey 1999, 147). Color is an excellent way to express a political message. Red, white, and blue are good patriotic campaign colors, priced as two colors with white as neutral background. Green could signal a candidate's focus on the environment. Remember that one color is usually less expensive.

Knowledge of the opponent's strategy and theme may allow a campaign to stay a step ahead. Incumbents often stick with a winning program, and tweak it to be current.

The placement of the candidate's picture on stationery or lawn signs is a judgment call. An attractive candidate is rarely a liability, but a picture will open the door to vandalism and graffiti. In the dark of night, few mischievous teenagers can pass up the opportunity to add a moustache, a goatee, and devil horns to a candidate's picture. Some may interpret the resulting image as an indication of a candidate's naivety and lack of political acumen.

Lawn signs usually have to be stapled two or three times to ensure stability, an added guarantee that a good wind, a passing eighteen-wheeler, or a well-placed dropkick does not dislodge them from the stand. Sign maintenance is important, and all sign locations should be revisited periodically by a member of the campaign. Weathered or damaged signs should be replaced.

Whether the candidate wins or not, meticulous attention must be given to the collection of all signs the day after the election. The timely removal of lawn signs offers a clear message about the campaign's organizational efficiency. Some municipalities assess heavy fines when campaigns do not remove signs in a timely manner. Leaving signs out after Election Day is not a class act, especially with a losing candidate, and displays false bravado with a winning one.

Perhaps a deal can be struck so that the other candidates also remove their signs. Having all candidates of the same party help remove signs will greatly increase effectiveness. Determine which candidates want to retain their signage for future use.

Sign Placement
Acquire the names of homeowners near the polling places, and target those houses for lawn signs. If residents do not want to place signs on their properties, ask them not to place signs for the opposition. Someone in the campaign or in the party may be able to reach out to a reluctant property owner on a personal basis to sway him or her to place a sign. Make challenging sign placement a topic for the weekly meetings.

Large, banner-type signs are great for major intersections and highways with a high volume of traffic. Identifying the owners of property at well-traveled intersections and along major roads and highways is very important. Party chairs and members who are real-estate agents are great resources. In an urban setting, bus-stop bench advertising may be popular; a fee may be required.

Target the main roads for signs, especially at the edges of the district near the town, county, or city limits. An abundance of strategically placed lawn signs is an indication of a highly organized and energetic campaign. The display of a candidate's lawn sign is a personal endorsement from the resident.

Transfer all personal contacts into lists: relatives, business associates, and people met through social and religious groups. Segment those lists into geopolitical areas (wards, precincts, districts). Do not forget those friends and relatives who own rental property. When placing signs on rental properties, remember to speak with tenants; they vote too.

There should be several designated locations throughout the district for sign distribution besides campaign headquarters. Lawn-sign storage depots should be easily accessible, such as homes or offices of key staff or party committee members. With such accessibility, volunteers can distribute signs 24/7, unencumbered by the hours of operation at campaign headquarters.

A fire, theft, or natural disaster might remove all the signs from inventory if they are housed in a single location. A network of multiple sign distribution points can help with security. Therefore, local political leaders and campaign representatives should each have a specific number of lawn signs allocated to them for distribution.

Remember, it is all about name recognition!

Intersection Rallies

In the final days of the campaign, it may be advantageous to form an energetic and vocal group of supporters for an intersection rally. Usually, the best time is during the morning or evening of the business day's commute. Use lawn signs and other signs stapled to small boards or sticks. This is a fun activity.

The campaign should provide the rally's volunteers with breakfast or lunch, as appropriate, as well as coffee and snacks. Furnish all necessary signage and supplies. Choose a busy crossroads or intersection for the rally, but not one that is dangerously busy. Choose a location with ample and convenient parking. In addition, ask the proper authorities if permits are required.

The campaign photographer should attend the rally. Notify the media, and supply them with "good photographs" when sending the press release about the event. The candidate or spokesperson should be prepared to offer a brief and substantive interview to reporters.

During weekly meetings, explore innovative ways to advertise the candidate's initiatives. Photos and video clips of rallies and sign waves, accompanied by a brief message, are always good material for the website and the unit manager's or communications director's blastcast e-mails.

Parades

Local municipalities may sponsor Memorial Day, Independence Day, and Labor Day parades. Contact the parade's organizer, and ask if a permit or fee is required to participate. Ensure that placement of the campaign staff and volunteers in the parade promote the candidate's affiliation with veteran or civic organizations, if appropriate.

Form a campaign parade committee, and acquire a properly adorned truck or convertible for the parade. Candidates with their entourages can walk the parade route, providing visibility and shaking hands. The distribution of literature—palm cards, bumper stickers, and buttons—may be prohibited or inappropriate.

> *Tip:* Make sure an adequate number of lawn signs promoting the candidate are visible along the parade route.

Enlist several young people to participate, as they often love parades. Parades are also a great time to show off the entire family. Remember, a political campaign is professional and energetic.

Coordinate the campaign's theme with the parade's theme. The US and state flags are always welcome. Research the proper way to display them, along with the ethnicity, content, and theme of the parade. The culture of every event should always be researched by the scheduling officer or advertising coordinator.

The campaign manager or candidate should approach the parade's organizer and ask if the candidate can speak at the event. Even if that is not possible, the candidate should be prepared to speak. Speaking at an event is usually an advantage held by an incumbent.

Billboards

Research the price of commercial roadside billboards. Professional billboards are often booked months in advance. If the campaign wants to rent billboard space for September through Election Day, the negotiations, contracts, and deposits should be completed and signed no later than the month of June. Other candidates may be vying for the same billboard space (Woo 1980, 87). Maintain the billboard placement until the day after the election. Some party members or the city or county chair may have an "in" with someone. Inquire!

Try not to employ the "construction style" flashing signs that are usually used along roadways to signal maintenance or a hazard, especially during races for sheriff, district attorney, or judges. In some districts there could be severe opposition and push back to this style of advertising.

Remember too that billboards, while higher above the road than lawn signs, are not completely immune from graffiti vandals. A contiguous message and theme is important, but a candidate's picture may be more appropriate for a billboard.

Photography

A smaller campaign can obtain high-quality pictures at a national retail chain store, such as Walmart, Sears, Kmart, Target, etc. A variety of background colors may be required for Internet usage, palm cards, and newspaper ads. Sometimes dark backgrounds are not newsprint friendly but are a classic touch in other mediums. The color and light intensity for backgrounds are also candidate specific. The palm card photograph in appendix F was taken at Walmart, and the fee was very reasonable. The expenses for a professional photographer may not be justified in a small campaign. Perhaps a high school or college photography student may be able to incorporate the experience into their curriculum—for credit.

> *Tip:* Different background colors may be required for photographs to comply with the Internet, newspaper, palm cards, and other advertising used in the campaign.

Candidate, team, family, and campaign-trail photos are essential in a larger campaign. Every candidate will need high-quality photographs for palm cards and advertising. Immediately upon the candidate's declaration of candidacy, three good pictures in different poses (frontal, standing, shaking hands with a voter) should be sent to all media entities with the candidacy announcement (see appendix D).

If the candidate does not issue a high-quality picture to the media, newspapers have a tendency to send a photographer to the first press announcement. The first picture that photographer takes could be one the newspaper will use as its file photograph. It may be very unflattering, yet the publication could use it time and time again. Therefore, it is important to be proactive. Send photos selected by the candidate at weekly executive committee meetings. Keep the media well supplied with high-quality pictures. Ship them by snail mail or e-mail, or have someone personally deliver them.

If a photographer is used, use a highly skilled professional. Photographers must know exactly what is transpiring before they can capture the essence and personality of the campaign, its staff, and the candidate. Evaluate new photographs at weekly meetings: select the ones to be used for advertising, the website, and e-mail blastcasts. Expect excellence from the photographer. Demand nothing less. It is results that counts.

Take photos of the teams during the campaign, but give them to team members only after the election. During the election cycle, the campaign's focus should be on the candidate, but the team should also get some exposure. It is the candidate's choice which outstanding team members should be recognized through media coverage.

Advertising with communal pictures of all candidates from a single party is a good way of expressing party solidarity. A candidate's association with popular incumbents may offer the electorate the perception of a strong united team. Strong teams win elections.

Newspaper Ads and Announcements

Many newspapers do print setups and usually charge for the service. If a graphic designer is on board, the quality of print advertisements may be greatly enhanced. It may not be cheaper or faster, but it will result in a higher quality product, with the campaign preserving a greater degree of control.

Most graphic designers can be contracted on an as-needed basis. The campaign may be able to find a new startup design company that would be interested in political experience. It depends on how much money the campaign has to spend. The advertising coordinator must oversee the quality of a product while facilitating communication between the design team and media.

Print ads must hone in on the candidate's four talking points and campaign theme. In addition, each article should deliver the candidate's message to the voters. If there are too many steps in any procedure, it may get cumbersome. A single design company offering continuous quality will enhance the theme continuum. The candidate's slogan and website domain name should appear on all advertising.

A different message every week will confuse the voters. The voter must be offered an unwavering central theme and message throughout the campaign, and it must be repeated time and time again.

Radio

Radio is not as big an advertising tool as it once was, but it is still important. Prime radio advertising time is usually during the morning and evening commute, i.e., 7:00 a.m. through

9:00 a.m. and 4:00 p.m. through 6:00 p.m. Lunch is also a popular advertising time. Some radio stations have audiences that listen during prime time. Match the candidate's talking points to the audience, stations, and times.

Most radio stations have loyal audiences, guaranteed slots, and fixed rate structures. TV and radio stations must also comply with FCC rules and regulations. Fill out the necessary forms, make copies, and file them with the stations well in advance.

Audio-file formats, like WAV, allow the candidate to record a political message and e-mail it to a radio station. A USB flash card or CD can be used in the same way.

Remember that some radio and television stations will broadcast beyond the political district. Make sure the selected stations' geographical broadcast reach blends well with the voting district's boundaries. Establish a rapport with a single employee at the station as point of contact.

Television

This advertising medium is very important to a larger campaign because it brings the candidate into the living room of the voters. It can articulate positive or negative sound-bite talking points (see Going Negative).

The candidate can hold a press conference to announce items of public interest, although this is another area in which an incumbent has the upper edge (Faucheux 2002, 201). Incumbents can make a big deal out of every dollar the government spends on roads, bridges, museums, and libraries. They often act as though they are giving away their own money.

There are many advantages to being associated with a major party. A popular incumbent in the same party may agree to combine some advertising. Keep tabs on incumbents' calendars, and try to be seen in the background of their photos, TV, or newspaper advertisements. The political party chair may be able to help with this process.

Slogan

Candidates should have slogans that encapsulate their candidacies in one bite, e.g., Restore Integrity, Leadership by Example, Experience Counts, Experience Money Can't Buy (Shaw 2000, 87). The most effective slogan stresses where the candidate is strong and the opposition is weak (Faucheux 2002, 184). The slogan should be synonymous with the candidate (Faucheux 2002, 176). It should appear at the bottom of lawn signs, palm cards, in all advertising, and on the campaign's website. The slogan should be used so universally in the campaign that it becomes almost a subliminal advertising agent itself.

Franklin Delano Roosevelt in 1932, Ronald Reagan in 1980, and Mitt Romney in 2012 all asked the American voters, "Are you better off now than you were four years ago?" (Campbell 2000, 70). General Dwight David Eisenhower, a hardened battlefield commander fresh from a World War II victory, appealed as a regular guy in the 1952 presidential race with the catchy slogan, "I like Ike."

> *Tip:* Spend the time needed to research a good campaign slogan. A large campaign may wish to hire professional help.

Logo

This symbol represents the candidate's campaign. A logo can be a pen-and-ink outline drawing of the city or town hall or a war memorial, bridge, library, or museum. It should be something immediately identifiable to all voters in the district and elicit a positive emotion at a glance. It should be a symbol of solid government—simple, yet effective (Shaw 2000, 92). Many candidates have cleverly incorporated their names as campaign symbols (McNamara 2008, 76).

The logo can also be used as a background symbol or watermark on letterhead and thank-you notes. The basic translation of the Greek word *logos* is "meaning." The campaign's logo should offer the electorate meaning.

Campaign Song or Tune

Connecting the candidate to a song or tune is a nice touch for the campaign. Some voters are more oriented to music than to pictures or speeches. Because voters like consistency, there should be one tune played when the candidate walks on stage or enters a room.

Graphic Designer/Illustrator

A good graphic designer can make or break the printed materials used in the campaign. For example, a designer can use photo-editing software to touch up digital images of the candidate. An illustrator or artist can use a photograph of the candidate to create a good pen-and-ink logo or pencil sketch, which then can be used in advertisements.

Palm cards and lawn signs have to be designed. Several functional managers, including the advertising coordinator, should review the graphic designer's products. However, there should only be one person in the campaign responsible for dealing with contractors such as graphic designers, illustrators, and photographers (Woo 1980, 69). Task assignments are done at the beginning of the campaign in forum at weekly executive committee meetings.

Business Cards

Business cards don't cost much these days and are a permanent and professional touch for executive committee members and functional managers. Many stationery stores will produce 100 to 250 cards at a reasonable cost and in a day or two.

The cards should match other campaign materials in color and design. The executive committee may choose to put the campaign's headquarters or the PO box as the address. One phone number on the card should be the headquarters. Voters may retain and refer to the business cards long after the election (England 1992, 28).

Tenet card
The candidate's business card can have key issues listed as bullet points on the reverse. It is an excellent addendum for the palm card during door-to-door canvassing with nominating petition and voter-registration drives. The bullet points should be organized in a question format. For Republican candidates, the list might be:

+ Do you want smaller government?
+ Do you believe in lower taxes?
+ Do you believe big government is too intrusive in your life?
+ Do you want a strong national defense?

This list gives the candidate an opportunity to place two or three key local issues before the voters and align those issues with party beliefs. The reverse of the business card cannot be busy or cluttered. It can be printed in black type or in the campaign's theme colors. Simple is better!

Democrats, Republicans, Libertarians, Independents, Conservatives, and Liberals can list their philosophies in question formats. Most political parties list their platforms on the Internet. Include at least one or two important local issues on the list.

The idea is to place registered voters on the same wave length as the candidate and their political party.

Letter of Support

The candidate and campaign manager will organize an effort to ask every prominent business owner, politician, and professional (teachers, doctors, lawyers, engineers, politicians, religious leaders) in the election district to sign a letter of support. Potential supporters should also include other community role models, such as key military veterans, influential community leaders, and prominent civic organization representatives whose influence and backing will be essential.

The advertising coordinator then will purchase a full- or half-page newspaper advertisement in the Sunday or Monday edition before Election Day, listing all of the people who signed the letter of support (Shaw 2000, 178). The more prominent the names are, the better it is for the candidate. This important initiative shows that these influential people believe the candidate's policies will help the district.

Try to entice the county or state party to pay for this ad; it may qualify as a campaign funds transfer or in-kind donation. There are legal campaign limits, but sometimes amounts can be shared between entities. Consult the campaign's treasurer, sage counsel, and state BOE.

Many people say they will sign a letter of support, but when it comes right down to it, they will not. It is best to actually have them sign a letter. The volunteer postcard also has a signature area set aside for this reason (see appendix A). A letter of support in the newspaper is similar in content to a letter of reference, espousing certain attributes and beliefs held by the candidate and the people who signed the letter. The letter should be brief and substantive.

Obtain signed letters of support or volunteer card signatures as early in the campaign as possible. Few professionals want to be associated with a hotly contested political campaign in its concluding stages. The Sunday edition letter of support is a very important document, an underutilized but extremely effective campaign tool (see appendix K).

Campaign Mailings

(See Campaign Mailings.)

Nuts and Bolts

- Research prices, ordering time, setup costs, availability, and procedures for purchasing all advertising items.
- Design or order preprinted envelopes, letterhead, and thank-you notes.
- Print advertising: order palm cards, lawn signs, and bumper stickers.
  - o Choose the same color and style for palm cards and lawn signs.
  - o Palm cards: quick reference bullet points (see appendices E and F).
  - o Lawn signs: assign one person to oversee distribution, including picking up signs, recruiting volunteers, and observing zoning laws.
  - o Lawn signs: distribute on main roads, near city limits, and close to polling places (within legal limits).
- Develop a rapport with all suppliers; log names, phone numbers, extensions.
- Use billboards and lawn banners in crucial areas, where land is available.
- Photography: use three styles of photographs (vary the backgrounds).
- Radio: match the message and broadcast times to audience.
- Television: hire an agency to deliver your message.
- Slogan: should encapsulate candidacy in one bite.
- Logo: use local or national symbol of good government.
- Graphic designer: a classy touch to a campaign for theme continuum.
- Personal business cards: order for executive committee and functional managers; be consistent in color and theme.
- Intersection rally: sign-wave campaign lawn signs on a stick.
- Support letter/testimonial: attempt to acquire signatures from all major local professionals.
- Campaign mailings: remember that direct and bulk mailings have different focuses (see Campaign Mailings).

VOLUNTEER COORDINATOR/RECRUITER

▼

The volunteer coordinator recruits campaign volunteers, manages their training, and assigns them tasks.

Recruitment

Recruiting volunteers is such a daunting task that it must be approached in stages. The goal is to harvest the low-hanging fruit from the tree of recruitment first and then methodically gather recruits from a predetermined hierarchical ladder. Exercising this model will divide the effort into manageable portions. The end result will be a diverse, highly motivated, and well-trained team.

As the campaign progresses, the number of volunteers will increase, offering the team a more diverse and trainable group for assignments. The ability of individual volunteers to perform a given set of tasks will depend on their skill level, dedication, and motivation rather than on when they joined the campaign. There can never be too many volunteers. There is a job for everyone (Pelosi 2007, 173).

Establish a master spreadsheet list with the contact information for all campaign volunteers during the early stages of the campaign. Use the categories on the volunteer card as fields. Update the spreadsheet on a frequent basis, and share it with the communications director (see appendices A, B, and C). Actively recruit volunteers during every phase of the campaign. Note: Time and money are finite resources, but campaign volunteers and staff are limited only by the number that can be recruited, trained, and managed effectively.

Vision Quest: The Ladder of Recruitment

Volunteerism is viewed here as a five-tiered hierarchy. The following example will help explain the recruitment process, segment by segment. Imagine a pond with a completely calm surface.

Now toss a pebble into the pond. The stone will strike the water's surface and create a splash, with concentric circles radiating outward. The splash will produce one, two, three, four, five diminutive waves in rapid succession. Hold that thought.

The epicenter of recruitment is symbolized by the pebble's first splash into the water: it contains the primary group of volunteers and supporters. This core group is composed of the executive committee and the candidate's relatives, close friends, neighbors, and business associates. Remember that ten people who are dedicated to work on a campaign is far better than a hundred people who are always too busy to pitch in and help. The number of volunteers is not as important as their quality and motivation.

The second ripple on the surface represents the political party's committee members. A political party is a cohesive unit that embraces and promotes a specific ideological platform. Its committee is an independent entity that works to further each candidate's goals and vision. During an election season, a dozen or more candidates may run under the banner of a single party. In this case, individual committee members may choose to support and circulate petitions for only those candidates they consider to be exceptional.

The third group of recruits is drawn directly from the core group of volunteers, the relatives, friends, neighbors, and coworkers of the campaign's executive committee and others in the inner circle.

The fourth group is formed by the members of civic, social, and religious organizations to which the candidate and campaign manager belong. This group also includes associates of executive committee members.

The fifth and final ripple includes people who have filled out volunteer cards, walk-ins to campaign headquarters, those who sign up online, and those recruited during campaign events and who generally make it known that they want to volunteer (see Computer Lists). Regardless of the hierarchical ladder of recruitment, the executive committee and staff should reach out to anyone who expresses an interest in volunteering for the campaign.

Many of those recruited during the later phases will gravitate toward the inner core of primary supporters as their eagerness to volunteer becomes apparent. However, some who were recruited first will not offer the campaign as much time as originally anticipated. Those volunteers should be reassigned to peripheral areas and to tasks that require a less intensive effort. Inactivity of core members must be addressed at weekly meetings and dealt with by the candidate or campaign manager. Conversely, volunteers who show exceptional abilities should be acknowledged, rewarded, and given more responsibility.

Current volunteers are an excellent resource for recruiting new ones. Volunteers' abilities to reach out to potential recruits are as unlimited as their own time and imagination. Make sure every person involved with the candidate in any way distributes volunteer postcards with postage stamps attached (see appendix A).

A volunteer recruitment drive may be required. Make sure volunteer cards are at every party, fundraiser, and function. Obtain names and make lists. Touch base with people on a person-to-person basis. It is easy to say no over the phone but more difficult face-to-face.

> *Tip:* A candidate may choose to explore their holiday card, wedding invitation, or other family or personal lists as a reminder of friends and relatives who might be receptive to donating money or volunteering to work on their campaign.

Never turn down a volunteer. An assignment can be found for everyone; volunteers should always be doing something. Remember, volunteering is a lot like fundraising. The subsidiary function of volunteerism is to have people buy into the vision of the candidate. Bring them all into the fold. They must feel valued and know they are contributing to the candidate's election.

Even someone who donates one dollar or works for fifteen minutes is part of the campaign. That person will vote for the candidate and recruit others. Volunteer assignments offer inclusion into the candidate's vision. It allows volunteers to be part of a movement that is making history.

Adjunct Special-Interest Groups

There may be one or more special-interest groups whose goals coincide with the candidate's, and those groups may agree to volunteer for the campaign. Those volunteers can be combined with other volunteers and staff or assigned a specific function, such as petition canvassing, literature drops (leafleting), corner blitz-intersection sign waves, or phone banks during GOTV efforts.

Another group may express an interest in volunteering, especially if the opposition candidate is an incumbent. These are the people who express an intense dislike for the opponent. This group may be a tremendous resource for behind-the-scenes work (O'Day 2003, 50).

Postcard Bundling

Charitable organizations often use postcard bundling for fundraising. This technique is also an effective tool for a political campaign. It can be used to generate donations and increase voter turnout on Election Day.

Many not-for-profit organizations have volunteerism and fundraising down to a science. Modeling success is one of the most useful strategies behind many businesses and political campaigns. Replicating proven techniques and best practices from iconic fundraising organizations can be extremely beneficial. Bundling is one of those techniques.

Offer every volunteer the opportunity to participate in the postcard-bundling project (see appendix C and Campaign Mailings). Give the volunteer a packet containing fifteen to twenty targeted political letters signed by the candidate, a donation letter, and volunteer card. At least half of the envelopes mailed by the volunteer should be labeled by the campaign and bear the addresses of base/core voters who live near the volunteer. The rest, the volunteer will address and send to supportive neighbors, friends, and relatives. In a larger campaign, the mailing piece may also include an area for credit-card donations or a pointer for donations on the website. The return envelopes, which will contain the contributions, should be addressed to the volunteer, who will consolidate donations in one large envelope and mail to the campaign's HQ.

Ask volunteers to compile lists of their friends, neighbors, relatives, and coworkers for the postcard-bundling project (see appendix J), noting those who may be interested in the neighborhood phone bank. Share those lists with unit managers and the communications director, who will add the names to the master spreadsheet and contact them during GOTV efforts. If volunteers do not have lists for postcard bundling, the campaign can furnish them with envelopes labeled with addresses from their areas, taken from its base/core voter and donor database.

Training

Volunteers' job preferences and degree of involvement in the campaign determines the training they will receive. A core team will slowly emerge over time. Traditionally, only 10 percent of the people who say they will volunteer will actually work hard on the campaign, but all who ask for training should receive it.

Functional managers are responsible for identifying the training their staff and volunteers require. They should list and note each person's area of expertise and previous training; then they should create a list of positions within the campaign and the training a volunteer will need to fulfill each job.

Coordinate Assignments

During weekly executive committee meetings, the functional managers should state how many volunteers they'll need in the future. Volunteer-recruiting goals will be determined by the tasks identified with each function.

The candidate should not deliver lawn signs, write newspaper ads, or perform other organizational grunt work. Of course, the candidate is the ultimate volunteer and should work shoulder-to-shoulder with volunteers on projects when there is time.

> *Tip:* Campaign staff and volunteers must believe that the candidate is the hardest worker in the campaign.

Envelope-Stuffing Party

This task requires volunteers to report to campaign headquarters (or a volunteer's home) and fold letters and stuff and label envelopes. When mailing to a specific group, the letters should be personalized and signed by the candidate or a designee. Note: With personalized correspondence, the name and address on the letter and envelope have to match. Great care must be taken to ensure this task is performed correctly.

It is always a good idea to order pizza or finger food and have nonalcoholic drinks available during these sessions. Bottled water, tea, and coffee should be supplied in abundance. An envelope-stuffing party is great for postcard-bundling and other targeted mailing projects. Note: Always remember that the candidate is subject to intense scrutiny, and no one associated with the campaign should ever drive under the influence of alcohol. Never take pictures with alcoholic beverage containers in view at any campaign function.

Door-to-Door Canvassing and Nominating Petitions

Analyze the data from the previous election, and find out how many signatures each committee member obtained when petitions were last circulated. Many county committees mandate that each member must obtain a minimum number of signatures. Some members will only get a dozen; some will get hundreds. Focus on enlisting the most productive members.

Praise the team members who are high achievers. Encourage and train those who achieve less. The volunteer who acquires only a few nominating petition signatures may have another area of expertise. Sometimes people cannot admit to a physical disability that limits their door-to-door activity. Find a less physically demanding task of equal importance for them to do. Note: Door-to-door canvassing is important enough to merit its own chapter.

Weekend Blitz: Literature Drop

Also called leafleting, this activity is extremely effective when done by a dozen or more people in several cars or a single large van, who focus on one geographical area and canvass door-to-door all at once (Joslyn 1984, 74). Teams working together exude a high-energy level, and this is felt by voters. Supply accurate door-to-door walking lists (if required), lawn signs, and campaign literature to every participant (see Computer Lists; Door-to-Door Canvassing/Walking Lists).

This type of activity can energize and rekindle a lagging campaign. The candidate or CM should energize the volunteers with a rousing speech just before their departure. The campaign also should provide bottled water and lunch for the volunteers. Note: Make sure leaflets are placed in a secure area near the resident's door. Wind-blown leaflets can be an unsightly mess.

Phone Banks

Using phone banks to deliver a candidate's message has long been considered a key method for encouraging constituents to go to the polls, despite statistical evidence to the contrary (Green and Gerber 2004, 125). Old political hands and media consultants often base their decisions on gut feelings, rather than on quantifiable evidence (Green and Gerber 2004, 90).

A campaign's finances are typically finite. Candidates and their campaign teams must choose the most appealing message and cost-effective delivery system available. Unfortunately, they usually have to include a dysfunctional, local, grassroots political committee over which they have little control. This committee may divide its time, energy, and resources among several candidates and not have the motivation or ability to establish an adequate support system for each one.

If that is the case, candidates may feel forced to turn to the least expensive and nearest means to maintain control, rather than spending the extra effort to sell their long-term campaign vision to the political committee and the electorate. The latter is the optimal route, but it is not the easiest. Candidates often grasp what is expedient (low-hanging fruit) and rely on the committee members who volunteer their services, rather than mine the depths of the committee for role models. The candidate must utilize the committee members who volunteer and appear on the surface for tasks. However, the most important task is to imbue the other members with enthusiasm about the candidate's vision, which will encourage the entire committee to offer its support.

Thanks to technology, telemarketers now have the ability to contact hundreds or even thousands of voters daily. Computer-generated lists targeted at a certain group can be incorporated into automated phone-dialing software, while tailored scripts can be added to voice-messaging systems. Consulting firms sometimes use local residents to deliver the candidate's message, giving the impression of a grassroots endorsement. The effectiveness of this system is one step up from robo-calls.

Robo-calls generated from a state or national political party have the least influence on voting habits. In fact, the influence is often near zero or as little as minus 1.6 percent (Green and Gerber 2004, 63). Having a well-known national or local celebrity record the message is slightly more effective. Robo-calls often target voters rather than households. Thus, houses with several registered voters are frequently inundated with these calls, sometimes alienating people who were once inclined to vote for a candidate.

However, positive results can be achieved with the proper use of phone banks. Gathering friends and neighbors at a central location—a business office or campaign headquarters—is the most effective organizational structure. Administrative oversight will be more inclusive and energetic, keeping volunteers on task and courteous without being demanding or intrusive. Volunteers will be motivated to deliver a more robust and personalized scripted message. Ensure that callers have a relatively private area to speak with voters, a place without background noise. Feedback from other callers will distort the quality of the message. Phone banks are more effective when callers engage in conversations beyond the scripted message (Green and Gerber 2004, 69). Future software advances may offer greater portability while still maintaining the integrity of a professional system. This type of a decentralized grassroots political advocacy is the best method for contacting voters by telephone.

Friends, relatives, and neighbors can create an efficient feedback loop in the phone-messaging script by asking questions about the voter's political leaning (polling). Local residents will be best equipped to respond to questions about local candidates. Comments concerning local issues and politicians can be used as feedback to redirect the candidate's emphasis on certain issues.

Whether a professional or a less formal system is used, a brief training session for phone-bank participants will be required. For example, the use of caller ID will be something the campaign must address, even though there is a gradual evolution underway from traditional landline to cell phones as the sole means of a household's personal communication. Voters will be more inclined to answer phone calls from relatives, friends, and neighbors. Note: Running a phone bank is one of the pool tasks that is shared by all functional managers for volunteer recruitment. Each manager may be requested to help fill recruitment goals.

Election Day Poll Watching (GOTV)

This is the final effort and push on Election Day and is one of the only times I recommend using telephones to contact the electorate (Pelosi 2007, 134).

Poll watchers are beginning to go electronic. Volunteers can highlight voters on computerized lists as they sign in at polling stations. Those lists will be mirrored at the campaign or phone-bank headquarters. Around five or six in the evening, someone at the phone bank will call people who have not yet voted, reminding them to go to the polls. The lists will concentrate on the candidate's party (base, core, and valence voters) and those identified as swing voters.

On the day of the election, every volunteer should call or e-mail close friends, neighbors, and relatives to remind them to vote for a particular candidate or issue.

The intersection sign wave, literature drops, door-to-door canvassing, and election-day events are very effective tools in motivating the electorate to vote. There is a synergistic effect to properly scheduling tasks, such as mailings, door-to-door canvassing, and phone calls. Remember, success is all about name recognition (see Advertising Coordinator).

Volunteer Packet

Create a packet, organized by task, for all volunteers. In a large manila envelope, include:

- Palm cards/handbills
- Nominating petitions, with instructions when applicable
- List of polling places, highlighting the district the volunteer will canvass
- Sheet of paper with the election date in big letters and the polling places underneath
- Candidate's résumé or biography (voters will ask questions about him or her)
- Bumper stickers and other campaign materials
- Walking list for the district (see Computer Lists)
- Voter registration cards, with instructions
- Absentee-ballot forms, stamped, with instructions (www.fvap.gov)
- Volunteer cards, with stamp (see appendix A)
- Accurate map of the territory (Shaw 2000, 126)
- Calendar of events, e.g., rallies and fundraisers
- List of acronyms and key codes used for polling and voter classification
- List of emergency phone numbers

The quantity of items included in the packet can be determined by usage in past elections and the area's political leaning and population density (Shadegg 1964, 133).

> *Tip:* Remember to ask seniors or people with disabilities if they need an absentee ballot or transportation to the polls on Election Day. Always follow up on voter requests. For

information about absentee voters in the military, go to www.justice.gov/opa/pr/2010/October/10-crt-1212.html.

Volunteer Media Kit

Offer a PowerPoint presentation to volunteers who want to be active in such areas as responding to pundits on radio talk shows, writing letters to newspaper editors, or posting positive notes about the candidate on a social media site.

Slide 1:
- Picture of candidate interacting with a group, usually family or voters (This will also offer the candidate the opportunity to target specific ethnic, senior, or veteran's groups within the election district.)
- A brief message from the candidate highlighting how vital a volunteer's active participation is to the election and the district
- Campaign slogan and logo
- Campaign website and e-mail addresses
- Headquarters street address and phone and fax numbers

Slide 2:
- Instructions for posting comments with online newspaper or political blog sites
- List of URLs for relevant newspaper and blog sites

Slide 3:
- Brief instructions about handling letters to the editor (see Letters to the Editor)
- List of all daily and weekly newspapers, including name, physical and website addresses, and editor's e-mail address

Slide 4:
- Radio call-in programs:
  o Radio station's acronym and website address
  o Physical address
  o Talk show host's name
  o Show's name and phone number

Slide 5:
- Instructions on how to log on and use Twitter, Facebook, YouTube, and other social media networks, including the candidate's four or five main talking points in any online dialog (Forming a strategy for social media networking is vital for the campaign and its volunteers.)

Voter Unit Chair

This is an example of a manager's position that could help define tasks in a larger campaign. Supervised by the volunteer coordinator and working in coordination with the campaign manager, this position would be in charge of absentee ballots, nominating petitions, voter registration, poll watching, phone banks, or other activities as assigned. Though time-consuming and important, these assignments are sequential and often are performed at different times during the campaign, allowing the voter unit chair the time needed to complete each one.

Consider establishing groups of off-site volunteers to handle specific tasks. Ward or precinct leaders can gather several clusters of people at one house, for example, and form phone banks to encourage fundraising or poll watching on Election Day. Using volunteers to cover neighborhood phone banks during GOTV efforts is an extremely effective tool when properly organized (see Volunteer Coordinator/Recruiter; Communications Director; and Phone Banks in this chapter).

Learning story
The Iroquois Nation was aligned militarily with Britain during the French and Indian War. At the Battle of Lake George, the Iroquois chief, King Hendrick, arrived with his warriors to help protect Fort Edward in upper New York State. When King Hendrick viewed the small British force he was to accompany, he said, "If we are to fight, we are too few; if we are to be killed we are too many." The French ambush, known as Bloody Morning Scout, soon followed in September 1755. King Hendrick was one of the many casualties (O'Toole 2005, 138).

The above narrative is a lesson to be learned by every campaign manager and volunteer coordinator. Aggressively recruit enough volunteers for nominating petition drives and GOTV efforts. The campaign cannot have too many volunteers.

Nuts and Bolts

- Solicitation and recruitment of volunteers
    - Volunteer postcards and lists
    - Volunteer sign-in sheets at all events
    - Envelope-stuffing parties
- Volunteer training hierarchy
- Postcard-bundling program
- Recruitment of special-interest groups

- Phone banks
- Election Day poll watching, GOTV efforts
- Door-to-door canvassing recruitment
  - Nominating petitions
  - Literature drops
  - Weekend blitz
  - Intersection sign wave
- Volunteer packet creation and distribution
- Volunteer media kit
- Voter unit chair (in a larger campaign)

FUNDRAISING CHAIR

▼

The fundraising chair (FC) is responsible for organizing all events and mailings that will solicit contributions from corporations, groups, and individuals to support a candidate for elected office. The person selected to fill this position must have proven managerial skills and the ability to organize key events with minimal oversight.

This functional manager must have the necessary temperament to deal with restaurant owners and vendors, volunteer staff, and campaign supporters since they will be interacting with a multicultural and economically diverse population. Fundraising events must be aligned with the campaign's theme and integrated with the other elements of the candidate's overall vision. FCs have the authority to seek out creative ideas and methods for fundraising; yet to ensure a successful event, they must be attentive to the slightest detail (see Fundraising Events).

In a smaller campaign, the FC's responsibilities can be shared with other managers, but quality is often born from a delineated job function. The FC should establish a tentative event schedule and budget as soon as possible and present it to the campaign manager and executive committee during a weekly meeting.

There are basically two types of insular campaign events in which the candidate will participate: fundraising events arranged by the FC, and civic and social events arranged by the scheduling officer or communications director. A financial donation is requested for admission to a fundraiser or financial contributions are openly solicited during the event. The FC's function is mostly concerned with soliciting campaign contributions. The FC may also work in tandem with the scheduling officer in areas such as hosting a party to solicit campaign contributions (see Fundraising Events).

Financial contributions will not usually be sought at other civic and social events; however, legal donations should never be refused at any time during the campaign. Speaking engagements, debates, and press releases are arranged by the communications director. The website, which solicits donations, and the Internet precinct are also the communications director's responsibility, but any activities that solicit funds should include the fundraising chair and the treasurer.

Responsibilities

+ Solicits contributions.
    o Manages fundraising events.
    o Oversees targeted first-class mailings to raise funds.
+ Updates fundraising lists: compiles, combines, and culls lists for duplicate entries.
+ Monitors the fundraising section of the website; works with the communications director and treasurer to optimize online contributions.

Skills and Components

+ Strong marketing and organizational skills.
+ Irregular hours (evenings and weekends).
+ Socially active, with clout in the community.
+ Working knowledge of the food-service industry.
+ Event-management skills.
+ Knowledge of US mail-sorting procedures, ancillary endorsements, discounts for address quality, and presort distribution.

Foundational Tasks

+ Engage the core volunteer group early.
+ Activate lists (to solicit funds and volunteers for events).
+ Compose and send targeted mailings with messages about raising funds.

Support Professionals

+ Communications director: letterhead, invitations, and thank-you notes.
+ Photographer: events.
+ Restaurant owner, manager, caterer.
+ Contractor for mail discounts.
+ Florist: table flower arrangements.

- ✦ Winery or brewery; use local vendors at events, particularly if they are affiliated with the party.
  - o Include small businesses when possible.

Cross-functional Manager Inclusion

- ✦ Advertising manager: advertises fundraising events.
- ✦ Communications director: generates computer lists and press releases, coordinates online contributions, manages the Internet precinct, in charge of handheld mobile devices for phone calls and texting.
- ✦ Scheduling officer: eliminates calendar conflicts; arranges candidate's transportation to and from events.
- ✦ Treasurer: handles deposits, donation limits and restrictions, postage.
- ✦ Volunteer coordinator: recruits and supplies volunteers.

Strategy of Fundraising

For the campaign to be effective, constituents must feel that they are a part of a candidate's initiative, not external to it. The entire process of fundraising is a fundamental building block that allows voters to gain stakeholder status by supporting a political candidate through monetary donations.

A political campaign is not viable without proper funding. Fundraising goes far beyond the ability to purchase canvassing literature, print ads, postage, or establishing an Internet footprint. As with nominating petition signatures, money is a way for voters to literally buy into the campaign and invest in the future of a candidate with their hard-earned currency. It is a pledge, like no other, to support a particular candidate or issue.

Many business gurus and heirs to fortunes have financed their own campaigns with millions of dollars, but then they were defeated because they did not understand this basic concept. People within the community want to donate and support their candidate. They must be offered an effective method of buying into the candidate's vision. Financial support is a basic building block within the political community.

The amount of money a campaign raises may be an indicator of the effectiveness of its advertising and the voters' acceptance of the candidate's message. People will not vote or donate to a candidate they feel is going to lose. There is a certain bandwagon effect with political campaigns. The candidates who project success may actually be successful (Campbell 2000, 243). The success of the fundraising initiative is an excellent voter feedback tool.

The key to securing the maximum number of votes on Election Day is embedded in targeted advertising through accurate voter and fundraising lists (see Computer Lists). The candidate's ability to deliver their message to like-minded people first will generate widening interest and then broader support.

Speaking ability, talent to solve issues, and organizational composition determine the candidate's ability to generate interest in their campaign. Interest generates money. Money enhances the ability to generate more interest, an upward spiral to success.

Fundraising events and targeted mailings are excellent fundraising tools. Contributions through the campaign's website are gaining in popularity. Money may be the root of all evil, but it is the foundation of a political campaign. Basically, there are six ways to raise campaign funds:

1) Fundraising events sponsored by the candidate's campaign, political party, organization, union, business, or individual (see Fundraising Events). If fundraising events are sponsored by the candidate's campaign, often there are few limitations on expenditures, but contribution limits for corporations, individuals, and family still apply.

   When another entity—such as a private individual, union, or business—sponsors a fundraising event, there are usually legal monetary restrictions on what must be reported as a donation. Ask the state BOE, campaign treasurer, and sage counsel for clarification.

2) Direct personal solicitation of funds by the candidate or campaign staff.
   a. Past donor-solicitation effort, with an emphasis on major donors
   b. New contributors
   c. PACs—political action committees
   d. Union or organizational contributions—usually through endorsement
   e. Political party's transfer of funds

   Candidates must create seed-money pledge lists for the personal solicitation of funds from relatives, friends, and coworkers who may be receptive to their candidacy (see Foundation: Getting Started). Some states have restrictions on certain elected offices, usually judicial, in which the candidate cannot personally solicit donations. Also, some positions (usually, judge, sheriff, district attorney) may have a window during which they can legally solicit funds before and after Election Day. Ask the BOE or sage counsel for election law clarification.

3) Direct marketing to a targeted audience, whether by the US mail, e-mail, or text messaging. Sending first-class mail or e-mail messages to a targeted audience is one of a campaign's best fundraising tools (Pelosi 2007, 134). Restrictions on style are usually

only limited by the creativity of the author, although pieces that will be delivered by USPS must conform to postal regulations (see Campaign Mailings; www.usps.com).

Key points of the candidate's message must be read within the ten to fifteen seconds it takes voters to travel from their mailboxes to trash receptacles. If, in that brief window of opportunity, the voter's attention is not captured, the mail piece may be promptly discarded (see Advertising Coordinator).

4) Online solicitation of campaign contributions is growing exponentially. New communications platforms are being developed every day. The one part missing in most online solicitations is the ability of the website designer to place the website before the voters. The website must be integrated on all materials associated with the campaign—depending upon search engines alone will not offer the most productive advertising doctrine. The website must be thoroughly integrated with every phase of the campaign's advertising program (see Internet Precinct and Communications Director).

5) In most states, the treasurer can accept personal loans from the candidate or others who guarantee to cosign loans. Direct loans from the candidate or spouse usually have few contribution limits. The candidate's immediate family may also have greater latitude on contribution limits or restrictions—consult state elections laws and sage counsel.

6) In-kind donations.

The use of the telephone and US mail as fundraising tools are slowly being abandoned in favor of the Internet. The one-on-one contact offered through door-to-door campaigning and traditional events like barbecues, clambakes, dinners, and picnics can never be replaced by technology. These events should be enhanced and augmented by technology whenever possible. All campaign events and milestones should be posted on the candidate's website, accompanied by select pictures and video clips.

Alternative Methods of Fundraising

Many creative methods can be used for raising money. Some county political committees have been very successful at raising money by publishing an "advertising booklet." Eighth-, quarter-, half-, and full-page ads are solicited from businesses and individuals who support a particular party, candidate, or issue.

The booklet should contain advertisements from a variety of small businesses in or near the political district. Often businesses include discount coupons with their advertisements. Coupon use may help indicate booklet circulation.

Tip: Encourage volunteers and staff to patronize businesses that support the candidate.

The advertising for the booklet is solicited before the largest fundraising event (usually a dinner), and the booklet is circulated at this event. Print enough so that copies can be distributed at markets and other places that distribute weekly newspapers and supplements, such as real-estate booklets. If legal in the candidate's state, an advertising booklet is an excellent fundraising tool.

Matching Funds

Matching funds has proved to be a very successful method of fundraising for some political candidates and not-for-profit organizations. It is an excellent vehicle for acquiring additional funds. Some people will contribute to a candidate if they know their funds will be matched by another contributor.

To achieve this, the FC must establish a base of major contributors to match funds, either a single sponsor or several donors acting in unison. It is an excellent way for an individual or corporation to gain notoriety. Sometimes a PAC or anonymous donor will cover the matching amounts, within legal limits. The campaign can advertise matching funds for contributions up to a specified amount or for ticket fees for certain events. For example, the ticket for the candidate's Independence Day barbecue is a donation of $100. The advertising for the event can state that all donations exceeding $100 will be matched by John Doe of John Doe Corporation or by an anonymous sponsor.

An anonymous sponsor may lead to a movement to reveal the person or corporation and draw them into the limelight. Since all donations over a selected amount are listed on the candidate's financial disclosure statement, it will not be difficult to narrow it down to a few donors if a determined effort is undertaken. An opposition candidate or the news media could undertake such an effort. Note: It is disingenuous and counterproductive to enter into a "matching funds drive" without there being a donor or anonymous sponsor as advertised.

Treasurer

All fundraising activities and events must keep the treasurer in the loop. Remember, there may be restrictions on fundraisers if an individual or organization other than the candidate's political committee is the sponsor of an event. Many people and businesses who innocently sponsor a political fundraising event may be completely ignorant of the state's election laws and its restrictions on contributions and in-kind donations. To include the treasurer only after the event is courting disaster.

Any and all methods used to raise money must comply with local, state, and federal laws. The campaign treasurer or sage counsel must research and train each functional manager on the legality of raising and disbursing funds, but the responsibility ultimately resides with the treasurer.

A large campaign war chest will help to discourage any number of prospective opponents in the campaign's early stages. Many financial statements are posted on the BOE's website, and candidates are fully aware of how much they or their opponents must raise to be competitive.

> *Tip:* The ability (or inability) of a campaign to raise large amounts of money is often the most telling indicator of broad-based support among constituents.

Direct-Mail Solicitation of Funds:

A first-class mailing to the candidate's relatives, friends, high-end party donors, and coworkers is key to obtaining the seed money needed to start a campaign. This population can be revisited later as the campaign gathers momentum (Shaw 2000, 83). Spend donations wisely (see Foundation: Getting Started).

> *Tip:* Never use the "occupant" approach for bulk mailing (see Computer Lists). Bulk mailings will often have only a 2- to 3-percent return, perhaps less than that. This is a shotgun approach used to capture people who have not been reached through events and other methods. Business bulk mail (BBM) should be used to solicit votes, not for fundraising (see Campaign Mailings).

People might want to donate to the candidate even though they are not eligible to vote in the election district. For example, owners of summer residences in the area may want to influence air and water quality, embrace a candidate's stance on crime and punishment, or support a pledge to lower property taxes. Since they may not be registered to vote in the candidate's district, donations may be one of the only ways they can support a local political agenda (see Campaign Mailings and Computer Lists).

A fundraising list might be used to solicit the entire membership of a country club or yacht club regardless of the members' political affiliation or residency. A current issue, such as the enforcement of zoning laws or water quality, may transcend the traditional political divisions found in such clubs. A large body of water may pass through or border several political boundaries. Water-quality issues in one part of a lake will affect the whole body of water. Similarly, a degrading quality of water may erode real-estate prices and downgrade businesses linked to recreation activities and tourism.

Another way that mailings can make money is to target a specific entity. For example, imagine there is a water-quality problem in a local lake or pond due to an invasive plant species or sewage leakage. Whatever the problem is, identify it. Align that problem with one of the candidate's talking points or campaign theme. Then seek votes and contributions on the highlighted situation. Water quality is just one of many issues that may transcend geopolitical boundaries (see appendix J).

In addition to monetary donations, people might want to donate office furniture, rental space, billboards, etc. Enclose a self-addressed stamped envelope (SASE) and volunteer card with every request for campaign donations or thank-you note (see appendix A). Note: a postcard-bundling project is also a great way to raise funds (see Volunteer Coordinator/Postcard Bundling).

In summation, a candidate seeks public office to identify and solve the problems of a community regardless of its members' ethnicity, religion, or social standing. Raising money helps candidates deliver their message to the electorate and offers voters the opportunity to become more involved in the political structure, a system that will ultimately determine their future.

Nuts and Bolts

- Establish and submit a budget to the CM.
- Organize, plan, and execute all fundraising events.
- Create targeted letters to solicit contributions by snail mail, e-mail, and via the website.
- Oversee and help create invitations for events, and maintain fundraising lists.
- Work with volunteer coordinator to recruit volunteers for events.
- Include the postcard-bundling project as a fundraising tool (see Volunteer Coordinator/ Recruiter).
- Form an event phone tree to enhance participation (see Fundraising Events/Phone Tree).
- Find event sponsors and keynote speakers.
- Utilize innovative technology to enhance the solicitation of donations.
- Explore alternative methods of fundraising, such as a campaign advertising booklet or matching funds.
- Employ the US mail or e-mail to target issues, civic organizations, and special-interest groups.

OFFICE MANAGER

▼

The office manager is a volunteer or paid position, who is brought on board by the campaign manager and the candidate, but who may also be interviewed by the executive committee to ensure compatibility. This person answers only to the candidate and campaign manager, but in truth accepts work requests from almost everyone and organizes daily chaos into cogent, sequential tasks at campaign headquarters.

The office manager is the first foot forward in the campaign. Many voters will be walk-ins to the HQ, and the first representative they will see is usually the office manager or a member of their staff. The old analogy, "you only get one chance to make a first impression," is true.

Tap youth adult groups, such as the Young Republicans or Young Democrats, for staff. In addition, local college students who are political science majors are good recruits for volunteers, as are party committee members and aspiring politicians. The candidate or campaign manager can present the campaign's mentoring program as one way college students can augment their formal classroom training with field experience.

Filling a work schedule with volunteers at HQ can be a daunting task for the office manager. Whoever is chosen should immediately initiate a recruitment drive among their friends, family, former classmates, and neighbors. Volunteers, staff, and the executive committee should be encouraged to have meetings or do any type of paperwork while sitting at the HQ's reception desk or telephone communications center. The people on the seed-money's foundation list (or their representatives) can work at the reception desk too, as they are among the candidate's base support group. This will increase the number of qualified volunteers available at HQ.

Lists are generated by the communications director, statistician, and other staff. While volunteers are seated at the reception desk, they can enter raw data from sign-up sheets into the computer databases. The person in charge of this work is the office manager. In a smaller campaign, which may not have an office manager, the secretary/scribe is responsible for all data entry. The secretary works directly with the CM and the candidate, and takes the minutes at all quorum-based meetings.

Back up computer files regularly, using a USB flash card or drive, or by sending an e-mail of files to be archived by the candidate and the campaign manager. The files should be stored in a password-protected file area on their computers or USB devices.

Headquarters

Many small campaigns do not require a storefront headquarters (HQ). However, if one is required, research vacant space, but also inquire with the county's party chair. There may be a loyal committee member with vacant commercial office space that he or she will make available free of charge or at a reduced fee. Such a contribution is usually considered an in-kind donation. If a campaign headquarters is required, inquiries into office space should begin before the candidate formally announces a plan to run.

If office space is obtained, try to acquire it for the candidate's exclusive use. A political party might seek to lease a common area for all candidates under one banner. If a common area is decided upon, computer and paperwork security could be a concern. Address those concerns at weekly executive committee meetings.

The perfect headquarters will have good access and visibility on a highly trafficked street. Choose a safe place with ample parking, both for visitors and for campaign workers who may need access to the premises on a 24/7 basis. Speak to local law enforcement in case extra security is needed.

Properly staffing the HQ with trained personnel is one of the most challenging tasks in a campaign and requires an office manager with strong recruiting skills. Ideally, there will be enough volunteers to staff the HQ properly throughout the campaign, but in reality there may be only enough available for the one or two weeks before Election Day, or only during critical hours.

Security can be a concern for two reasons: to protect staff and volunteers and to prevent illicit access to computer files. There are many ways to protect the HQ building from intruders (using items such as motion sensors or webcams) and data files from hackers and thieves. Password protection can be a big help, especially when passwords are only provided to select users. One of the first purchases for the HQ should be a paper shredder.

The HQ is the depository for most of the physical campaign materials: lawn signs, palm cards, bumper stickers, etc. Create information packets for walk-in visitors that are specific to each interest or task, e.g., absentee ballots, voter registration, and candidate position sheets. Volunteers should document all voters calling into the HQ in a permanent log that includes dates, time, phone numbers, requests, and follow-up conversations. There always should be a sign-in sheet near the door for walk-ins and prospective volunteers (see appendices A, B, and C; Volunteer Coordinator/Recruiter).

The HQ is a central meeting place and training area. Information about available training should be prominently posted along with maps of the election district that use color codes to note canvassing progress, party enrollment, and voting histories (Grey 1999, 81).

> *Tip:* Do not store all of the campaign's supplies at the headquarters. Placing literature and signs throughout the district will enhance distribution and minimize loss in case of fire, theft, or natural disaster.

Requirements for Headquarters

- Regular hours of operation posted on window or door
- Clean and neat
- Well lit, safe inside and out
- Functional, not busy or cluttered
- Toilet facilities
- Sufficient electrical outlets
- Good location, safe, convenient
- Food facilities nearby
- Includes an area for computers and phone banks
- Storage area for campaign literature and office supplies
- Display area for maps, calendar
- TV and radio, desks and chairs, coffee machine, document shredder, computers, phones, folding tables and chairs
- Adequate parking, safe access 24/7

Nuts and Bolts

- Manage HQ volunteers, staff, and reception desk.
- Work with the secretary/scribe.
- Recruit volunteers to staff HQ.
- Organize HQ meetings and events (with scheduler).
- Keep track of campaign materials and literature, as assigned.
- Staff phone banks.
- Convert raw data to organized lists.
- Create informational packets for volunteers and walk-in visitors.
- Help select HQ building.

UNIT MANAGER

▼

The unit manager is a member of the executive committee and reports directly to the campaign manager and the candidate. This manager has complete control over all fundraising events, advertising, volunteer recruitment, scheduling, and other tasks within a specific political district, as assigned by the campaign manager. The unit manager is a grassroots political whip and maximizes the knowledge base developed through the functional-manager support system.

The position's title must have a unique name to reflect the area it represents, such as Greene County Coordinator, Ward (or Parish) Four Coordinator, or the Town of Jackson Coordinator. In this way, unit managers can maintain integrity and forward momentum by taking advantage of the preexisting political infrastructure and geographical boundaries.

In this campaign model, the functional managers are the field experts who are dedicated to a specific discipline and guarantee knowledge and professionalism in their areas of expertise. The unit manager utilizes the methods, database models, and techniques established by the functional managers to support staff and volunteers working on tasks, such as the organization of a fundraising event. Grassroots feedback from staff and volunteers at weekly meetings is also an important characteristic of this campaign model—the unit manager must explore every opportunity to interact with the campaign staff and the electorate.

The engagement of an expert for a specific task by the unit manager is arranged through the functional manager, who may assign a photographer, computer specialist, graphic designer, event specialist, or other expert whose services have been contractually arranged at the macro-campaign level.

For example, the communications director is the functional manager of the graphic designer and photographer. In the case of a fundraising event, the fundraising chair assigns the key staff members. The unit manager manages the event and supplies most of the volunteers, who should be recruited locally when possible. It is important to have local grassroots support for staffing. Functional managers only offer their expertise if needed on tasks common to all events, such as invitation wording and printing, seating arrangements, ticket donation amount, menus, and other professional touches.

The unit manager must cultivate an extremely good rapport with the functional managers in order to take full advantage of their expertise. The campaign cannot be a bastion of personal egos and domain infringements, nor can any manager view a request for help as a "fire and forget" missile. Requests for assistance and staff assignments must be monitored from the time of application to implementation.

The candidate or campaign manager must directly assess questions of productivity with the affected unit managers. The style and expertise of each may vary greatly. It is results that count, not the micro-process or personality. One unit manager may be more effective than another in their assigned geographical areas. Each manager must gather data and perform activities in a uniform manner, and areas of success should be replicated by the campaign manager. Unit managers must not compete for resources.

> *Tip:* Functional managers are resources for unit managers. Dispute resolution between the functional managers and unit managers is handled by the campaign manager.

Social Media Networking

As many as three levels of electronic information are disseminated to voters. The first is distributed locally through unit managers. The second originates from the central campaign; it is both grassroots, bottom-up, and administrative, top-down, information gathering and dissemination (Pelosi 2007, 15). The third level of information is from a state or national party, which may influence local elections. This third level includes PACs or businesses who advertise independently, either for or against a particular candidate or issue.

The unit manager's staff and volunteers must collect e-mail addresses from constituents by utilizing every available means at fundraising events, campaign speeches, door-to-door canvassing, luncheons, meet and greets, etc. (see Computer Lists). The unit managers send the information to the central campaign's computer section. The communications director collects, coordinates, and sorts the data for distribution to the intended audience. The information can be used to target appropriate areas of focus, including veterans, seniors, educators, homeowners, and business owners. The central campaign will have many resources, such as a website, for collecting e-mail addresses and data that may not be available to the unit managers.

Weekly Blastcast

Online communications at the neighborhood level should be similar to those of a media representative. There will be pushback if voters feel they are being bombarded or spammed with biased political advertising. Therefore, information disseminated to voters should be in the form of an informative newscast.

Unit managers can direct volunteers to send information to potential voters who reside within certain geographical areas or who are in their personal e-mail address books. Avoid spamming constituents and friends with verbose, unwanted information. Strive to craft high-quality, newscast-style information about the candidate and campaign that would be of interest to friends, neighbors, and the people in organizations to which they belong. It is very important to make the candidate's talking points timely by sprinkling them with current events.

Do not present the same uninteresting format time and time again, or people will automatically delete the e-mail without reading it. Instead, formulate a blastcast that will be informative, trendy, and interesting to read. The method of delivery should reflect emerging trends in communications technology.

Unit Manager Responsibilities

+ Serve as the candidate's local representative.
+ Coordinate activities with the campaign team to maximize candidate's time.
+ Partner with the county, town or city political committees for a unified effort.
+ Design a plan for campaign administration to visit all municipalities to meet with local officials and voters.
+ Assemble a team of volunteers to handle a variety of responsibilities.
+ Develop and execute a communications plan to build awareness of the candidate's platform to ensure proper representation of views and talking points.
+ Organize fundraising events, participate in mailings, and acquire constituents' e-mail addresses.
+ Research and provide key facts about county and communities.
+ Coordinate fundraising activities and target high-end donors.
+ Cultivate grassroots fundraising efforts on a person-to-person basis.

Community activities
+ Provide candidates in the defined area (county or district) with a responsible, professional, positive, and visible presence for accurately representing their views.

- Maintain a dialogue and liaison with the political party's committee.
- Attend local events and club meetings, e.g., Rotary Club, Elks, and Kiwanis.
- Find and recruit key advocates to attend clubs and meetings (list clubs and members).
- Find and recruit key military veterans and senior citizens.
- Enter into an ongoing dialogue with important business, civic, and community leaders.
- Coordinate volunteer activities.
- Establish a first line of defense to cull well-intended but overly time-consuming or negative political counsel; manage people's access to the candidate and the dissemination of information.
- Coordinate the acquisition and advertisement of polling data through the campaign's statistician.

Coordination with functional managers
- Work with campaign manager and scheduler to ensure that the candidate has regular presence in the unit manager's assigned area.
- Maximize the candidate's time in the area by putting together a full, productive schedule.
- Ensure the campaign is up-to-date on announcements, policy statements, and other news.
- Relate plans and activities through ongoing conversations with local political advocates and party chairmen/women.
- Coordinate campaign efforts by motivating and communicating with volunteers.

Assembling the team
- Approach and identify dedicated people who are willing to work on the campaign.
- Create an advisory board of key people within the unit manager's district.
- Assign team leaders for various functions (events, ethnic representatives, seniors, veterans), who will report to the unit manager at weekly meetings.
- Develop a reporting mechanism for voter and staff feedback to keep efforts on track.
- Keep the campaign manager and functional managers notified of developments.
- Seek out endorsements, and work with political parties and unions who have endorsed the candidate.
- Supervise and train nominating petition signing teams by geographical areas; this will be an important forerunner to successful door-to-door efforts later in the campaign.
- Energize and schedule nominating petition circulation drives as well as new voter registration and absentee-ballot efforts (Key 1966, 25).

Communications planning
- Public relations: build relationships and maintain an ongoing dialogue with important news media.

- Editorial team: coordinate ongoing submissions of editorials, letters to the editor, and op-ed articles to support the candidate and party, with an emphasis on educating the electorate on issues.
- E-mail blasts: send e-mails on weekly or biweekly basis to an ever-increasing list of likely voters. Discuss the best approach for keeping in continuous contact with voters, without resorting to intrusive spamming tactics.
- Advertising: create a localized plan.
- Determine budget and continuously upgrade cash flow through fundraising initiatives.
- Mailings: compose and provide plan and budget for bulk and targeted first-class mailings.
- Voters: target records from the county or state BOE to identify registered voters with a history of supporting the candidate's platform.
- Grassroots: visit all municipalities in the city or county, and work with the party to get people to cultivate grassroots enthusiasm for the candidate.
- Identify key events through the scheduling officer.
- List groups to contact, noting leadership advocates for support (see Computer Lists).
- Organize fundraising events: dinners; train, bus, or boat rides; rallies; picnics.
- Demographics/research/fact finding: establish economic-development advisors for the campaign; research demographic information and statistics; top employers—address, phone of president/CEO; number of employees and products (see appendix I).
- List e-mail addresses and websites of municipalities and elected officials (city, county, state, federal).
- Maintain contact with loyal volunteers through e-mail, coffees, rallies, local networking.

Targeting

The concept of targeting is controversial in some political circles, and yet no other word can capture the essence of the need to hone in on specific areas of the campaign during critical phases of the election process. It is the campaign manager's job to identify times to target specific areas, e.g., during the circulation of nominating petitions, or when to focus on a group of people, such as veterans or seniors. It is the unit manager's job to take advantage of the training offered by the campaign and gather and motivate an effective workforce for the candidate's successful resolution on Election Day.

SECTION 3

Strategy and Function:
The Heart and Soul of the Campaign

- ☞ Alternative Voting Methods
- ☞ Crisis Management
- ☞ Door-to-Door Canvassing
- ☞ Endorsements
- ☞ Going Negative
- ☞ Internet Precinct
- ☞ Mentoring
- ☞ Swing Vote
- ☞ Voting Blocs

ALTERNATIVE VOTING METHODS

▼

The American political system is always in search of innovative ways to enhance the electorate's ability to cast a secret ballot. Several states have turned to alternative voting methods (AVMs) in an effort to make the process more convenient and to increase the number of participants.

AVMs can be defined as any voting that takes place outside of traditionally designated polling places or time designated as Election Day. These include early voting, vote-by-mail, mobile voting, weekend voting, or the use of voting centers. Exciting alternatives on the horizon include voting by phone, computer, and television.

Alternative voting methods are being used in nearly every state in America, but their degree of success are highly dependent on each jurisdiction's demographics, culture, election laws, and organizational standards for recruitment and training of personnel.

Early Voting

This is a process in which voters cast a ballot at a traditional brick-mortar polling place before Election Day. Texas was one of the first states to implement early voting and has done it effectively since 1987. Thirty-two states currently allow some form of early voting, based on the idea that greater flexibility and convenience will yield a higher turnout (Elliott and Kuhnhenn 2012). That has not been the case (Rodriguez et al. 2008, 6). Historical data on the process in Texas has determined that early voting only gives voters who normally would have voted on Election Day more flexibility and convenience. There is no way to actually tell if the number of voters would have decreased had early voting not been implemented. Since early voting is much more expensive than traditional methods, its overall value must be weighed by the constituency it serves.

Absentee Ballots

Absentee-ballot voting was initiated during the American Civil War to allow military personnel the opportunity to cast a ballot when they were serving away from home. Many states have extended absentee voting to anyone with a valid excuse. Several states also allow "no excuse" absentee ballots, which is a precursor to voting by mail.

Voting by Mail

The opportunity to vote by mail has been offered to Oregon residents since 1981. Oregon now administers all elections exclusively through the vote-by-mail process. This controversial method has increased voter turn out to almost 90 percent during presidential elections. In-person, precinct-based elections are more expensive, mostly due to the costs associated with personnel training and rent of polling places.

Oregon has perfected its three-tiered, secret-ballot system. Those who administer the Oregon election process believe that current electronic signature verification technology ensures sufficient ballot integrity. Accurate voter-registration lists are continuously updated using returned mail. The US Postal Service also makes an extra effort to collect ballots at a specific time at specified locations on Election Day. Ballots not requiring postage can also be dropped at designated sites.

Voting Practices

Many states do not require voters to show identification, and several progressive states, such as Vermont, have extended voting eligibility to certain felons. Puerto Rico also allows incarcerated felons the right to vote (see appendix H for an election law inquiry on a state-by-state basis).

Campaign Strategy

Nearly all alternative voting practices are advantageous to campaigns that are highly organized and efficient. They allow constituents an opportunity to vote before Election Day only if the extra effort is expended. The candidate's campaign must extend poll watching for the entire period to determine who has voted. This will often leave the late deciders, typically the swing voters, as the main focus in the final days of the election (see Swing Vote and Voting Blocs).

For further study, search online for the following:

- Help America Vote Act of 2002 (HAVA)
- US Election Assistance Commission (EAC)
- US Code Title 5 Section 6103(B)
- alternative voting methods
- Texas Election Code (TEC)
- federal Voting Rights Act
- Election Day state holiday

CRISIS MANAGEMENT

▼

Conflict! We all manage some type of turmoil nearly every day, either in our working environment or personal lives. However, very few of those incidents threaten our survival and develop into a crisis.

It is inevitable that during campaigns or terms of office, someone will verbally or even physically attack candidates, their staff, or their families. Crisis affects everyone differently. There are few metrics categorizing threat levels as there are with homeland security. A crisis team must be assembled during the first days of the campaign to train staff and deal with problems as they arise. In this campaign model, the communications director creates and manages the crisis team. However, the CM may choose to modify job descriptions and assign tasks to fit the personal strengths of individual managers.

The external or internal assault may be a direct threat to candidates' electability or to the status they hold in the community. Times of intense personal crisis will demonstrate to everyone what the candidate stands for and who they really are. The people and groups that survive a crisis are those who are well trained and have a coordinated plan. They respond quickly because they've prepared for catastrophic situations through training and rehearsal.

These defining moments of stress can actually be intensely beneficial and garner support from circles that were once out of the candidate's reach.

Political Threats Are Often Opportunities in Disguise

Winners never retreat from a good battle. Do not let the people attacking the candidate take the high ground and control events. The perception of reality, in the eyes of the electorate, is what the campaign must deal with in addition to possible litigation.

If candidates have something dark or unsavory hidden in their past, most likely our political system will ferret it out. People of questionable character should not run for political office, but many do and are elected and reelected. The campaign's survival depends on the degree of infraction and the manner in which the indiscretion is displayed before the public.

There are few secrets in politics. If a person running for office harbors a secret, such as infidelity or a DWI, there will usually be a sad awakening. Crisis strategy is essential when campaigning for political office; however, the violation of any election, civil, or criminal law needs to be addressed through the legal system. Immediately inform law enforcement authorities if there is a physical threat to candidates, their families, staff members, or volunteers.

Preparation
Hurricanes are often a seasonal crisis to the residents of America's coastal regions, but they are neither unpredictable nor unexpected. America's coastal residents know that a community's survival is directly proportional to the degree of its preparation and knowledge. They expect the best, but prepare for the worst. When handled properly, a crisis can unite opposing factions.

Candidates under attack usually call a meeting to strategize their counterattack. They arm themselves and their loyal followers with a plethora of verbal weapons, beginning with a statement that the accusation is unfounded and without merit.

Some of the biggest scandals in political history have gotten legs because candidates were not honest and forthcoming after their first encounters with the media. It is a normal response to defend someone in a crisis situation, but this may not be the wisest course of action if the goal is political longevity. A "circle the wagons" mentality is usually a harbinger of disaster.

Both the candidate and the campaign team should be cool under fire. Always tell the truth, even during those rare occasions that require an outright admission of wrongdoing. There must be only one spokesperson—the candidate. The campaign manager becomes the spokesperson if the candidate is unavailable, and "unavailable" does not mean "in hiding."

First and foremost, it is important to get a handle on the accusation. Is it a questionable rumor, or will the accusation be on the front page of the morning newspaper?

Today, a picture or video clip can be captured on a cell phone and displayed on the Internet within seconds. In a matter of minutes, the campaign will be asked to address an accusation of wrongdoing. What is also true is that, in today's electronic environment, nearly any medium can be manipulated or altered.

Have an active crisis-management plan in place. Establish a united front and unified vision *before* a crisis occurs.

The Attack

- ◆   Confirm that the attack is real and not a whisper campaign or rumor (which could lead to other problems). Is it a real threat, or an overblown perception?
- ◆   Does the accusation have substance?
- ◆   Is the attack a distorted truth?
- ◆   If possible, identify the originator. Who made it, and why?

Spending the campaign's energy and resources on an attack makes it real. Once the campaign team addresses the accusation, then they have made it real. In politics, perception is often reality. Do not hit an ant with a sledge hammer, but adequately plan a course of action in the event it is required.

If not stopped at inception, the solitary and inconsequential voices of the few may soon become an onslaught of the many. Deal with small problems before they become a Niagara Falls of accusations. This may mean to simply form an internal strategy in case there are accusations. Like automobile recalls, sometimes accusations of wrongdoing will build very gradually over months or years until there is a major event in the media.

The other end of the spectrum is *mokusatsu*, which in Japanese means "to kill with silence." If something is not addressed, then it does not exist. If candidates believe the accusation is totally without merit and will not become a future problem, they may choose not to address it at all. Accusations, true or false, that will not become future problems with the voters, should be left to wither on the vine.

To address any issue or allegation gives it merit and a certain degree of substance and validity. The quote from Hamlet, "The lady doth protest too much, me thinks," is a reminder that if someone vehemently denies an inconsequential accusation, it may lead people to believe there is more substance to it than was previously thought. By addressing an attack, the entire focus of the campaign can shift from offensive to defensive. The campaign wastes time, money, and resources by defending unfounded accusations when the focus should be on getting the candidate's message to the voters. *Mokusatsu* is a very effective policy when properly used.

In the event of an attack on the candidate's policies, issues, or morality, the entire executive committee may take a perceived indiscretion as a personal violation. The campaign team's reaction should be unified. The impact of any accusation, even if completely unfounded, may deeply affect the candidate's team. Every substantive accusation from the opposition must be addressed internally by the executive committee, which consults with the crisis team. Communication of a crisis to the management team should always be through verbal communication, never by text, e-mail, or other written methods.

Most substantive accusations, from the opponent or elsewhere, will challenge a candidate's qualifications to hold public office based on past events. The opponent may cast aspersions on the candidate's judgment, honesty, or integrity in an attempt to shift the public's attention away from campaign issues, especially if the opposition's stance on those issues is soft. Identify and address the opposition's drift from substantive issues and lack of a viable platform (see Going Negative).

Qualifications

Perhaps a candidate for sheriff has been accused of having a DWI or a speeding violation. Perhaps a candidate's claim of having a specific educational degree is under investigation. These are different than if a candidate is engaging in an extramarital affair or if doubts are cast on a candidate's sexual orientation.

A DWI or speeding ticket brings into question one's qualifications for the office of sheriff, and the claim that an educational degree or combat experience that does not exist (Shaw 2000, 211) is an attack on a candidate's honesty and integrity. Both accusations are quantifiable.

A candidate's false claim of military medals, combat service, or educational degrees may be leaked by the opposition to the media only days before an election, when the candidate has very few hours to respond. Quantifiable video clips, phone tapes, and photos must be addressed immediately. Remember that in today's world any photograph or video can be modified, altered, enhanced, or taken completely out of context (see Going Negative).

Personal Attacks

Attacks on family or personal traits are the most difficult to combat. They are subjective and in a nearly all-gray area. Even though the alleged character flaw may be baseless, it may cut the candidate and their family to the quick.

If it is a personal matter, view it in the light of what it is: a baseless accusation and not a qualification for public office. Candidates and team members cannot be judged on what their families do. For instance, if the candidate's seventeen-year-old, unwed daughter is pregnant, it should be off-limits. It does not affect the candidate's ability to hold public office or reflect on their leadership skills.

Even an unfounded accusation can drive a permanent wedge into the heart of a once-harmonious family. Every family member must be well versed to potential dangers. Reactions to any accusations should follow the outline of the crisis plan; reactions should be passionate but not unprofessional or venal. Attacks on offspring can provoke a "father or mother bear" style of response. Candidates should never lose their composure under any circumstances.

There are basically two ways of dealing with this type of crisis: If true, candidates can admit it and attempt to project it in a better light. However, if false, candidates or campaign spokespeople should deny the accusation and identify it as baseless. Then, they should immediately refocus on campaign issues and the candidate's qualifications.

Whether true or false, an accusation is the most damaging when it surfaces one or two days before the election. This gives the candidate little time to gather evidence that refutes the accusation. To avoid such a situation, the candidate should gather college diplomas and transcripts, birth and marriage certificates, military discharges, etc., before the campaign begins.

When addressing an accusation:
  + form a crisis team early;
  + put a crisis plan in place;
  + identify the specific problem;
  + centralize the information that flows out;
  + expand the information that flows in;
  + develop worst- and best-case scenarios; brainstorm;
  + remember: in politics, there's usually little to no chance of containment;
  + put the problem in perspective; and
  + communicate a remedy.

The way candidates deal with a difficult situation will determine their ultimate fate on Election Day. If there is an open dialogue during weekly meetings and the proper feedback loop is in place, it will be unusual to have an unexpected crisis. Even hurricanes give some type of warning. In politics, too, there are often several types of warning signs. Minimize the negative impact on the voters and also on the campaign team.

Feedback from the team is vital. Address problems before they become crisis situations. There is often an opportunity to out a candidate's impropriety before the opposition has the opportunity to create a major issue around it. Be careful not to expose anything that may otherwise go unaddressed by the opposition.

One of the best forms of self-preservation is to use a practice example during a brainstorming session of the executive committee. It will give the CM and the crisis team an opportunity to enhance their facilitator training. Activation of the crisis team may be needed after a natural disaster or crisis. For example, September 11, 2001, was primary Election Day in New York State.

The following are possible crises:
+ unforeseen events or actions
+ attack or criticism by the opposition, electorate, or media
+ media investigations: undercover and unflattering reporting of campaign operations
+ media criticism: targeted and sustained condemnation
+ legal threats: petition errors, campaign law violations
+ errors of judgment
+ arrest or imprisonment of campaign team members
+ confidentiality breaches: the leaking of sensitive information
+ legal action: proceedings that put candidate or staff in the spotlight
+ negligence or malfeasance: professional negligence claims
+ candidate-involved accidents: serious injury or death
+ other accidents: serious injury or death where a team member or member of the candidate's family is involved
+ candidate- or staff-involved theft
+ financial problems: candidate, family, or staff (IRS, mortgage, credit card)

An apology is to admit wrongdoing and should embody several characteristics:
+ truthfulness and sincerity
+ apologies to all stakeholders who are offended; identify each one
+ timely and well strategized
+ acceptance of full responsibility
+ expression of regret
+ plan for mending fences

Mending fences involves the following actions:
+ asking for forgiveness
+ seeking reconciliation with injured parties
+ providing full disclosure, i.e., transparency or at least translucency
+ offering corrective action
+ providing adequate compensation

The following consequences can result:
+ devastatingly negative media coverage
+ low staff morale
+ altered or severed relationships with the electorate; loss of voters' trust
+ downward spiral for fundraising
+ potential criminal or civil charges

If criminal or civil charges may be filed, an apology may be considered an admission of wrongdoing by a court of law. Consult with the sage counsel (attorney) if there is even a remote possibility a law has been violated.

Note: The crisis-management team may also be utilized as an adjunct advisory board for case-specific topics or to explore a subject when the executive committee does not have the time or expertise to do so. However, the team should not divest the candidate or campaign manager from accepting responsibility for controversial decisions.

DOOR-TO-DOOR CANVASSING

▼

The most cost-effective tool in the candidate's tool kit is walking door-to-door to meet and establish a personal dialogue with the voters. Direct exposure to constituents offers the candidate an opportunity to gain grassroots support, name recognition, and the vital feedback required to tweak campaign strategy and update computerized voter and fundraising lists. Door-to-door canvassing is also critically important for reaching out to voters who might not be accessible by other campaign methods (Thomas 1999, 33). A personal door-step introduction by the candidate with a registered voter is the gold standard for political campaigns.

The Elements of Canvassing

There are a variety of technological advancements that can enhance the process of door-to-door canvassing. However, they may only enhance the acquisition and clarification of data; they do not circumvent the three distinct phases involved in the strategy of door-to-door canvassing.

The first and arguably the most important factor in most elections, other than GOTV, is the time allocated for the collection of nominating petition signatures. Most candidates need to gather the number of signatures required by law within a specific time frame for their names to appear on the ballot. An absentee-ballot program and voter-registration drive may be introduced at this time and fully activated during the summer canvassing cycle.

The method used to introduce the candidate to the electorate will set the tone for the rest of the campaign. It is easier and less costly to persuade residents to vote for the candidate in the early stages of the campaign than to dissuade them from voting for the opposition at a later date.

The second phase is the summer and early-fall initiative, a slow, methodical canvassing drive in the election district that introduces the candidate to as many voters as possible.

The third phase is the GOTV stage, which begins in the final forty-five to thirty days of the campaign. The door-to-door GOTV program revisits the voters who signed nominating petitions and those who were visited during the summer canvassing program. Pay special attention to people who were not home during those earlier initiatives.

The GOTV phase is equal in intensity to the nominating petition effort but has a different tone. This is the final push by the candidate, volunteers, and campaign staff to personally contact voters before Election Day. GOTV is most effective when designed to reintroduce the candidate to the electorate in a positive way, to maximize the candidate's exposure through canvassing, advertising, e-mail, texting, and social media. The sequencing of multiple advertising disciplines during the campaign's final week could offer voters a synergistic effect (Green and Gerber 2004, 96).

The Canvassing Team

Due to population densities and cultural differences, door-to-door canvassing in a rural setting is much different than it is in a city. Suburban housing developments and residential clusters also pose challenges for canvassers, where in a city canvassers could be denied access to secure apartment complexes. In a rural setting the same could be said for gated communities. Many jurisdictions have their own cultures and require canvassers to adopt slightly different techniques. Whenever possible, volunteers should be assigned areas familiar to them.

The candidate or canvassing volunteer should be accompanied by at least one other team member in most settings, and especially when walking door-to-door. This provides both safety in numbers and also someone who can jot down the voters' needs, which is a good indication of team cooperation. To enhance coverage, some canvassing teams like to divide odd- and even-numbered residences.

If the candidate has been endorsed by a political party, its committee people will usually have been assigned specific areas for coverage. Those districts, wards, precincts, and parishes are their assigned responsibility. Connect the campaign's canvassing effort to the political party's committee and coordinate efforts as much as possible. A mentor or guide may be required to act as an intermediary with the committee to coordinate work flow and schedules (see Mentoring).

People are voting for the candidate and their team. Americans often have compassion for and value a maverick's stance; yet they realize that only a strong political team can bring about substantive long-term change to government. To become an effective politician who can deliver results, the candidate often needs to build bridges and form alliances where there once may have been only rigid barriers. A resourceful candidate with a good team can offer long-term political stability.

Personal Appearance

Personal appearance is highly valued by most voters. Take the old adage to heart: a person only has one chance to make a first impression. Many candidates feel that shirt and tie is required when they are knocking on doors, while casual dress works best for others. The affluence of the election district and the office being sought also determines the style of dress worn by candidates and their representatives. A candidate for district attorney or judge may want to project a more professional appearance than one running for the city council.

> *Tip:* All the people who represent the candidate during door-to-door canvassing should wear a campaign identification badge pinned to their jackets or shirts (Grey 1999, 81). The design of the badge should reflect the campaign's logo in theme, color, and style.

Porch and Stoop Etiquette

1. Knock on the door, or ring the bell, then step away from the door. Give the occupants their personal space.
   + Never wear tinted or reflective lenses, and do not wear sunglasses.
   + Never make any threatening gestures or rapid hand movements.
   + Never, ever, say a four-letter word.
   + Be articulate and speak clearly.
   + Respect voters' need to be heard; listen to them.
   + Never denigrate an opponent, even if the voter does.
   + The right hand is for shaking, not for carrying items such as bottled water or papers.
   + Refrain from chewing gum or smoking.
   + Never canvass before 9:00 a.m. or after dusk.

2. Introduce yourself. Look at the walking list, and call the person by name. This is where time spent on walking-list data comes to fruition. Say, "Hello [or Good morning/afternoon]. My name is John Doe and I am the candidate for mayor of Whatville." Or "My name is Jane Doe, and I am here representing candidate John Doe, who is seeking the office of mayor of Whatville."

3. Promote your candidacy and team using the palm card's talking points. Training will offer consistency and esprit de corps among canvassers.

4. Do not talk for long periods. Be professional and brief. Use the four talking points on the palm card to answer questions from voters. Listen to voters. Do not ever disagree with them.

Describe in a positive way how you, or your candidate, will deal with their concerns and the problems confronting the community.

5. Speak only about issues related to the office being sought. Do not become mired in national issues or issues beyond the candidate's scope.

6. Hand people your palm card; if they are receptive, they may take a lawn sign or bumper sticker. The voter should place it in the yard, unless they specifically request you to do so, or if you request to do so.

7. Be aware of nonverbal messages from voters: facial expressions, the way they hold their head and hands or fold their arms. Body language cues are signals to you. Watch them, and they will tell you what subjects to emphasize or abandon (Andreas and Faulkner 1994, 148; Grinder and Bandler 1976, 32).

8. Dialogue is a two-way street, a six-lane highway. The voter has five lanes.

9. Never argue, especially if you sense the slightest hostility. Instead, ask voters what they would like changed in the district, town, or city. Ask how you can help them. You are knocking on their door to help them.

10. Do not take signs of rejection personally. People may have a cake in the oven, a baby that needs changing, or they may be in the middle of a project (Grey 1999, 199).

11. Ask the resident to vote for you! Come right out and say, "Joe or Jane Resident, I need your support on November 4th. Will you please vote for me?" Shake people's hands firmly. Don't stare, but look them right in the eye the whole time. Be sincere.

12. There will be a time when people become receptive, and you feel you have their vote. At that point, stop talking!

13. Take a mentor with you the first few days. The mentor will tell you how you are doing and offer advice. Use breath mints and carry bottled water (leave it in the car).

14. Elderly residents or people with disabilities may need rides to the polling place. College students, snowbirds (northern or southern residents who migrate with seasonal changes in climate), and military personnel may need absentee ballots (Pelosi 2007, 202). Inquire. Look out for handicapped ramps and military or college stickers on cars or doors. An RV in a driveway might indicate a snowbird lives there. Pay attention to people's needs, but focus on the population most sympathetic to your cause and central theme. Follow-up is important.

15. If no one is home, hang a personalized palm card (handbill or door hanger), along with a brief note, on the doorknob. Mark the residence down for a revisit. It is against federal law to place any campaign literature in a mailbox.

   Tip: The socially accepted hours to canvass are between 9:00 a.m. and dusk.

Speaking with Voters

While canvassing, the candidate and volunteers should always remember that they are imposing on people's homes, their castles. Again, and this cannot be stressed enough, when speaking to people, the most important thing is to listen. They will usually share their areas of interest and concern.

When asked a question, make sure you understand what is being asked (Grey 1999, 122). Do not presuppose what the person is thinking or interrupt. Think about the question and decide if it can be answered using one of the candidate's four talking points. Then, answer in one to three sentences, offering statistics and quantifiable evidence to support the candidate's position. Strategically guide the voter down an issues-related path.

Volunteers who have not been trained in canvassing can be instructed not to talk to people about the candidate's political agenda or stance on issues. Instead, they can refer questions to the candidate, campaign manager, headquarters, or the website. Personal contact is recommended.

Do not beat around the bush. Offer an articulate, courteous, and well-informed reply. If you do not know the answer, say so and get back to the person later. Follow through, or at least one vote will be lost. Do not forget to directly ask people for their votes.

A moment will come when you sense that there has been enough conversation and that the voter wants you to leave. That is the time to wrap it up. Call their attention to the literature you handed to them earlier, ask them if they have any questions, and then leave.

The secret to door-to-door communications is to leave people with the knowledge that you have listened more than talked. You are there to help them. Sell the candidate's unique attributes but know when it is time to leave on an upbeat note.

The Invisible Thread

Candidates are always in search of the "invisible thread" that indicates a common interest and trust with a voter. This bond can be established in several ways:

+ through the introduction of a friend, relative, neighbor, coworker, role model, or community leader (see Mentoring/Unlocking Social Structures with Guides)
+ through hobbies, membership in a civic group or social organization, or military service (see Computer Lists)
+ through a shared political ideology, party membership, or advocacy
+ through endorsements that demonstrate communal acceptance of candidates and their vision
+ through advertisements and speeches that target specific talking points of interest to constituents

The Internet precinct's tools, lists, canvassing, events, speeches, and many other tasks and vehicles help to identify and create a common bond between the candidate and the voters. They help to establish a bridge of trust and build a relationship that allows individual voters to share a candidate's overall vision for future governance.

Mapping Strategy

Start the walking campaign on the main roads first. Place lawn signs on all the main arterials during the first few days of the campaign. Next, canvass the residents who live near the polling places for nominating petition signatures, and ask them to place signs on their lawns. Follow this with visits to the prominent people in the community. Branch out from there. Start calling people as soon as candidates announce their intent to seek elected office, or even before, to solicit pledges of seed money, volunteers, and lawn-sign placements. Make lists!

Walking door-to-door in the country may not accomplish a great deal given the amount of time spent in the endeavor. In a rural setting, try and meet as many people in one location as possible, such as at a library, a senior center, a landfill/recycling center, or a farmer's market. Include someone who is a role model and has commonality with the group attending the event; someone who is well known and respected in the community is always a helpful guide. Even the most densely populated states have sparsely populated areas and an hour of work going door-to-door may only result in a meeting with five or six voters. Spend time wisely.

Get a feeling of how well party committee members will cover the district based on what they have done in the last two or three elections. Find out how many signed nominating petitions they have harvested in the past; that number will usually mirror the number of votes attained for a candidate in a particular district. When a voter signs a candidate's petition, in a way, it is a subliminal pledge to vote for them. There is no downside to an active petition drive. To circumvent legal challenges, the campaign should gather at least three times the minimum number of signatures required by law. Conversely, opponents may be vulnerable in areas their campaigns do not properly canvass. Note: A copy of an opponent's nominating petitions, to determine their areas of strength and weakness, may be obtained from the BOE. A copying and FOIA fee may be charged.

Volunteers and committee members should notify the volunteer coordinator of small local events that might be off the team's radar. Notification is a two-way street. In turn, the campaign should notify volunteers and party committee members of events inside and outside their districts. An event calendar should be included in every volunteer's packet.

If committee members are not receptive, then place the campaign's canvassers in their areas "to assist them." Go through the proper chain of command, and be careful not to step on toes, but also remember that the qualities of efficiency and drive are honored in politics.

But remember, this is politics. People may promise to assist the campaign using a passive method of evasion or subversive tactics. Most people are in politics to help the party's endorsed candidates, but some people only want to further their own agendas or causes. Identify the volunteers who work hard; reward them with praise and thank-you letters. A volunteer should rarely be terminated; reassign them if their work is substandard in a particular area.

The campaign manager or volunteer coordinator may want to assign certain volunteers to specific areas. A senior's high rise is one example (Simpson 1972, 127). The campaign might seek out a senior citizen who is popular and a leader within that age group as a guide during the canvassing effort. However, seniors love young volunteers. They like the attention and exuberance that youth offers. Having a popular senior canvassing with young volunteers might work very well.

The volunteer coordinator should furnish everyone who canvasses door-to-door with a packet. It will contain walking lists, maps, campaign literature, a calendar of events, and schedules. Canvassing must be done with military precision (see Volunteer Coordinator/Recruiter).

Grassroots politics in America involves person-to-person contact and that often means going door-to-door, day after day, in blistering heat or thunderstorms. Many incumbent politicians lose direct contact with the voters, which leaves them vulnerable to being dislodged by a hard-working candidate with an organized campaign. Note: Canvassers should take special note of households with three, four, or more voters who are enrolled in a party sympathetic to the candidate's ideology and stance on issues. Those households may also be prime targets for absentee ballots, for the residents might span several generations—elderly, college or military (Thomas 1999, 50). There is also a "household effect" where active voters will encourage others in the residence to vote (Green and Gerber 2004, 38).

America is a bottom-up republic. There is nothing more important than one person's vote. Elections can be won or lost by one vote, one district, and one precinct. Build a foundational support base one vote at a time through incremental steps. Align a voter's interests with the candidate's theme and talking points. Ensure that each volunteer has a thorough understanding of the one-person-one-vote concept (Green and Gerber 2004, 3).

Statistics and Demographics

Yes, there may be more voters in high-density population areas, but there may not be more votes for a particular candidate. A candidate may be able to call on dozens of households per day in a city, but canvass only a few in a rural setting. People who are sympathetic to your cause and vote frequently are the ones you seek.

Walking Lists

If the BOE (county clerk, state department, elections department, political software contractor, or political party) furnishes walking lists to the candidate's campaign, ensure they include specific data sets.

The walking lists should be organized by ward, parish, precinct, and district. The lists should be further broken down by odd/even street address, last name, first name, party, gender, age, and recent voting history. If the source of lists follows the Voting Rights Act, ethnicity may be an option to be selected (Green and Gerber 2004, 26). Another style of list may be preferential, but whatever is required, be specific. Ask what type and style of list is available from the BOE or the campaign's supplier. A political party endorsement may offer the candidate access to databases that combine voter history with an assortment of techniques, such as precinct mapping.

Copy and divide the lists into assigned geographical areas for dissemination to volunteers. Remember that a cluttered list may confuse some volunteers. If there is a primary, highlight the names of people who are eligible to sign nominating petitions and vote for your candidate. Remember too that the odd- and even-numbered houses on the same street may be in different districts or even different states.

There should be a space on the list where the canvassing volunteer can evaluate the voter's loyalty to the candidate (polling) using a code on a scale from zero to five, for example. Zero would indicate that the voter intensely disagrees with the candidate's policy; five would mean that the voter will definitely vote for the candidate. Whatever code is used, it must be uniform throughout the campaign and party.

Include a sheet with all the codes in the volunteer's packet. The way polling questions are phrased is vital; therefore, the same format must be used universally. It may be advantageous to have people periodically monitor canvassing progress in specific areas; they can also collect petitions or deliver materials, such as lawn signs and palm cards.

Canvassers should update the walking lists since they are the "boots on the ground." If volunteers are organized into groups, those people should meet at the end of the day to be debriefed and hand-in their walking list revisions, absentee-ballot and voter-registration requests. Volunteers also must hand in their signed petitions. Updated and current voter lists are invaluable to the campaign. The raw data updates may be done by the statistician, communications director, office manager, or scribe. Updated lists and the door-to-door poll from the voter's opinion survey are vital tools, used by the executive committee to tweak the candidate's future advertising messages and initiatives (Woo 1980, 56). This data will aid in voter mapping, which will help target areas in need of extra attention.

Maps

Obtain county maps from the appropriate source. A city, town, or county engineering unit may have GPS/GIS mapping in several formats: political, roads, and sewer and water lines. Some elected offices, such as judicial positions, may hold jurisdiction in as many as ten to twelve different counties that may be divided capriciously, perhaps from an ancient gerrymandering.

Perform a search for reasonably priced and current maps at the BOE, county or city clerk's or county engineer's office, library, department of public works, or at a local stationery store. At campaign HQ, post a map that notes the progress of the door-to-door canvassing efforts for all staff and volunteers to see. Again, a candidate's endorsement by a major political party may offer the candidate useful software for mapping, statistics, and voter histories.

Note: Political districts have boundaries. Each school district, city, town, and county also has distinct judicial, legislative, and congressional districts (McNamara 2008, 9). Each candidate might have different territorial concerns.

You Are Out There Anyway, Do Something!

Door-to-door canvassing should not be a one-way street with the candidate or staff only talking about politics. Do not pass up the opportunity to help people. One task, for example, might be to inform property owners of tax exemptions for which they may be eligible. In many communities, veterans and seniors are offered property or school tax exemptions that can save homeowners thousands of dollars. Some communities offer an unmarried widow of a veteran the same exemption as an eligible living veteran. Perhaps water and sewer bills are difficult to understand. Seniors and disabled veterans may also want an absentee ballot or to register to vote. When canvassing, there is a real opportunity to do some good for residents and to take the candidate's message to them. Do not pass it up.

Training

A training regimen is an important door-to-door canvassing tool. For example, specific election laws govern the creation and circulation of nominating petitions. The sage counsel should be included in developing this portion of the training.

Walking door-to-door is a daunting task for people who feel insecure about the thought of addressing total strangers, especially when a vote for their candidate is at stake. One easy way to help people get past this uncomfortable feeling is to have two people experienced in this activity role-play a typical door-to-door scenario. One person plays the canvasser; the other plays the voting resident. They can show by illustration and improvisation the various kinds of reception that can be expected. It will be fun. It will be amusing. And it will quell the nerves of jittery neophytes as they begin to grasp how they might deal with certain situations.

Another good idea is to provide a script for the volunteer to follow, but everyone must be enthusiastic and appear spontaneous. Prepared canvassing scripts should be personalized. The pair of volunteers who will canvass a neighborhood together can practice their lines and evaluate each other. A positive and helpful remark can remove stress and uncertainty. Remember, everybody should have fun.

Canvassing volunteers will find the job much easier if they are prepared. Volunteers should be properly equipped with maps, address sheets, a legal-size clipboard to secure the sheets, a pen, some paper for taking notes, and a highlighter to mark the areas they have visited. A sheet of plastic wrap or plastic sheet protectors will protect the nominating petitions and walking lists from rain during inclement weather. Palm cards and lawn signs are also staples for canvassing volunteers.

Assignments should be matched to individuals. If an area has an ethnic flavor try to match it with the appropriate canvassing volunteers. If people prefer to walk alone, they should be offered that opportunity. Although it is safer to walk in pairs, sometimes there are not enough volunteers available to do so. Volunteers who reside in the area they canvass may feel more comfortable walking alone. After a few houses, they will each develop their own rhythm and style.

This campaign model stresses the importance of establishing a positive footprint in the candidate's election district early in the campaign through an effort to attain the maximum number of nominating petition signatures from eligible voters. Next, update voter residential lists, create an absentee voter list, initiate a voter-registration drive, and obtain polling data to highlight areas and groups of voters in need of targeted advertising. Then, during the summer initiative, broaden the scope to try and reach every enrolled voter in the election district.

The GOTV effort will focus all the campaign's resources—door-to-door canvassing being an integral part—until Election Day. The synergistic effect of many advertising disciplines in repetitive unison will offer the electorate optimal exposure to the election process. Remember, only a strong team can offer long-term political change and government stability.

ENDORSEMENTS

▼

Endorsements are foundational building blocks for political candidates seeking elected office (McNamara 2008, 85). Candidates must set a strategic path at the beginning of their campaigns to outline a theme, talking points, and major issues to be addressed with constituents (Grey 1999, 62). Their platforms will resonate with specific segments of the population. One of the executive committee's first meetings should address which endorsements will be most advantageous for the candidate to seek. Eventually, the campaign website will list the people and organizations whose endorsements the candidate has accepted.

Types of Endorsements

+ Political: from a political party, an incumbent, or the politically influential
+ Personal: neighbor, friend, relative, local people of distinction
+ Professional: business associates; local professionals, such as doctors, lawyers, engineers, and religious leaders, etc.
+ Media: daily and weekly newspapers*
+ Union: police, fire, public employees, electrical workers, miners, etc.
+ Organizational: industrial and business development, veterans, seniors, ethnic groups, civic, social, educational, etc.
+ Corporate: employers in the election district
+ Political action committees (PACs)
+ Celebrities: the Oprah effect (Dalton 2006, 115)

  * FCC rules generally prohibit TV and radio stations from openly endorsing political candidates.

A working or active endorsement, especially from a political party, may offer a host of advantages: advertising, donations, volunteers, membership rosters, and, most important, a distinct following of loyal voters. The CM can use membership lists of organizations that endorse the candidate for targeted fundraising messages and GOTV efforts as Election Day nears.

However, a passive endorsement is often only a symbolic statement of the alignment of issues and the intended degree of support. Either the working or passive endorsement from an individual or organization will give both constituents and the opposition the perception of a positive wave of acceptance for the candidate within the election district.

Note: People rarely endorse a losing candidate. Thus, endorsements send a strong, harmonic message of support that will be felt throughout the district. The campaign manager must reignite this effect at definitive stages during the campaign by targeting specific populations with the candidate's message.

Targeting

Honing in on a specific population allows the candidate to target strategically designed messages to a group of individuals. Message targeting also allows the candidate to explore secondary issues that are only loosely tied to their central campaign theme. This approach would leave the rank-and-file voter untouched and unconcerned about issues they may consider irrelevant, but are of great interest to the targeted population. Isolating or layering a group within a population is called micro-targeting (see appendix J).

Party Endorsement

A political committee's main function is to endorse candidates for elected office, solicit members to go door-to-door with nominating petitions, and raise funds to support endorsed candidates. Political parties generally endorse candidates at committee meetings and caucuses.

If aspiring candidates are members of a party's city or county committee, many opportunities for endorsement will be open to them. If they are not committee members, the first item on their to-do lists should be to obtain membership. Sometimes they are appointed by the party's town, city, or county political chair. In most states, a committee member is an elected official and, at some point, must run for office. Aspiring candidates often must perform foundational work for committee membership a year or two before their candidacy.

Political committees usually have numerous vacancies. The candidate's campaign manager should acquire a copy of the committee's bylaws before endorsement selections are made. Consult with the campaign's sage counsel for legal advice.

Tip: In some political cultures, the mere request for written rules and bylaws could be viewed as a threatening gesture. Be diplomatic.

Once candidates have joined the party's committee, the next step is to have several family members and core supporters elected or appointed to the committee as well. This will help them establish a power base for future endorsements—not only for their candidacies but for their supporters as well. Establishing a bloc of committee votes also enables the campaign to form internal political relationships and alliances from a position of strength.

Typically, the party's committee will endorse a candidate before primary elections, in January or as late as June. As a result, there is usually an opportunity for candidates to present their platforms before the committee in open forums or among party leaders in executive sessions. However, candidates may find that the committee has someone else in mind. That means a primary fight.

Some parties endorse candidates behind closed doors through an executive committee vote. Some chairmen/women endorse candidates during golf games or libations at the country club, without seeking the advice or consent of anyone. Welcome to the world of politics.

Candidate Selection Process

+ Caucus, a group of committee members, selects candidates for endorsements
+ Governing (or executive) committee from a party selects candidates
+ Open vote takes place at party committee meetings with a quorum of members
+ Party chair selects whoever they believe is the most competent
+ Delegates are selected by the committee to represent a political area

The candidate must be presented as a strong leader with solid credentials and firm beliefs; a team player; and someone with demonstrated leadership qualities. Candidacy within a political party requires a different skill set than candidacy in a partisan election. This is one reason why some endorsed candidates are icons within the party, but may not capture many votes on Election Day. Candidacy takes diplomacy, knowledge, money, forethought, and time.

The candidate should always be professional and courteous and should not burn any bridges, which may affect future endorsements.

Be prepared. Vacancies for elected office sometimes occur very rapidly due to the unfortunate death or injury of an incumbent. Some officials wake up and decide that today is the day they will retire. People who are poised for candidacy may need to start their campaigns upon a moment's notice. Ask the state and county BOEs about the appropriate procedure for getting on the ballot in primary and general elections. Do not rely on a political party or its representative to perform this task unsupervised.

If offered the opportunity to present before the party committee, the candidate should present a concise platform in a five- to ten-minute speech. Individual time allocation also depends on how many candidates are seeking endorsement during that meeting. At this time, never say anything against the opposing candidate(s). The perceived common dislike of an incumbent, opponent, or issues, which may seem prevalent among constituents, may not be the view of that party's committee members or base voters (Thomas 1999, 9).

In many states, it is permissible for a candidate to seek an endorsement from more than one political party, if a party does not have a registered candidate seeking election to the same office. However, most states do not allow cross endorsements. Certain states also offer what is called a "right to ballot," which offers a candidate from one party an opportunity to run on the primary ballot of another party. Some cases may require a notary public to circulate nominating petitions. Endorsements across political parties are not only possible but frequently sought after in some states.

Union and Social Group Endorsements

If one of the candidate's talking points is "law and order," police and fire union endorsements are crucial. As mentioned previously, the downside to any endorsement is that opponents will say that candidates owe allegiance to those who endorse them.

> *Tip:* Prepare talking points to defend endorsements, but only address the issue if the opposition brings it up. Be prepared.

Unions and organizations endorse candidates because their philosophies and goals are closely aligned. Candidates must weigh the advantages and disadvantages of union or organizational endorsements before seeking them. If endorsements are obtained, the CM should try to obtain membership rosters from the organization to enable the solicitation of volunteers, votes, and donations.

Large organizations and national unions usually endorse the safest bet, and that often means the incumbent. Nobody wants to endorse a losing candidate. With this in mind, endorsement from a major newspaper may indicate which candidate has the best chance of winning—at the time of the endorsement. If things get dicey, some people or organizations may withdraw their endorsements.

Endorsements may create an opportunity for free advertising; contact the media through press releases issued by the communications director. At the same time, the executive committee should filter endorsement requests carefully. Some organizations hold extremely negative connotations, and their statements of support are known as "pariah endorsements."

Newspaper Endorsements

After a political party endorsement, a newspaper endorsement may be the most important for a candidate. Most newspapers in the United States openly endorse political candidates through their editorial boards. Fairness doctrines, written or implied, often allow equal exposure for candidates seeking endorsement. However, depending on the publication, there may be a cognitive dissonance between the perception and the reality of fairness.

Unlike other corporations, media conglomerates have unlimited access to a public platform through which they can present their self-interests in the guise of being watchdogs that protect the citizenry. Many reporters have biases just like everyone else. If a paper endorses a particular candidate, that person is at least tacitly beholden to it, and in many cases the newspaper has predetermined its news coverage for the future. Few newspapers turn on their endorsed candidates after the election; instead, they offer them every opportunity for success. If an endorsed candidate fails, it reflects poorly on the editorial board's judgment. Either way, constituents may not be represented fairly when a newspaper endorses a political candidate.

The Pygmalion effect

Psychologist Robert Merton developed central elements in the science of sociology and coined phrases such as "unintended consequences," "role model," and "self-fulfilling prophesy." Peter Senge built on the self-fulfilling prophesy concept to form a social treatise known as the "Pygmalion effect," in which positive opinion about (endorsement of) candidates offers them a greater sense of accomplishment with faith in and optimism about future achievement. Henceforth, marginal or even substandard performance will most likely be met with positive reinforcement (Senge 1990, 80).

Unendorsed candidates, however, are *expected* to perform poorly because they were not chosen. They venture through social minefields of negative labeling, lower self-esteem, and anticipated poor performance. But a candidate's future is never preordained. Endorsed candidates may choose not to optimize their favorable position and sit on their laurels; unendorsed candidates may be spurred on to try much harder.

Conclusion

Candidates should never assume that they will get an endorsement from a particular party, union, newspaper, or organization. They should always conduct research and the required networking to ascertain which way endorsements are heading.

For instance, let us assume that a Conservative/Republican candidate running for a county supervisor's position is a retired assistant district attorney from an adjacent county. One of the candidate's four talking points is law and order. Other than the military, there are few organizations more conservative than the rank and file of police and fire unions (McNamara 2008, 79). The Republican's central talking points also include the proposal for a smaller, more efficient government with lower taxes.

However, the police and fire unions may endorse the Liberal/Democrat as their candidate because the unions believe in larger government with more services, that higher pay and an enhanced benefits package will attract better higher quality applicants to the police and fire departments. The same scenario might be said of teachers or any other public employee or trade union.

As a rule, constituents do not trust politicians. Congress's approval ratings are often in the low teens. The quality or quantity of endorsements a candidate receives may be the deciding factor for many people, especially swing voters.

Note: Pay attention to the new laws governing social media and not-for-profit organizations concerning political endorsements. Conduct an online search for FTC Endorsement Guide and endorsement laws governing nonprofit, 501 (c)(3) organizations (http://ftc.gov/os/2009/10/0 91005revisedendorsementguides.pdf).

Organizations may be reluctant to relinquish their membership lists, even to an endorsed candidate. If so:

+ the organization may be willing to send a letter written by the candidate to its membership;
+ the candidate will compose, envelope, and stamp the letters; the organization will label and mail them to the members;
+ the candidate also could write an article for the organization's membership newsletter; or
+ the candidate could write an e-mail to the members.

Tip: All correspondence from the candidate should include the campaign's physical, e-mail, and website addresses.

For many Americans, philosophical and organizational endorsements have merit. However, when citizens endorse a candidate by placing lawn signs in their yards, those endorsements vouch for the candidate's personal quality at a grassroots level. Personal endorsements from friends, neighbors, and community role models have a great influence on the number of votes a candidate receives on Election Day.

GOING NEGATIVE

▼

The entire focus and forward momentum of political campaigns lie in building a positive model for candidates based on their education, qualifications, and experience. In essence, a candidate runs *for* an elected office, not *against* another person.

The candidate should place their credentials before the voters in a positive, upbeat manner. People need to know about a candidate's education and experience to determine who is best qualified to fill the elected position and deal with constituents, tasks, and social challenges. The candidate's qualifications far outweigh an opponent's political apathy, moral indiscretions, or intentional misrepresentations.

Therefore, candidates must develop a positive long-term vision that projects their personal attributes and the party's foundational tenets, ideas, philosophy, and unity from the first to the very last day of the campaign.

Another option is to go negative. This often shifts the campaign's spotlight to the opponent and may encourage voters to focus on short-term issues rather than on the candidate's long-term vision.

I have never been in favor of negative campaigning, but there are times when voters must be informed about certain facts concerning the opposition that might otherwise go unaddressed. The methods used to raise allegations of impropriety will reflect on the honor and integrity of both the accuser and the accused.

The public's litmus test for candidate malfeasance may open a floodgate of controversy that crushes an opponent's election bid. Or it may boomerang, and the candidate will be viewed as having so few attributes that negative campaigning was their only course of action (Shaw 2000, 224). Going negative is usually the last-ditch effort of a losing candidate. What is truly disheartening is that sometimes negative attacks destabilize the opposition's campaign momentum or instill doubt in the voters' minds. Most elections are won by very narrow margins.

The most famous negative advertisement in US electoral history was produced during Lyndon Johnson's run against Barry Goldwater in the 1964 presidential election. It is known as the "Daisy Spot" and is available on YouTube. The commercial opens with a small young girl with freckles in a field, innocently picking petals from a daisy, haphazardly counting down from ten to one. A deep male voice takes over the countdown; at zero, an atomic bomb explodes—a mushroom cloud advances skyward. Then a voice states, "Vote for Lyndon Johnson on November third. The stakes are too high for you to stay home" (Joslyn 1984, 2; Campbell 2000, 242). The "Daisy Spot" aired only once, but Barry Goldwater was instantly labeled a war monger who would start a third world war, if elected. Less than two months after his oath of office, on March 8, 1965, in response to the Gulf of Tonkin incident, LBJ (the reelected president) landed the Third Battalion Ninth Marines at Red Beach Da Nang, Vietnam—starting the Vietnam War (Hoffman and Crumley 2002, 544). The Vietnam War killed more than fifty-eight thousand Americans. The "Daisy Spot" shifted the entire focus of the 1964 election, and was instrumental in altering world history.

The goal of negative campaigning is to shift the opponent's campaign into a defensive posture, requiring it to spend energy, time, and money to cover past indiscretions rather than to look forward to building a positive, issue-based campaign. To describe this style of campaigning as wholly unsavory paints this method with a wide brush and fails to take into account a full menu of options. There are several ways of approaching the realities of negative campaigning. Conversely, campaign staff should know when negative tactics are being employed against them by the opposition.

Note: Voters rely on an informed and unbiased news media to reveal political malfeasance. However, certain candidates seem impervious to media criticism, and direct intervention may be required (see Endorsements/Pygmalion effect). Sometimes people seeking elected office have had lapses in moral judgment severe enough to raise questions about their qualifications to hold public office. In these cases, it may not be a question of whether to reveal the transgression, but who will do it, and when and how.

The candidate could wait and confront the opponent at a debate, but this type of public ambush may not be viewed as being appropriate by the electorate. The grandstanding shockwaves of a direct confrontation may gain the candidate momentary popularity but may later stain the campaign as venal rather than politically adept. Negative campaigning will forever change the complexion and tone of the race. Once a campaign's negative genie gets out of the bottle, it is impossible to put back.

Of course, a candidate may choose to take the high road, exude a professionalism that is impervious to daily mudslinging, and never say anything negative about the opponent in public. Meanwhile, their campaign staff will leave no stone unturned and clandestinely do exactly the opposite. A good attack advertisement will not directly attack an opponent (McNamara 2008, 95).

Nearly all candidates have something they would prefer to remain private: past or present addictions, nonpayment of child support, sexual dalliances, traffic violations, DUIs or DWIs, or worse. The litany is endless. Perhaps the opposition candidate has been convicted of fraud or embezzlement. Certain types of indiscretions should be taken before the people. Let them decide. Any severe infraction that may affect a person's judgment in office should be placed before the voters. The American political system is designed to expose such injustices and not to do so may actually be a disservice to the public (Shaw 2000, 211). Voters should be kept informed of all the facts in order to make a sound decision on Election Day (see Statistician/Researcher).

Each allegation that surfaces must be true beyond any shadow of a doubt. However, the procurement of documents to substantiate allegations cannot tread upon a citizen's privacy rights. In this light, most incumbents are before the public for their entire term in office and are much more vulnerable to negative campaigning (Faucheux 2002, 198).

The Positive and the Negative

Most incumbent politicians eventually vote themselves pay increases, which could be brought to light by the opposition in several ways. One way would be a letter to the editor praising the incumbent, sent to the newspaper by a concerned citizen. For example:

> John Doe has worked hard for his district as a city supervisor and the $180,000 a year
> he is paid by the city is well worth his tireless devotion to his job. He only voted himself
> a $6,000 pay increase this year, which is only a 3.3 percent increase. If he were employed
> in private industry he would be making twice that amount.

Voters could be outraged and a harmonic ripple effect flood the newspaper with a firestorm of indignation, or it will die a natural death of disinterest. In this particular case, it is likely the incumbent will be forced to justify their salary and pay increases, shifting the focus of their campaign and denying them the time to discuss issues vital to their reelection (Shadegg 1964, 89).

This may be one of the only times when an incumbent is at a disadvantage. One of the best negative advertisements is when candidates' own words are used against them. Everyone makes mistakes. With politicians, those mistakes can be played again and again every evening on television. Dirty politics ensues when this tactic is followed with an issue that is not true, particularly when it is just days before the election when there is no time for an adequate defense or response.

Tip: Going negative and going dirty are two different things. This book does not propose either, but using negative advertising sometimes has excellent results. However, if it is not done properly, negative advertising can boomerang very quickly. It is often the last, desperate tool used by a losing candidate.

Links

If negative campaigning is employed, it should be a targeted effort that focuses on only one or two areas where the opposing candidate is vulnerable. Sometimes, there is a vocal coterie of people who may dislike the opposition candidate. This group may be a valuable resource for information, volunteers, and donations.

Another successful method is to link opponents to unpopular figures they have supported in the past or to an issue they championed that has gone south or to past platforms and policies that have failed. Success or failure of a policy is often in the presentation.

How aggressive does the campaign want to be? Once it starts, there is no telling how far it will go. The subject may acquire legs and a body of its own.

It was once a treasure trove for the opposition and news media to gain information on a politician's sexual transgressions. Since the 1990s, however, voters have shown disinterest in reports about infidelities by candidates of every persuasion. It is unfortunate that many politicians have lowered the morality bar so grievously. Politicians are human. They have frailties and prejudices, and have on occasion made grievous errors. However, the press often seems to selectively tolerate chosen candidates on both sides of the aisle. Books have been written outlining the relationships between morality and individual character.

A political campaign may feel that issues of morality are subjective and should not be considered unless they are illegal. Issues of sexual orientation or infidelity should not be pursued by the campaign team unless they will affect the opposing candidate's ability to govern.

Do attack ads work? Sometimes, but more often than not negative campaigning displays the character of the accusatory candidate rather than the person being attacked. If a campaign resorts to negative advertising it may soon overshadow each candidate's true qualifications for office and the real concerns of citizens. Negative campaigns usually lower voter turnout on Election Day (Green and Gerber 2004, 60). Many candidates have won elections and lost the values they once held dear.

INTERNET PRECINCT

▼

The Internet precinct is a bridge that connects the campaign to the electorate by utilizing modern communications tools and data-collection methods. It not only offers voters a window into the candidate's political initiatives but enables the campaign to collect vital information about residents in the district. At the heart of this effort is the campaign's website, but the Internet precinct is active on many levels. This network is constructed by the coordinated efforts of the campaign manager, communications director, computer specialist, and statistician.

There are basically two complementary efforts in progress, similar to what a military general would call the air and ground campaigns. The air campaign is the electronic platform. The ground campaign consists of the canvassers, staff, and volunteers of the political party's committee who merge existing political support networks with the candidate's campaign initiative.

The air campaign consists of the website and other electronic technology the campaign uses for communication and data collection. The website puts the candidate's best foot forward, giving residents the opportunity to know him or her. It also serves as a vehicle for citizens who want to donate or actively participate in the campaign.

For people to access the website, they must know it exists. The Internet precinct is not a stand-alone electronic initiative, but a tech-savvy platform for reaching out to every voter in an attempt to establish common ground. All campaign advertising should include the campaign's website address.

Create an Electronic Platform

+ Build a website using the campaign theme—candidate's vision and talking points.
+ Implement credit-card acceptance for fundraising (e.g. Paypal).
+ Develop an e-mail-forwarding tree, starting with staff and core supporters.
+ Publish a weekly e-mail blastcast (e-newsletter).

+   Video or webcam the candidate's central message and "hot issue" responses at events and debates for upload to the website.
+   Utilize every available tool to collect the e-mail addresses of constituents.
+   Post a changing photo montage of the candidate interacting with voters.
+   Create a useful resource that helps constituents navigate the government's labyrinth of agencies.
+   Ensure that all campaign literature and marketing materials contain the website address.
+   Create a spreadsheet to capture demographic and polling data collected by door-to-door canvassers, through the website, and via other methods, such as event sign-in sheets.
+   Employ modern communications technology for volunteers and staff as tools for interacting with the electorate.
+   Use GPS mapping to aid and track canvassers.
+   Assist the poll-watching effort on Election Day and during GOTV efforts.

The key to an Election Day victory is embodied in the interaction of the air and ground campaigns, i.e., and the optimal utilization of the political party's support network during the door-to-door canvassing phase. Many candidates start their campaigns too late and are forever playing catch up in trying to make up for lost ground.

If endorsed, the candidate and the campaign manager must decide to what degree, if any, the canvassing initiative will interact with the local party's committee. The political party will circulate petitions for every candidate on the ballot. Each candidate's campaign team will also circulate petitions. A deal may be struck to help a select group of (endorsed) candidates also running for elected office with canvassing and the distribution of their petitions, quid pro quo. Note: If candidates have not been endorsed by a political party, they must mirror the party's framework as closely as possible and create their own political base from scratch. This is a Herculean task, but doable.

The canvassing initiative (ground campaign) and electronic footprint (air campaign) must coexist with the candidate's political party initiative. The campaign manager must establish a rapport with the party leadership and rank-and-file members but also establish a somewhat independent campaign structure.

>   *Tip*: Political cultures and party rules are different within each election district. Party members often work long hours for no pay and few rewards. However, in some areas an antiquated hierarchical structure may be in place. Party membership will sometimes include a few individuals in honorary, nonworking positions. If this is the case, an astute mentor may be invaluable help by encouraging trained canvassers to assist less enthusiastic committee members.

A united canvassing effort will help to build an Internet precinct and establish

- the maximum number of nominating petition signatures
- polling of voter interests to modernize the campaign's theme and talking points
- updating of voter databases and walking lists with physical and e-mail addresses; these are required for successful voter-registration drives, the engine of growth
- introduction of the candidate to the voters
- advertising of the campaign's website through the distribution of palm cards (handbills/door hangers), yard signs, and campaign literature
- updates of the absentee-ballot registry that identifies students, military, seniors, people with disabilities, and snowbirds who might not make it to the polls (Pelosi 2007, 201)
- an early voting program, if sanctioned in the state; thirty-two states now sanction early-voting practices (Elliott and Kuhnhenn 2012)

To ensure a successful resolution on Election Day and that the Internet precinct is an effective tool, voter data must be current. The Internet precinct assumes more of a background role during the canvassing cycle. However, as the campaign gains momentum, it will move into the foreground during the summer—gaining prominence in the early fall and during GOTV efforts as voters realize its usefulness.

People who vote are the target of the campaign's initiative, in a hierarchical ladder of importance as to their political party and voting frequency (see Voting Blocs). Nevertheless, the demographic data on voter residency (USPS or other vendor) gathered by the statistician should be compared to the BOE's rosters to identify unregistered residents. The statistician's identification of unregistered residents is also connected to the canvassers' work to update the voter rolls. Unregistered voters are a huge reservoir of untapped potential. Initiate a voter-registration drive to enroll residents who fall within this category. Newly registered voters usually vote if special attention is offered them during GOTV efforts.

> *Tip:* Residents may be hesitant to share their personal e-mail addresses with a total stranger. Canvassers must direct them to the candidate's website, which should also have an area dedicated to issues such as property tax exemptions for eligible seniors and veterans, documentation on food stamp eligibility, or other items of prominence to aid residents in the election district. In addition to being a vital political and advertising network for a candidate, the campaign's website can be a valuable resource for voters. Canvassers should mention this resource during their door-to-door programs to entice constituents to participate.

Building a Data Collection Network

An Election Day victory requires the campaign manager to use every available tool to update voter residency lists to properly advertise the candidate's political agenda. The campaign will coordinate the effort to update and collect every e-mail address, voter address, and phone number within the election district using the BOE's lists, residency lists, and emerging technology. The computer specialist and statistician will establish a database to support the generation of mailing labels, e-mail communication (blastcasts), and directories for phone-bank use.

Currently, the most reliable tool for obtaining and updating information is through door-to-door canvassing, which then is refined and expanded to collect voter data through the website, rallies, hosting of parties, and many other areas. As technology evolves, there will be new ways to collect e-mail and physical addresses, but the utilization of canvassers to collect data does not incur an additional expense and touches base with every voter on a personal level (Shadegg 1964, 125).

Building an Effective Internet Precinct: Challenges and Advantages

The techniques used to build an Internet voting network are similar to the way politicians still build their base constituencies—by knocking on doors throughout their districts. Unit and campaign managers will ask staff and volunteers to gather e-mail addresses by mining networks of friends, family, membership rosters, neighbors, party committee members, coworkers, and business associates (Pelosi 2007, 39). The updated residential and e-mail lists obtained from volunteers and canvassers will enhance the accuracy of voter lists obtained from the BOE or political parties.

Newspaper articles deliver yesterday's news to an ever-decreasing customer base. Television is no longer effectively reaching the number of voters it once did. The six o'clock news is viewed by many as being neither current nor unbiased, and it requires a viewer to accept a one-way communication at a specific time and place.

Conversely, online news articles are continuously streamed, and evolve from second to second, offering the distinct advantage of hyperlinked text for further research (Morris 1999, 92). The transition from newspaper snippets and television or radio sound bites to in-depth and instant Internet coverage is as profound as the change from silent to talking pictures. However, this new frontier of connectivity is currently unregulated, unpredictable, and in a continuous state of flux.

Access to the Internet allows the voter to be politically active and attend a candidate's rally or debate online in real time. Within seconds, an attendee's experience can be shared by thousands or maybe millions of like-minded people through a multitude of social networks like Twitter, YouTube, and Facebook. Furthermore, the candidate's message itself has become an interactive real-time experience with the campaign website offering a candidate's résumé and biography, video clips, current political news, as well as volunteer and donation icons. The person in control of an election's outcome has always been the voter. Today, the cyber-citizen influences not only the outcome but also the direction of a political campaign.

The Internet offers every person who supports a candidate the opportunity to be a campaign worker. Each political party member with access to a modern communications device has the ability to forward e-mail messages or newscasts. The political candidate need only tug at a contemporary issue popular among the electorate to enlist an army of frontline party supporters and behind-the-scenes activists. If requested, people who read interesting political articles will share them with friends and relatives.

If a relative or friend composes or forwards an e-mail article, it may be more readily accepted than when a political campaign spams a given population. It is a matter of trust. Voters will trust relatives, friends, coworkers, and neighbors before they will trust a stranger. This style of interaction is also a characteristic of the swing voter's decision-making process (see Swing Vote).

Exploring the Roots of the E-mail Tree

Candidates want voters to accept, view, and read their messages; agree with them; relate to them; and forward the messages to others. The campaign must have all volunteers, managers, and staff members start address books on their computers exclusively for campaign use.

People who forward blastcasts and campaign articles should not use their entire address books for this purpose, but select only the recipients who may be receptive to the candidate's message. The activity of e-mail forwarding and re-mail forwarding will send the candidate's message to an exponential number of constituents. And it is nearly free.

Note: If unit managers modify the blastcast solely for the distribution to their areas, the message should be cleared by the communications director to ensure the announcement is congruent with the candidate's talking points and central theme—a discussion for weekly executive committee meetings.

The computer specialist can outline the procedure for forming an address book for campaign usage on computers or mobile devices. Staff and volunteers will use the e-mail programs they already use on their computers, such as Gmail or Hotmail. Training seminars, hard-copy instructions, and a helpline must be set up for this purpose.

Dual Membership in the Candidate's Campaign

An opportunity exists for a political campaign to offer dual membership to constituents by capitalizing both on the existing political structure's framework and a second, united front through an electronic partnership—the Internet precinct. Utilizing the existing political structure will promote traditional political activism at the ward and precinct level to encourage beneficial contact with the party committee members who participate in door-to-door canvassing and personal interaction with the electorate (England 1992, 55). Door-to-door canvassing, with direct personal contact, will solidify the base and core party constituents as well as establish a new personal dialogue with valence and swing voters (Pelosi 2007, 15; see Door-to-Door Canvassing). Likewise, using the Internet and cutting-edge communications tools forms a dual front of information dissemination and gathering that is distinctly separate from but works in unison with the traditional political infrastructure and its advertising doctrine. The Internet effort will maintain the interest of the base and core voters, but allow the campaign to establish a new cutting-edge dialogue with valence, unaffiliated, independent, and swing voters (see Swing Vote; Voting Blocs).

There may also be another type of campaign initiative in progress, especially during presidential and gubernatorial elections: when PACs, super-PACs, and national political committees (DNC, RNC) overlay their campaign models on top of a local candidate's effort (McNamara 2008, 95). PACs and state and national political committees may utilize robo-calls, canvassing, newspaper and Internet advertisements, radio, television and mailings without the inclusion or expressed consent of the local candidate, often sacrificing the grassroots campaigns for national interests. Unfortunately, such initiatives often take the form of negative advertising, even though it may directly conflict with the local candidate's campaign.

The Candidate's Newscast

The candidate's newscast originates from the central campaign's communications director. E-mail recipients should never be spammed but should receive one informative newscast per week from the campaign, except during the GOTV initiative. The straightforward, timely, and informative newscast message should be sent to all the e-mail addresses collected at the campaign level. However, a larger campaign has the flexibility to utilize its unit managers, who will redistribute modified newscasts with local flavor to their e-mail address books, allowing for a more personal correspondence to their areas of influence.

Historically, few small political campaigns have the resources or knowledge to mount a professional effort through the Internet, but the ease of use, increased knowledge, and lower costs are allowing every campaign some form of online presence.

Compared to snail mail, modern communications technology is amazingly effortless and cost-efficient. But the campaign must understand that traditional methods of advertising—newspaper, direct mail, and door-to-door canvassing—may reach one audience, while electronic communications may reach another one entirely.

A great number of voters work full-time, commute, have children and family obligations, hobbies, club membership, and a variety of other commitments. They are pressed for time but want to be kept informed of major political news that will affect their lives. The campaign's weekly e-mail newscast is designed to network with this population.

The American political scene is modernizing and undergoing continuous change. The train of electronic information cannot be stopped, but it can be directed to different tracks. There are untold rewards for candidates whose campaign managers embrace technological innovations.

Moore's Law for computer systems states that computer memory size and speed (performance) will double every eighteen to twenty-four months. This has been an amazingly accurate prediction, and was true even before 1965 when the term was coined. With this in mind, it is projected that the computer technology and communications tools available to aid political campaigns will evolve much faster than humans can adapt to them (Senge 1994, 69). This is one of the many reasons why only broad terms and not specific technology are addressed here.

Conclusion

The campaign uses the existing political structure to gain access to the electorate through traditional means, such as door-to-door canvassing, neighborhood phone banks, and the US mail. However, the Internet precinct addresses a new cultural norm in fostering change through technological advancement by integrating conventional methods with contemporary tools. Effective integration of both initiatives will reach distinct audiences and form the fabric of a strong union and a winning campaign.

MENTORING

▼

Mentoring, coaching, and teaching embrace their own educational and business purviews, but political mentoring is distinctive. Political campaigns have their own lexicon for thought, language, and deed. Mentoring teaches the language of politics and experiential campaign literacy.

Finding an adept mentor is one of the first steps in a novice's retinue. There are basically two ways to accomplish this goal: through a formal, structured mentoring program or with an informal, more conventional style of instruction. They both have strong points as well as drawbacks. An effective political mentoring program is a hybrid of both but designed to fit the needs of a particular candidate and election.

Mentoring is especially helpful in politics because the political system is a unique environment. Few friends or relatives of the candidate may know a great deal about the internal workings of the political structure, yet the candidate is expected to grow and prosper in this unfamiliar territory. An aspiring candidate often experiences a compressed time frame and a lack of political expertise.

A candidate is often in desperate need of unbiased advice from a person with knowledge and experience. The primary emphasis for mentoring in a political setting is to educate a new candidate who offers great potential but has few internal contacts or experiential knowledge. Mentoring is most effective when augmenting a candidate's existing knowledge. *Political Tool Kit* presents ideas and proven techniques for the mentee to bring to the mentor/candidate table for discussion and implementation (see Foundation: Getting Started).

Expectations and Agreement

The first meeting between the candidate and mentor must set expectations and outline objectives in a concrete manner. The mentor's primary task during this meeting is to critically evaluate the candidate's intellectual and political acumen to ascertain what tools, knowledge, and professional contacts are needed for their success.

An informal agreement between the two is often a good starting point. It will establish goals and clearly define the relationship and should include a limited confidentiality agreement. The agreement between mentor and mentee is not a binding document or contract. Rather, it is an outline of what is expected and should transpire in the future—a tutorial wish list. It will help to eliminate the candidate's fear of the unknown by identifying the steps needed to form a competitive campaign. The campaign's goals and projected training can be modified later upon mutual consent. A political party chair may have the authority and resources to implement a training program of this type.

A formal mentoring program
- Chooses a mentor coordinator (usually the party chair or a designee)
- Recruits and interviews prospective mentors; notes specialties
- Has a mentor coordinator, who evaluates the need to improve relationships
- Monitors the mentor and candidate's progress at periodic intervals
- Encourages mentor and candidate to maintain a journal to record campaign progress, experience, and use of resources (see Candidate/Logbook)
- Targets "nests of need" for mentoring: election laws, fundraising, advertising, etc.
- Provides a feedback loop to help redesign the program for future use

A mentor
- Identifies and cultivates the candidate's positive attributes
- Serves as a positive role model
- Provides support and encouragement
- Shares the candidate's and the party's vision
- Initiates best practices, drawn from experience
- Predicts outcomes; has political intuition
- Ventures beyond stated obligations
- Inspires the candidate to reach higher
- Uncovers and develops a candidate's latent talents
- Passes on hidden informal political language and characteristics
- Teaches through informal methods, such as "learning stories"
- Bridges the cognitive gap between fact and intuition

Mentor tasks:
- Recommends ways for the candidate and campaign staff to perform a specific task
- Serves as a proactive resource and confidant, especially when problems occur
- Identifies "one shot" intervention techniques for individual tasks

+ Acts as a source for information regarding the campaign's strategic direction
+ Gives feedback on observed behavior and reported performance
+ Maintains contact for feedback, as needed, to ensure success
+ Seeks information and assistance to resolve questions or problems
+ Agrees to a no-fault conclusion of the mentoring relationship
+ Observes political and economic trends; offers feedback
+ Establishes time-management guidelines (realistic task time frames)
+ Helps to eliminate fear of the unknown

A mentee

+ Identifies the mentor's source political base: candidate establishes their own network—replicates success
+ Protects confidentiality

Tip: The mentee (candidate) is a partner not a subordinate. If requested by the committee, a successful mentee will become a valuable resource and a possible mentor in the future.

The Mentoring Program

It is not important how the candidate and the mentor come into contact, by happenstance or assignment. However, there must be a bond of common political interests and personal rapport between the candidate (protégé or mentee) and mentor (coach or teacher). A mentor often becomes a long-term political friend and confidant who will offer good advice and direction without bias.

It is also invaluable for the candidate to have an impartial sounding board during critical phases in the campaign. There is a cognitive dissonance between wanting to do something and having the tools to do it. A mentor can close that gap. Elected office and government administration is often insular, and leadership is lonely. A mentor is a person who can offer out-of-the-loop discourse, and unbiased advice during crucial times.

When mentors are selected, they must take the candidate under their wings. This act implies that knowledge and training will be offered to the candidate as well as a certain degree of protection from adversaries and predators while under the mentor's tutelage. Mentoring does hold a degree of risk for the candidate because few mentors who are veteran politicians have no adversaries. It is both the mentor's and the candidate's job to only take the good away from the relationship (Andreas and Faulkner 1994, 147).

Candidates must always be wary of unwanted influence and aware that some political people may have an urge to control them and their ideas or to at least channel them into alliances that may prove unrewarding. Candidates should not be clones of their mentors and must learn to forge their own paths and methods. Any increase in political knowledge and acumen will greatly benefit the candidate's constituency and the political party the candidate represents.

The candidate's alliances and support system are strengthened by the mentor's knowledge, friends, and contacts. A mentor's positive model can be extremely empowering.

A Formal Mentoring Program

A mentoring program for aspiring politicians established by a city, county, or state political party is an effective tool. An established program offers a considerable degree of professionalism and structure. A structured program exposes a candidate to several mentoring choices. A strong candidate will mobilize the entire ticket on Election Day (Green and Gerber 2004, 3), and a successful candidate will be a professional representative of their political party.

Mentoring can surge a campaign forward in the first few days, helping to overcome the imbalance associated with a fledgling candidate's lack of experience. Mentors can be strategically placed where they have an overall view of the entire campaign. On the other hand, select mentors can specialize in one-shot mentoring for a given area, like advertising, mailing, computerized lists, nominating petitions, and door-to-door canvassing. These mentors often possess hands-on experience that can help circumvent the high fees charged by advertising agencies, political consulting, or public relations firms.

A mentoring program will also enhance and broaden the party chair's own base of support and political power. An active mentoring program will enhance political relationships and foster new pathways for internal alliances. Alliances within a political party become blocs of votes.

Alliances and voting blocs are the foundation of party unity for political endorsements and support. A party chair should aspire to be in the enviable position of directing alliances to a particular issue or candidate. An active mentoring program will enhance party solidarity, while the chairman/woman dispenses knowledge and resources. Several campaigns under one party's banner can be integrated through a mentoring program to weave a universal thread, offering a united front to an opposing party.

A formal mentoring program can be as short-term and casual as an employee orientation, or it can be as structured as an internship for medical doctors, nurses, or teachers. The mentor/

mentee relationship can even be as brief as someone showing a new employee the lay of the land and location of their offices or the wash room.

Formal political mentoring is not nearly as structured as other mentoring programs involving some type of certification, but the process should include a timetable and goals. It is designed to bring the new candidate on board with an introduction to the political landscape. It informs them of the informal and hidden language of candidacy and the posturing of specific individuals on both sides of the aisle.

Mentoring is also beneficial to the party in general by guiding the new candidate through potential minefields of mistakes. A well-informed professional candidate reflects well on everyone in the political party.

> *Tip:* A latent fear within a candidate may be that today's confidant and ardent running mate could become tomorrow's most vitriolic opponent (Pelosi 2007, 25).

Unlocking Social Structures with Guides

The political environment touches every class of society, social strata, and civic organization. No matter how worldly or well versed candidates are, they still carry the attributes and baggage of their social class and education. Hidden rules are cloistered within every ethnic, business, or social group (Payne and Krabill 2002, 20). Candidates must remove barriers and build partnerships with each group in their districts. This form of in-depth social interaction can only be accomplished through relationships.

The best way to understand unspoken cues within a social group or class is to have a guide from that faction who will act as an interpreter and representative. The candidate's guide will be the key to unlocking the door and outline a framework of accepted and exceptional behavior within that class. Acceptance within the group will allow the candidate and their representatives freedom of movement within the class but also a limited degree of protection from opposition candidates who may also try to gain admission.

The campaign manager or mentor must select a well-respected role model from within that social class or civic organization to serve as a guide. Organizations with large populations—such as military veterans, senior citizens, and religious or ethnic groups—should be represented in the campaign if those groups are well represented within the election district.

Guides must know the lay of the land and be honored and respected among their peers. The choice of a political ambassador and gatekeeper within the identified social group may be one of the most critical decisions facing the campaign manager and candidate. The guide will pave the way for the candidate to be offered what is tantamount to tribal membership in that group.

A Cup of Tea

A cup of tea or coffee is an informal meeting between the candidate and the mentor, and the dialogue between them is a two-way conversation. A time limit should be set with all meetings.

Empowerment has become a trite cliché in today's business lexicon, but it is the only word to properly describe the benefit that can be achieved from the advice of a seasoned mentor during a political campaign. The mentor must establish a rapport with the candidate that builds relationships of trust and loyalty that encourage people throughout the campaign to take greater risks and responsibility. A good mentor is an invaluable tool.

Political mentoring builds a learning cycle on complex issues, such as the need to establish relationships and coalitions; budgets, strategy and vision; the campaign team's training and development; and the skills needed by the candidate and members of the executive committee. The guide system will help the candidate form productive relationships in areas that otherwise may have only harbored mistrust and alienation.

Topics for Meetings

+ Address what has transpired since the last meeting.
+ Address main issues in order of importance.
+ Improve the candidate's skill set: leadership and presentation.
+ Improve and establish new relationships.
+ Close the meeting with an objective view of the campaign's direction.
+ Establish a time for the next meeting (using the same day and time is helpful), and outline a proposed agenda.

What Is a Mentor?

A mentor is a person who has "been there, done that," is most often (but not always) older than the mentee, and the veteran of several political battles. Mentors are usually respected on both sides of the aisle for their knowledge and expertise. They are resources of information and teachers and guides who help remove barriers, often before problems materialize. Mentors are honored for their expertise and sage advice, and yet some of the best mentors may not be candidate material themselves. Even a formal mentoring program in politics should have the ambiance of informality.

The mentor/mentee bonding process is very important and should have a no-fault disposition where either one can walk away from the relationship without liability.

To help raise the candidate's profile for effective leadership, a mentor should try to teach through learning stories whenever possible. These stories are often funny but embody a strong message of what to or not to do without directly stating specific objectives. A learning story is a parable, and each candidate can take away a lesson matching their own level of understanding. Learning stories are often timeless messages embraced by the cultures embedded within every social stratum (Underwood 1991, 11).

What a Mentor Is Not

Under perfect circumstances, a mentor should not receive any monetary reimbursement or appointment. The relationship between mentor and candidate is one of adult interaction, trust, and a shared, long-term political vision; it is open and honest. It does not completely preclude a reward of some type for the mentor, to honor hard work, but designing a reward into the project may jeopardize the mentor's objectivity.

A mentor cannot
  + criticize or demand
  + have a savior syndrome
  + act like a parent
  + project superior knowledge or insight (even though they may possess it)
  + assume the role of a rescuer
  + have a haughty, arrogant, or adversarial approach

A mentor cannot play personal counselor regarding the candidate's
  + marital or family difficulties
  + financial problems (external to the campaign)
  + drug and alcohol abuse
  + depression or personality disorders
  + complex problems of a personal nature

The campaign manager and mentor must also have a good working relationship, but the mentor should be focused on the candidate's personal growth and development. The campaign manager, whose focus is primarily on the campaign's forward movement, optimizes the candidate's existing attributes and identifies areas that need improvement.

One-shot mentors who have a particular specialty are also in the campaign manager's tool kit. The entire mentoring purview is designed to increase performance of executive committee members, not to directly perform tasks and assignments. Mentors are advisors and teachers, not campaign workers.

Note: Candidates alone are responsible for decisions made during their campaigns. They should not seek, choose, or accept mentors with whom they are not comfortable.

SWING VOTE

▼

Every political statistician, guru, or pundit has a method for determining a party's voter makeup or the illusive swing vote. This chapter addresses the swing voter's multifaceted internal characteristics as does the section on voting blocs. After years of evaluation, I have determined this to be the best and most expedient model.

Rather than gradually shift to the left or right, the swing voter's dominant characteristic is to embrace political change as it arises, free from the tether of a major party's endorsed candidate or predetermined canon. Swing voters are continuously refining their knowledge of issues and candidates, often right up to the moment their votes are cast (Dalton 2006, 11). The swing vote has become a deciding factor in many elections because voters are becoming more and more disenchanted with the effectiveness of the two dominant political parties, once defined exclusively by socio-economic status (Lazarsfeld, Berelson, Gaudet 1968, 16). Voters have begun to migrate to what were once considered nontraditional political alternatives. As partisanship weakens, candidates often seek less-refined platforms to attract swing voters, which further weakens a party's resolve (Wattenberg 1991, 2).

An increasing number of voters are more open to a wider range of alternatives when addressing the challenges facing their communities and the nation on a daily basis. Consequently, the swing voter's nonalignment with partisan politics requires more information and deliberation in their selection of a candidate. The swing voter seeks unbiased discourse separate from a candidate's typical methods of advertising via the media, e-mail, or direct mail. Swing voters may deliberate longer. Their search for political options is often marked by the perception of indecision because of their intended disassociation from established political ideologies, infrastructure, or dogma (Wattenberg 1991, 31).

Many election districts in the United States have more voters eligible to be placed in the swing voter category than are registered as Democrats or Republicans (Dalton 2006, 15). Since the 1940s, there has been a slow migration from party- to candidate-centered politics (Wallenberg

1991, 12). As a consequence, the political structures that were once icons of stability and traditional American ideals appear to vacillate in a modern global society, in which long-term party ideologies are often sacrificed for short-term candidate survival (Wattenberg 1991, 21).

Information being disseminated by major news channels is no longer judged as unbiased or for its in-depth coverage. Instead, news networks reveal their political leanings when reporters interpret and then dispense the news in swift sound bites (Joslyn 1984, 11; Jamieson 2000, 187). Swing voters often solidify their opinions based on what they consider reliable and unbiased sources: friends and neighbors, radio talk shows, op-ed articles, letters to the editor, newspaper editorials, parents or siblings, and professionals they trust, such as doctors, lawyers, and religious leaders.

Swing voters have the opportunity to cast a wider net in a search of the most perfect candidate. Voters who do not rely on partisan-political largess have the opportunity to establish a more stringent framework for what they desire in a candidate (Dalton 2006, 95). Even though the swing vote is comprised of an amalgam of several ideologies, a successful candidate who captures the swing vote must extrapolate and target the specific composition of the adherent's divergent tendencies—divergent only in their ideologies but often convergent in their final voting booth decision (Dalton 2006, 58).

Identifying Swing Voters

Swing voters are sometimes identified as crossover voters, maverick voters, floating voters, late deciders, switchers, indifferent voters, fence sitters, smart voters, pushovers, persuadables, or ticket splitters (Faucheux 2002, 151; Key 1966, 16; Shadegg 1964, 23; Woo 1980, 63; Shaw 2000, 112). A host of other names have been used in an attempt to bracket their specific voting tendencies. However, the act of naming a group of voters is an attempt to define and restrain its characteristics for ease of use.

Voters registered as blanks (i.e., without party affiliation) and independent voters have no political fidelity. Blank registrants and independents are the nucleus of the swing vote. Their votes are often unpredictable, open to alternatives. Their allegiance, if there is any, floats between party and antiparty doctrine, candidates, and current "flavor of the month" issues.

Most swing voters register with no party affiliation, with the emerging Independence Party, or have affiliation with groups such as the Tea Party or the Occupy Wall Street movements. This act implies a certain amount of disdain for the mainstream political structure to which many once subscribed (Joslyn 1984, 8). For every voter, the act of casting a vote requires purposeful intellectual engagement, decision making, and community involvement. The intent to *cast a decisive vote* is more prominent with swing voters.

Swing voters are often depicted as mavericks, but they are more fluid and trending than stalwart. Votes are often utilized by citizens as their only way of expressing disenchantment with or acceptance of current political policy and trends. The swing voter floats on a trending sea of political ideologies and current issues. Their numbers often fluctuate tremendously from election to election (Wallenberg 1991, 79). Rather than embrace a specific ideology, swing voters often have negative responses to a party platform or doctrine, such as a stance on abortion, same-sex marriage, or troop deployment.

Swing voters often revel in their maverick cloak, taking great pride in their individualism and detachment from the mainstream political parties. The swing vote is considered by many in political circles and the media to be a deciding factor in propelling a candidate to victory. A large percentage of elections are won by the narrowest of margins, and nearly everyone associated with the political system is aware of the swing voter's value and power. Many among this group wait to be courted by a political candidate, knowing full well that their votes are highly prized.

Strategies for Capturing the Swing Vote

Traditionally, a candidate facing a primary fight would focus on the base vote of their party and then expand to other voters (voting blocs) who are likely to participate in the election. A message should be tailored from the candidate's existing talking points to target the group in question, based on the results of the campaign's door-to-door canvassing, and telephone and online feedback and polling.

If a primary is open to voters other than those in the candidate's own party, a different strategy can be employed. The practice of allowing open primary voting may result in an unopposed candidate in one party mustering supporters to select the weakest candidate in another party as the opponent in a general election. In my opinion, allowing crossover voting in a primary election rarely produces two strong candidates, which, in the end, does not benefit the electorate.

It is rare for a base party voter to cross over and vote for a candidate of another party, but do not take the base vote of your party for granted. In a 1986 survey, only 14 percent of the voters admitted to voting only along party lines (Wallenberg 1991, 34). Nevertheless, the party's base voters are usually the main reason for a win in a primary election, while swing voters often influence a general election - depending on state laws and who is allowed to vote in the primary.

Don't waste time and money on trying to attract the base voters in the opposition party, unless that party has an overwhelming voter-enrollment superiority in the election district. Supporters of the opposition party will nearly always try to lure a candidate into frivolously spending time and money in their direction.

Voters can also be further selected by seniors, veterans, property owners, special-interest or ethnic groups, religious and community groups (Rotary Club, Elks, Kiwanis), and areas of social and economic class definition (see Computer Lists). Volunteers, staff, and supporters of the candidate should be assigned lists from this data to directly connect with the people with whom they may be associated.

Endorsed Candidates

Candidates who are endorsed by major parties carry their party's foundational attributes to the electorate as well as a certain amount of unwanted baggage. The media will often selectively focus on a candidate's baggage rather than their qualities, causing even greater indecision among voters. Connecting candidates to a political party opens them to universal condemnation and criticism, even though they may not champion every issue supported by their party.

One of the functions of a political party's committee is to research, interview, deliberate on, and then select the best candidates to endorse. Party endorsement can eliminate the time and energy base/core voters need to expend on candidate research. It will also help to diffuse some of the personal responsibility of the party's members. Base/core voters may not fully embrace every issue but will inherently trust their party's selection of a candidate because they are closely aligned with the party's ideology. However, swing voters may be more distrustful of the established political infrastructure. Cross endorsements are allowed in some states, and the candidates selected by those parties may be represented on several ballot lines. A cross endorsement will allow swing voters to select a candidate endorsed by a major party but also to express their maverick nature by voting for that person on a nontraditional ballot line (see Voting Blocs).

Swing voters who are enrolled in a political party but choose to question their party's endorsed candidates are defined in this campaign model as valence voters. Registered voters who opt to remain unaffiliated (blank), also accept more of an individual responsibility for their votes. They must dedicate time to independently researching the qualifications of each candidate (see Endorsements).

But as many parents have said to their offspring, "The road to hell is paved with good intentions." Most voters today are stretched to the limit with jobs, family, and a shelf load of other commitments. Every moment is packed with decisions; every waking hour filled with unresolved issues. Even though this group of voters fully intends to gather the research necessary to make an informed decision about a candidate, Election Day still manages to sneak up on them.

Consequently, many swing voters find themselves standing in line at the poll, unprepared, and asking themselves, "Which candidate do I select to best represent me?"

Get Out the Vote

In the last days of the campaign, many undecided voters are not undecided through apathy but by design (Dalton 2006, 11). Voters have molded personal criteria for their candidate to fit into, but the candidate has yet to convince them there is a match. This group of voters will need to be more deeply persuaded by the candidate. They may require further empirical support to make up their minds. A nonpolarized political race may leave the majority of valence and swing voters in an undecided gray area up until the last moments on Election Day. A nonpolarized election may also have a low voter turnout and a large under-vote (see Voting Blocs).

At this crucial juncture in the final days of the campaign, the cumulative effect of advertising also plays an important role with voters on an unconscious level (Green and Gerber 2004, 96). Having momentary exposure to a candidates' billboards in passing while tuning in the car's radio, lawn signs on the way to work, and television commercials as they walk from one room to another may not have had a conscious impact on them at the time. However, all advertising affects the voter's final voting booth decision (Dalton 2006, 58).

Valence and swing voters may wait until the last week before the primary or general election to make up their minds. These late deciders are the principal recipients of GOTV initiatives in the final days and hours before Election Day. A large portion of the campaign's budget should be sequestered in reserve for the final GOTV initiative. The larger the swing and valence vote, the greater the GOTV initiative. Be innovative and technologically savvy when contacting this group. Their votes could very well determine the campaign's outcome (Green and Gerber 2004, 96).

Anyone can judge the swing vote the day after the election. To capture a voter's interest, candidates must build quality into their campaigns by refining their presentation skills and speaking ability, and clearly defining and properly addressing current issues (Wattenberg 1991, 3).

Conclusion

There is a question about whether individual research and following one's heart yields a more qualitative vote than aligning with an established party and partisan infrastructure. This is the basic question before any aspiring candidate and campaign manager. Political candidates who seek the swing vote must embed their campaign's tool kits within the framework swing voters utilize for research. Unfortunately, as a result of time constraints and other compelling factors, political campaigns or the media will often dumb down advertising messages to slogans, sound bites, and snippets of information, rather than offer voters an engaging discourse on concrete issues (Dalton 2006, 26; Faucheux and Herrnson 2001, 150; Morris 1999, 83).

When the smoke clears, voters must emerge from the voting booth satisfied that they have cast a decisive vote, instead of being consumed by lingering doubts.

VOTING BLOCS

▼

This campaign model segments the voting population into four groups that can be targeted for specific emphasis: base voters, core voters, valence voters, and swing voters. People are placed in each defined category, or voting bloc, based on party affiliation and voting frequency. This enables the campaign to produce varied messages in an effort to capture constituents' support (Shaw 2000, 110). The theory is that the greater their voting frequency, the more voters will align with their party's basic ideology and endorsed representative. A political ideology's most faithful adherents are people who frequently use the ballot box to express their concern about issues of governance.

The heuristic method (see below) and under-vote analysis are guides for more finely tuning the base, core, valence, and swing segmentations of the electorate. Polling is a feedback tool that gauges a candidate's degree of support among constituents.

Voting blocs can be determined in four ways:

a) Obtain an individual's voting history, and prioritize the database records (see appendix H).
b) Track polling data from door-to-door, telephone, or Internet canvassing, using a spreadsheet (see the section on polling below and appendices B and C).
c) Analyze voter affiliation from past elections (see sections below on heuristics and analyzing voter pathways).
d) Analyze the under-vote; calculate the number of votes given to unopposed and exceptional candidates.

Note: Items a and b are the two areas most campaigns will utilize to define voting blocs; item a may be the sole criteria required in a small campaign. Items c and d are mentioned here only as examples of the numerous methods available to a campaign in its continuous quest to analyze trends and voter allegiances.

Voting Bloc Characteristics

The categories below are based on the analysis of five general elections. The executive committee determines the exact composition of each voting bloc by using the four criteria listed above in items a-d. The polling data from canvassing (item b) will reveal the degree of support for the party's endorsed candidate and issues.

1. *Base voters*

These are the registered voters from a single political party who vote in primary, general, and nonpartisan (school board, library trustee, etc.) elections religiously (Key 1966, 16). These people vote even if there is a hurricane or an earthquake. They are a political party's strongest advocates.

In this example, base voters have voted in four out of five and five out of five elections. They are very likely to vote for the party's endorsed candidate and in nearly every primary and special election. The goal of every political party is to increase its base voters.

2. *Core voters*

The base voter's and the core voter's philosophical characteristics are very similar in that both strongly adhere to their party's philosophy, and the campaign manager may decide to combine them in a single aggregate. However, the core voter votes less frequently. A portion of the core vote could be influenced by an extremely exceptional opposition candidate. In that instance, this group of voters may be considered swing voters.

Core voters, in this example, have participated in two or three out of the last five general elections. They will only vote in *select* primary, special, and nonpartisan elections where they have a special interest. Unlike base voters, their need to vote may be temporarily displaced by work, family, or other pressing requirements.

3. *Valence voters*

These voters adhere loosely to their party's ideology but may believe that the party has temporarily wavered on one or two issues, such as candidate endorsements, the economy, employment, troop deployment, unfunded mandates, etc.

Instead of rushing to the polls to voice their opinions, they are usually apathetic and shy away from addressing social issues. Young voters (those under twenty-five) often fall within this category as do niche voters, who only venture to the polls during a presidential election or for a specific issue, such as gun ownership, abortion, same-sex marriage, or taxes.

Valence voters will vote in greater numbers if they are specifically targeted. Targeting can only be accomplished by defining specific groups and voting blocs, as suggested here. These voters often respond to a high degree of external influence from opposition candidates and gravitate to hotly contested issues. They may be prime candidates for cross-over voting and could be considered part of the swing-voter category.

4. *Swing voters*
   + Blank: a registered voter who is not enrolled under the banner of an established political party. This voter may also be labeled as unaffiliated or undesignated.
   + Independent: registered with a third party, such as the Reform Party associated with H. Ross Perot or the candidacy of Governor Jesse Ventura of Minnesota in 1998.
   + Independence Party, a designation similar to Democrat, Republican, Liberal, or Conservative (see the Independence Party's Architecture section in this chapter). Including Independence or other nontraditional party members in the swing vote is a decision that must be made by the campaign's executive committee.

Explanation of the Valence Model

A model that works in one discipline can be used effectively in another. In the example below, matter, in the form of an atom, is used to represent similar characteristics among voting tendencies. Note: Such examples are identified in this book as Vision Quest learning stories (Underwood 1991, 11).

All matter has substance or elements, which are comprised of atoms. An atom in turn is composed of protons and electrons in partnership within a nucleus. One of the major differences between elements is the number of protons and electrons. That number gives each element a unique signature and a measurable atomic weight (as noted in the periodic table).

In chemistry, electricity, and electronics, there is a phenomenon known as the valence. Usually the outer electron shell of an atom, the valence determines the degree to which the substance becomes an electrical conductor or an insulator, based on how easily the atom's electrons can be dislodged from their normal routine. The more electrons in an atom, the easier it is to remove them, to entice them from complacency.

In electronic technology, the outer valence electrons of a semiconductor material, such as silicone or germanium, are excited through the use of applied power (heat/power, volts/amps). When power is applied, some of the electrons might be dislodged from an atom's outer shell. If they are, this electron movement from one atom to another creates a type of power valve enabling the transistor and microchip technology we have today.

In political parlance, there is a type of valence in which applying power—i.e., exciting the electorate through a variety of means—moves votes to a different candidate or issue. Voters have a tendency to remain stable (complacent) unless they are disturbed by an opposition party candidate or a hotly contentious issue. The closer they are to the party's base, the less prone voters will be to external influences, and the less likely it is their votes will migrate to the opposition.

Unlike the swing voter, who has nomadic tendencies, the valence voter subscribes to a political party and its basic ideology (Dalton 2006, 9). This allows the candidate to tailor a message specifically to this group of voters. Your party's valence voters must be identified, awakened, reenergized, and brought back into the fold through door-to-door canvassing, advertising, e-mails, texts, direct mail, outreach on the website, and GOTV efforts.

Valence voters from an opposition party must be challenged in their beliefs to entice them to cross over. In essence, the valence voter is a political party's swing voter. Campaign managers, however, must not treat the opposition party's valence voters the way they do their own party's valence during GOTV efforts. Note: This analysis is dependent upon near-equal enrollment ratios between Democrats and Republicans. If an election district's voter composition is skewed to favor one political party, strategies may have to be adjusted (Faucheux 2002, 152).

How to Code Data

If the candidate has been endorsed by a major political party, the party's database may be available to the campaign team for mapping, voter histories, demographics, and statistical analysis. In that case, the data acquired may not be alterable.

If database lists are built from scratch or can be transferred to spreadsheets, following the model below may prove helpful. Data in this campaign model are segmented into the four voting blocs (base, core, valence, and swing) and into cross-functional categories using an additional spreadsheet field for seniors, veterans, homeowners, ethnicity, and organizational membership. This will help target the specific needs of voters (see appendix B).

Once all the data on registered voters in the election district have been collected, input the information into spreadsheet fields that can be coded and sorted. One spreadsheet field must also include the polling data obtained from door-to-door, website, or telephone canvassers. Identify registered Republicans or Democrats as base, core, and valence voters based on how frequently they vote. There should be one field for party affiliation and an adjacent field for voting history, although the two fields can be merged if space is problematic. Swing voters will need their own spreadsheet field and code. For example, 2R could be the designation for a Republican who voted twice in five years; 4D could be a Democrat who voted four times in the same period; 3S would be a swing voter who voted three times.

Methods of coding will be determined at the executive committee's weekly meeting. It will be the campaign's decision whether or not to merge voting frequency and party into one field. If other parties—such as the Working Families Party, the Liberal Party, or the Conservative Party—have large enough populations within the election district, the statistician should also subdivide these parties into separate fields on the spreadsheet.

Excel pivot tables, for example, allow the campaign to track specific groups, such as twenty- to twenty-five-year-old married female Democrats, or seniors of a specific age, or veterans of a specific war. More enhanced sorting methods may become available as technology develops.

Polling

Polling the electorate will identify issues of concern among voters as well as their degree of support for a candidate. Polling data can be collected in a variety ways, but two of the most common are door-to-door and telephone canvassing. Direct-mail surveys, e-mail messages, and the campaign's website can also be utilized to poll constituents. However, traditional or cyber-savvy polling methods may capture different audiences. The integrity of the data obtained from website sources might be questionable; Internet polling is vulnerable to flooding (one group or person responding hundreds of times), which will skew data unless precautions are implemented. Whichever method is used, polling questions must be uniform and comply with the spreadsheet format/fields used by the campaign (Iyengar 1990, 20).

Note: A state's election laws may have restrictions on the public release of polling data; consult the BOE and the campaign's sage counsel.

Heuristics: Analyzing Voter Pathways

Heuristics is a trial-and-error method for obtaining a rule-of-thumb estimate rather than a statistically quantifiable doctrine. The method outlined below may be used in conjunction with voter-history statistics to determine a party's percentage of base, core, valence, and swing voters.

To initiate the process, first identify the best and worst candidates the Republicans or Democrats have endorsed to run in a contested general election within the last five years. This may include two elections for the office being sought (Grey 1994, 30).

The best- and worst-candidate case scenario should be a relatively well-known fact among the politically astute within the election district (Shadegg 1964, 15). Verify (quantify) each category by obtaining voter data from the state or county BOE by district, ward (precinct), county, and for the entire election district. This will allow a fine sort analysis, if one is desired.

The difference between the best and worst candidate's voting data can help determine the maximum number of obtainable swing votes. The minimum number of swing votes available may be determined by analyzing the difference in votes from a hotly contested race between two popular candidates.

This heuristic method of analysis will reduce the need to perform complicated in-depth statistical computations (Shaw 2000, 111). However, it will introduce several areas for further study and refinement, which will be required if the candidate needs exact details about the swing voters' characteristics. In-depth analysis to identify an incumbent's strengths and weaknesses could be accomplished by the statistician using the BOE's or party-supplied voting-history data, such as voter turnout by sex, age, education, homeownership, ethnicity, etc. Such an analysis may determine that the swing vote is mainly comprised of a specific gender, ethnicity, and age.

Use percentages, rather than the actual number of votes, in the analysis, rounded to the nearest whole number. Every election will produce a different set of numbers, but percentages are more user-friendly and easier to interpret when matching one election year to another. The data will be in flux during the election, but static afterward.

How long does an analysis of this type remain valid? It depends on the voter composition within the district and how rapidly political trends change. The polling data created from door-to-door, telephone, and Internet canvassing is usually candidate-specific and can be extrapolated if it has been segmented into a separate spreadsheet field.

In addition, turbulent economic times might force a migration of the electorate as the employment picture changes throughout the nation. A county in upstate New York, New Hampshire, or Maine may have very little change in voter enrollment over a two-year period. At the same time, parts of North Dakota, Texas, New Mexico, Florida, or California may change very rapidly due to dependence on the oil and gas industry, farming cycles, immigration, or in the wake of a natural disaster, such as a hurricane or earthquake.

Under-vote Calculations

To many politicians, the under-vote is a defining characteristic that determines trends and change. An under-vote occurs when a voter chooses not to vote for a candidate on a ballot, often because that person is running unopposed or when two opposing candidates do not clearly define the issues (Shaw 2000, 114, 142).

Unopposed candidates present an interesting alternative for the opposition party's base and deeply committed core voters. They do not offer voters many alternatives; yet a vote for them is considered a vote of confidence for their platform. Many consider a voter's abstinence as a no vote for the candidate. The number of "no confidence" votes a candidate does or does not receive may be a telling indication of trends or that the electorate is not fully supportive of a single candidate or a specific issue.

In essence, candidates who have no opposition in either a primary or general election should still keep in contact with their constituents. People who vote often do so year after year, and the unopposed candidate should not appear aloof or uncaring. An under-vote will be a clear signal of a candidate's waning popularity and weakness. However, an election district may have finite resources for candidates, and an unopposed candidate may choose to assume a low profile and, as a team player, refrain from taking resources from a party in need.

The composition of an under-vote may be very complicated. This book's analysis is intended as a quick-reference guide to help a candidate, not as a complex, in-depth examination. If that type of analysis is desired, a candidate should consider hiring a firm that specializes in this area.

Note: Evaluations of the under-vote phenomena are especially useful during the decision-making stages of a candidacy. They can be used by the aspiring candidate to determine which elected office they are qualified to fill and which one may be the most vulnerable to a challenge.

The Independence Party's Architecture

The Independence Party is as much of a political party as the Republican or Democratic parties. Many Independence Party members incorrectly believe they are listed on the voter rolls as a blank, with no party affiliation. That is one reason why Independence Party voters and blank registrants are categorized together here, but Independence Party inclusion in any aggregate will require executive committee or CM approval.

The Independence Party's platform is a partisan alternative for voters who seek political independence but do not want to be set adrift in a sea of ideologies. Even though this party is currently only represented in New York State, a viable third-party alternative may continue to gain momentum in all fifty states and territories. An alternative party offers the voters more of a "flavor of the month" policy than the "set in stone" doctrine that is believed to exist within established political parties, even though the Independence Party does have a well-defined platform (www.ipny.org/platform.html).

Independent/Third Party

Being an Independent is often associated with a single candidate seeking elected office. The news media frequently refers to the swing vote as the Independent vote, which it is not. Theodore Roosevelt could not obtain the Republican Party's endorsement for president in 1912, so he reformed his followers under the banner of an independent, progressive party called the Bull Moose Party, thereby splitting the Republican Party's vote (Wattenberg 1991, 47). The split allowed Democrat and "peace candidate" Woodrow Wilson to become president (Campbell 2000, 166).

A similar incident took place in the 1992 presidential election with H. Ross Perot, who split the Republican ticket headed by George H. W. Bush. William Jefferson Clinton was elected as president (Campbell 2000, 103; Jamieson 2000, 161). Swing voters and first-time voters are credited with placing Jesse Ventura as governor of Wisconsin in 1998. Governor Ventura, a former Navy SEAL and professional wrestler, ran under the Independent Reform Party as a "down to earth—outside the beltway" candidate (Dalton 2006, 115).

Energizing a third-party candidate may be one of the only methods for decreasing an opposing party's base vote. The contemporary political system offers third-party candidates very little chance of actually winning an election (Faucheux and Herrnson 2001, 155). Most third-party candidates run for office to bring certain issues to center stage. Examples include Ralph Nader's unsuccessful presidential runs in 1992, 1996, and 2000 with the Green Party, bringing environmental concerns to national prominence. In 1999, however, Audie Brock did win a state assembly race in California under the Green Party's banner (Faucheux and Herrnson 2001, 94).

Some argue that many Conservatives and Republicans have given support to Ralph Nader's campaigns with the goal of destabilizing the liberal side of the Democratic Party (Shaw 2000, 210). Conversely, some Democrats may have at least tacitly supported H. Ross Perot's presidential campaign for a similar reason, to draw base voters away from the Republican candidate.

Archiving Historical Data

The party chair should gather and archive data on candidates so they can be compared with future elections and analyzed for voting trends. Presidential and gubernatorial elections have special meaning because they usually add percentages to the swing vote rather than to the base.

Polling statistics for local candidates are sometimes unavailable, unless the county chair has established data collection uniformity and has archived the information.

Polling data are usually candidate-specific, but it would be invaluable to archived data for future elections by office. Changes in demographics and the party's voter enrollment should be noted as well as overall trends and specific issues. The analysis of historical data may help to identify emerging political trends.

Conclusion

Polling data will help define the voting blocs built from voting histories. Further refinement is also possible through a variety of other methods, such as the use of heuristics and under-vote analysis. After voting blocs are defined by the executive committee and statistician, an appealing message and method of delivery must be designed to specifically reach each cohort.

S E C T I O N   4

Tool Kit: Resources for the Team

☞ Budget
☞ Letters to the Editor
☞ Campaign Mailings
☞ Computer Lists
☞ Fundraising Events

BUDGET

▼

A campaign's budget is not complex. It is a straightforward, prioritized list of expenses. The most important component of a campaign's budget is the interaction between the functional managers, the CM, and the treasurer to identify reasonable expenditures according to a realistic schedule. The synchronization of time and money will set the rhythm of the campaign. It is this finely tuned proactive orchestration that helps to win elections.

The proper identification of prioritized issues and assessment of expenditures is an essential and often an experiential craft, born from the treasurer's knowledge, which is gained from past campaigns. The treasurer's framework for building a new budget for the campaign is to research the BOE for financial disclosures from the most recent election for the office in question. The treasurer need only compare a list of expenditures from that election to those of a similar election to properly assess the minimum that will be required.

Each functional manager must submit a budget request to the CM before the end of the third weekly executive committee meeting. Realistic appraisal of the functional manager's and unit manager's individual funding requests are also based on past practices and current technological innovations and requirements. The initial expenditure for items such as lawn signs and palm cards can be increased over time as door-to-door canvassing reaches a crescendo and proceeds from donations and fundraising events offers the campaign greater financial stability.

If additional knowledge is required, the CM should find a candidate or someone who has served as treasurer on a similar campaign within the election district as well as research the BOE's recent archives for relevant financial disclosure statements. As mentioned, budgets from similar campaigns will serve as a framework and point of reference for the CM and treasurer (Pelosi 2007, 164). Advertising methods and campaign expenditures change very rapidly in the contemporary world in which we live.

The campaign manager and treasurer will offer the candidate a realistic appraisal of line-item expenditures and the revenues required to build a winning campaign. Money is not an intangible asset or promise, but the electorate's corporeal investment in the candidate and their vision for future governance. The philosophy of fundraising is a tapestry that is interwoven with the candidate's ability to share their vision with the electorate. The degree to which he or she can share their vision will be reflected in the amount of money being raised and how it is spent.

The campaign cannot spend funds it does not have. Lack of funds will deny, or limit, the candidate's ability to deliver their message to constituents. There is no downside to incrementally building an overflowing war chest of funds. Financial strength offers candidates a larger menu of options for delivering their messages to voters, especially during GOTV.

Few candidates have lost an election because their campaign had too much money. Conversely, losing campaigns often lack the monetary resources needed to adequately deliver the candidate's message to the voters. The lack of financial planning may leave the campaign without resources in the most crucial final days of the campaign.

Bulk-item discounts are important, and the campaign can focus on one product's purchase while only maintaining the stock in another. In an extreme emergency, palm cards can be scanned and printed on home computers with card stock; lawn signs cannot. Scanned palm cards can also be incorporated in e-mail advertising (consult the sage counsel for possible infringement on copyright issues). Prioritize expenditures.

The campaign manager's awareness of the effect of time and technology on financial and human resources is also vital to success. Establishing a dialogue among the treasurer, candidate, campaign manager, and sage counsel is crucial for a smooth-running campaign. In addition, it is important for the treasurer to establish an excellent rapport with vendors. The proactive expenditure and acquisition of resources will help to create a seamless workflow. The lack of financial planning creates emergencies that redirect the campaign's role to putting out fires (small emergencies) which may sap the campaign's strength and forward momentum.

Campaign managers should remind the team to solicit in-kind donations for furniture and other office supplies. Allowing constituents to buy in to the candidate's political vision is an important part of the campaign process. When the campaign needs housekeeping items—office supplies, furniture, rental space, computers, coffee, phones, etc.—the CM should touch base with loyal party committee members, the candidate's relatives, and business people who have interest in the candidate's political initiatives. Every item gained through in-kind donations will free money and people to solicit votes.

Newspapers are gradually losing effectiveness as an advertising tool. Print media is often very costly, but it currently reaches a select group of constituents who may feel abandoned without it.

The technology-adept cyber-citizen who relies on mobile devices for daily communication and information gathering may not take the time to peruse newspapers each morning with coffee. Money will be required to deliver the candidate's message to all constituents. Lifestyles will present distinct audiences, and the campaign must use innovative ways to gain access to them.

Highly contentious races cost more. Core seed-money donors and personal loans from the candidate must be explored at the campaign's startup and revisited, as needed, during the GOTV phase. At least 30 percent and often as much as 40 percent of the campaign's budget should be held in reserve for the GOTV initiative in October and November. This money can be raised throughout the spring, summer, and fall through fundraising events.

Note: Replicate success. Prioritize essentials. List expenses in a spreadsheet, in categories with a linear timeline divided by month. A sound financial strategy is an essential component of a winning campaign (see appendix G).

Some spreadsheet categories and budget line items are:

Advertising	Board of Elections (BOE)	Consulting firm
palm cards	voter walking lists	strategy
lawn signs	voter lists	specialty events
bumper stickers	donor lists	
literature	maps	**Staff**
mailings	demographics	salaries
newspapers	statistics	expenses
radio	financial disclosure filing fees	taxes
television	nominating petition fees	
printing		
graphic designer	**Computer section**	**Insurance**
photographer	website	
letterhead and postcards	Internet (ISP) fees	
thank-you notes	credit-card acceptance fees	
billboards		**Fundraising**
misc., buttons, etc.	**Transportation**	deposits
	expenses: gasoline, food	events
Headquarters	mass transit (public)	excursions: boat, bus, train
rent, lease		food
utilities: heat and lights	**Mailings**	entertainment
phones	direct, first-class	decorations
computers	bulk, business	site rental, lease
furniture	mailing-house fees	beverages
supplies: envelopes, pens	postage	permits, fees, licenses
copying, printer		parking
postage		custodial fees (cleanup)
labels	**Legal and accounting fees**	rentals: chairs, audio system
parking fees	permits and licenses	misc.
food	fees	
	consultation	
	bookkeeping	
Training fees		**Door-to-door canvassing**
personnel		polling
audio/visual	**Miscellaneous**	research
media training	gifts and donations	focus groups
absentee ballots	entrance fees	identification badges, buttons
voter registration		
GOTV		
early-voting program		

LETTERS TO THE EDITOR

▼

Writing a letter to the editor is a great way to share an opinion about articles, reports, or editorials published in a newspaper or magazine. Whether the political issues are local or national in scope, editors look for timely, well-written responses to what has appeared in their publications, or a unique perspective on a different issue.

Many letters contain relevant viewpoints that may otherwise go unaddressed. They can also build a base of support for people who have a similar mind-set. The main reason to write a letter is to inspire readers to join a political movement or support a particular candidate or issue (England 1992, 85).

The letter to the editor has a strategy all its own: it is an opportunity to clandestinely "go negative." This type of letter may help a campaign bring unknown issues into public view without creating a direct relationship with an organization or candidate (see Going Negative).

When written and submitted correctly, the letter to the editor can shift public opinion to or from a particular candidate, amendment, or school bond issue. Letters are the best free advertising available, but some newspapers literally receive thousands daily. To improve the chances of getting a letter published, here are a few helpful tips.

Know the rules
Review the policy on letters to the editor. Look for guidelines on the publication's website or on the second inside page of the print edition. The length of the letter is important. Most newspapers will specify a word limit. If the letter is one word too long, the editor may not publish it or, worse, may alter it in undesired ways. Avoid that pitfall at all costs.

Newspapers have a cut-off date and will stop printing political letters one or two weeks prior to an election. Few newspapers are politically middle-of-the-road publications. They will espouse a particular credo, either overtly or covertly, especially if the newspaper endorses a candidate.

There are limits on the number of letters to the editor one person is allowed to submit, either involving new topics or in reply to earlier published letters or articles. Writing more than two letters a month may place a person in the category of a political activist rather than an average concerned citizen. Show good judgment; follow the rules.

Some newspapers accept only typewritten, double-spaced paragraphs. Be aware that the larger publishing houses receive a high volume of letters daily and may promptly reject the ones containing the slightest infraction of the rules! The newspaper's guidelines are often posted on the publication's website, but it is always a good idea to phone the newspaper to obtain the rules and a best-methods approach for submittal. Be tactful; remember that the paper's editorial team may not share a candidate's ideology (Joslyn 1984, 11). It is advisable to send letters by e-mail for reasons of convenience, economy, and archiving. Always keep a copy of the letter for reference.

Write an outline
Gather cogent thoughts together in an outline, with items numbered by order of importance. Maintain focus on one subject. Don't ramble. Too many talking points will reduce the statement's impact and dilute the importance of the subject matter (Jamieson 2000, 53).

The tone of the letter is most important. Educate the readers. Keep the letter as short as possible but always support a position with statistics, citations, or other factual evidence. A factual message should be offered to the readership with passion and feeling. Escort the reader through the stated points in a lucid manner to impart a logical conclusion.

   Tip: Only one main point or topic is preferred for a letter to the editor.

Prepare the letter
The lead paragraph is very important. Use it wisely to capture the reader's attention and then to immediately make your point. Your letter is competing with dozens of other letters and must stand out to be accepted. It cannot be just good; it must be great.

A letter to the editor is a succinct comment and must be composed as efficiently and rapidly as possible while the topic is fresh in the writer's mind. It is a good idea to write it one day, reread it, and submit it the next. Have someone proofread the letter, if possible. Seek the advice and unbiased criticism from someone knowledgeable on the subject to enhance the letter.

If your letter is in reply to a specific article or editorial, reference the original by its title and the date it was published. When responding to previously published material, the content of your message must stand on its own. Not all of the publication's readers may have seen the original letter or editorial to which you are responding.

The purpose of a letter to the editor is to educate the readers, not to verbally assassinate anyone. Refrain from insulting or attacking an opposition candidate, a reporter, the newspaper, or the author of the article to which you are responding (Grey 1999, 187).

A positive and upbeat letter is most effective. Identify and quantify the problem you seek to illustrate and then offer a solution. Do not claim anything you cannot prove.

A possible opening statement might take issue with a comment from a previous interview, editorial, or opponent's comment. Add to the discussion by pointing out something the readers will benefit from learning. Alternatively, disagree with an editorial position, or point out an error or misrepresentation made in a previous article.

Know your candidate and the opposition. Detailing your candidate's attributes often exposes the opponent's lack of knowledge in certain areas without specifically expressing it. Conversely, do not tout your candidate's bachelor's degree if the opponent has a master's or a doctorate. Accentuate the unique qualities of your candidate.

Lead the reader down a creative path and connect the dots by being assertive and passionate, not emotional, obnoxious, or rude. Add personal experiences and anecdotes. Connect social issues like poverty and crime in a political format related to a candidate's platform or stance.

Close the letter with a memorable thought that will linger with readers. Concentrate on the central point you hope people will take away with them. Educate readers; do not talk down to them.

If you are associated with a group of people, coordinate your efforts and encourage them to compose and submit their own letters to the editor. Persevere in the effort, knowing that not all of the submissions may be printed by the newspaper.

Some politicians and policy gurus read the letters to the editor, op-ed articles, and editorials to gauge the views of their constituents. The views expressed in letters to the editor are a good metric for defining hot topics and current issues of concern to the public. Your letter may inspire a fellow reader or reporter to pursue an issue further with a more in-depth article. Many politicians and analysts view the volume of letters to the editor dedicated to one subject as a statistical sampling. The volume of letters on one subject may alter an election's focus or outcome.

Your letter could get legs and generate an op-ed article. Post your work on any type of Internet forum that is available to you: the campaign website, blogs, etc., with links on Facebook or Twitter, if appropriate.

Authors of letters to the editor must include their names, street addresses, and phone numbers, although only names will be published. Editors guard against false identities by contacting writers for authorship verification. Letters and articles should always be signed when sent by snail mail and e-mail (they can be electronically scanned). Newspapers will not print anonymous letters.

CAMPAIGN MAILINGS

▼

Americans have been successfully using the US mail for political advertising for more than two hundred years. Even though this method of advertising is slowly being supplanted by technology, direct mail, delivered to a resident's doorstep by a human being, has few equals in its persuasiveness.

Mailing campaign literature to constituents is an attempt to touch base with those missed through door-to-door canvassing, the Internet, and other advertising methods. A mailing also reintroduces the candidate to people who were reached during the canvassing cycle, reinforcing the depth of the campaign's initiative. Even though e-mail is rapidly gaining favor over traditional snail mail, it often reaches a different audience. A fully engaged cyber-citizen will rely on the Internet and mobile devices more frequently than traditional methods of communication.

The US Postal Service offers both the option of first-class and bulk mail. Whichever method is utilized, for optimal coverage, it may be wise for the CM to recruit a retired postmaster or postal employee who is familiar with sorting, delivery, pricing, and the addressing format required by the postal service (see http://pe.usps.com/businessmail101/).

A candidate should never do a bulk mailing addressed to "occupant." In many areas, some bulk mail labeled occupant is discarded as waste by the postal service. Such mail will also be delivered to people who are nonvoting residents and reach only a small percentage of people who actually vote. Bulk mail is a shotgun approach to marketing, but it does have a niche in the campaign's tool kit if the proper voter lists are utilized.

A rapid calculation will determine that more money may be spent on bulk mail than might have been spent on first class. A first-class mailing is the most cost-effective vehicle for reaching a targeted audience with a time-sensitive message (Faucheux and Herrnson 2001, 46). First-class mail also offers many features unavailable with other classes of mail, such as automatic forwarding (McNamara 2008, 85; see Computer lists; Volunteer Coordinator/Recruiter; appendix J).

Ancillary Service Endorsements

The postal service has a feature called "ancillary endorsement," which offers ways of correcting a mailing list. Ancillary service endorsement is a fantastic service for political candidates or political parties, and is available on request, often only for a small fee. Here is how it works:

An imprint placed on a designated area of the mail piece is used by the campaign to request notice of an address change. The imprint selected by the campaign determines the type of service to be provided and fee assessed, if any. The service varies by class of mail and determines if the mail piece will be delivered to the new address and how the campaign will be notified of the recipient's address change. There are currently five types of ancillary-service imprints:

- address service requested
- return service requested
- change service requested
- forwarding service requested
- electronic service requested

> *Tip:* The CM, communications director, advertising coordinator, and statistician should determine what type of voter this service should target: absentee or unregistered voters, snowbirds, etc. If a fee is assessed, the campaign must pay for the service requested (see http://pe.usps.com/businessmail101/addressing/specialAddress.htm and www. usps.com).

At first, perform a test using a portion of the campaign's mailing list, to show the return rate. If the entire mailing list is used, the return rate might be overwhelming. The sample mailing will also indicate the accuracy of the address or barcode quality in the mailing list or labels obtained from the BOE and other suppliers. Also, fine tune the mailing lists incrementally. Use only a portion of the voter lists with ancillary endorsements each week to prepare for the GOTV phase of the campaign cycle. This will also help to synchronize mailings with door-to-door canvassing, phone-bank calls, and other advertising.

The USPS's business model is changing very rapidly. The postal service has modernized many of the products it offers. Updated residency lists may be available through the USPS, for a fee. If so, the campaign statistician can compare those lists to voter lists supplied by BOE or their political party. The resulting list produced would be a roster of all residents within a particular geographical area who are not registered to vote. This list should be available for voter-registration drives and offered to the door-to-door canvassers as another tool for enrolling new voters. New voters must have special treatment during GOTV.

Mail Pieces

The design of the candidate's advertising mail pieces should follow the campaign's theme in color and style. The candidate's message and talking points must be lucid and concise, articulated with bullet points and emphasized by color. A semi-glossy, single-sheet, postcard mailing, addressed directly to a voter offers the best message (Thomas 1999, 48). However, a standard letter is often utilized to target a special-interest group, such as property owners, military veterans, and seniors, or concerning a single subject, such as water quality, playgrounds, property taxes, or crime and punishment (see appendix J).

Note: The design should be legible and bold enough to catch the recipient's attention. A voter should be able to read the entire mail piece within fifteen to thirty seconds, the time it takes to get from mailbox to trash receptacle. The candidate's website address should hold a place of prominence on the mail piece.

Working with a Mailing Contractor

Many private contracting companies specialize as the middle men between the campaign and the postal service. The local postmaster, bulk-mail specialist, county political party chair, or letter carrier may know about the best contractors that provide this service within the election district. Many small business private mail contractors are former postal employees. The mailing company may request that its postal permit number be printed on the mail piece for the proper discounts with the US Postal Service. Since the design must comply with postal regulations, both the contractor and the USPS might want to proof the design.

COMPUTER LISTS

▼

Several key foundational drivers embedded within a political campaign can move it forward seamlessly to greater heights. Clearly, list generation is one of the most important. Volunteer rosters, nominating petitions, enrolled-voter data, fundraising activities, and the general organization of the campaign are completely dependent upon the quality of generated lists (Faucheux 2002, 149).

Computer-generated door-to-door canvassing lists, volunteer lists, and fundraising lists will make or break a campaign. Scheduling and calendars are all done on computers and can be linked to cell phones and handheld mobile devices as well as GPS maps, e-mail, and other digital applications. To enhance contact with voters, technology must be embedded within the campaign's core organizational structure, not attached to it as an afterthought (Creech 1995, 46).

Voter lists enable the campaign to identify and categorize the registered voters who reside within a set geographical boundary (Shadegg 1964, 158). Sorting, merging, culling, or comparing the voter lists with organizational membership rosters will produce target fundraising and voter mailing lists.

Accurate voter and fundraising lists represent political power at the highest level. This fact cannot be stressed enough. The ability of volunteers and staff to legally capture a diverse platform of lists will determine the quality of fundraising and voter mailings. Acquire every possible list of residents in the election district (Pelosi 2007, 49).

The campaign's effort to exhaust every means possible to obtain lists cannot include any methods or practices that may be deemed questionable or immoral. Politically like-minded individuals may generously provide membership lists from their organizations for campaign use upon request. It would be disastrous for the campaign to embroil itself in any activity that was remotely tainted or illegal.

Voter lists from the state's BOE should be updated by door-to-door canvassers. The BOE database is the foundational driver for the creation of voter lists. However, computerized lists and electronic aids can never be fully divested from the art of door-to-door grassroots canvassing (see Door-to-Door Canvassing). While the door-to-door canvassers are updating voter lists, they are also creating a feedback loop by inquiring how constituents feel about the candidate and issues (Pelosi 2007, 100; see appendix H).

Accurate polling data collected by door-to-door canvassing volunteers can be used to formulate strategic direction during weekly executive committee meetings. Accurate lists and voter feedback are seminal to a successful campaign and an Election Day victory.

> *Tip:* The framing of a polling question is very important. Alterations to the wording or form of the survey question can produce dramatic variations in answers. For instance, physicians and patients alike were considerably less attracted to cancer surgery when the statistics describing results were presented in terms of mortality rather than survival rates (Iyengar 1990, 20).

Note: Polling data can be used for many different reasons. President Ronald Reagan used polling data to better sell his beliefs; President Bill Clinton used polling data to determine what to believe (Drew 1999, 152). Instead of deciphering public sentiment, the Nixon Administration used polling results to try and manipulate public opinion (Jacob and Shapiro 1995).

Adopt one basic format for voter and fundraising lists. The spreadsheet format and fields used by the BOE is a good starting point. If the fields from campaign lists and spreadsheets are not similar, it will be nearly impossible to merge them to create mailing labels and eliminate duplicate entries. Touch base with the campaign's computer specialist for he or she may have input as to the best format. If there is a coded spreadsheet field for seniors, homeowners, veterans, etc., it will be easier to mail-merge labels or e-mails to target a specific group for votes or contributions (see appendices B and C).

Types of Lists Used in a Campaign

I. Operational, internal organizational lists
    a. Volunteers (see appendix A)
    b. Campaign team members and executive committee
    c. Media contacts for TV, radio, newspaper, and magazine reporters; advertising, letters to the editor, distribution
    d. Vendors: suppliers of palm cards, lawn signs, and business cards, noting point of contact—with addresses and phone numbers

II. Lists that generate votes
   a. Door-to-door walking lists from BOE or party database such as voter vault (see http://votervault3.gop.com/)
   b. Petitions (generated from signed nominating petitions, thank-you notes)
   c. Lawn signs (lists of who has one and who wants one)
   d. Absentee ballots, obtained from BOE and door-to-door canvassing lists
   e. Registration drives, obtained from door-to-door canvassing and new voter lists

III. Fundraising
   a. Contributors: those who have donated or may donate
   b. Mailing lists: includes snail mail, e-mail, texting, etc.
   c. Invitation lists: fundraising events, speaking engagements, and home parties

IV. Demographics and statistics: raw data for capturing volunteers, voters, and donors
   a. Volunteer postcards
   b. Sign-in sheets at events and HQ
   c. Party committee membership rosters
   d. Membership lists from service and civic organizations
   e. Relatives and friends
   f. Online sign up
   g. Identify support groups and form clusters of volunteers for specific tasks

Dissemination

I. Operational documents and lists:

These lists are internal and dedicated for organizational use only. They may defy merging. In any case, there will be no need to merge items such as news media contacts with executive committee members.

To facilitate better communication between the campaign and the media, list contacts for radio, television, magazines, and daily and weekly newspapers with names, addresses, and phone numbers. Do the same for contacts for letters to the editor, advertising, press releases, and distribution (McNamara 2008, 17). Vendors for palm cards, lawn signs, and business cards are also in this category. A vendor list may be available for those corporations doing business with the city, county or state; it could be used for a targeted fundraising initiative (see Communications Director; Statistician/Researcher).

II. Voter lists:

a) Walking lists

The average walking list contains:
- registered voters' full names (all voters residing at a given residence/household)
- street addresses, separated by odd and even numbers for walking ease
- party of registration (Democrat, Republican, Independent, etc.)
- gender and age of voters
- voting history/frequency during the last five to seven years, with an emphasis on presidential and gubernatorial elections
- phone numbers and/or e-mail addresses—a GOTV requirement
- county, ward, district, parish, town, or city (down to the finest geographical sort)

BOE and other voter lists contain several fields of data, which are usually abbreviated with codes or acronyms. The key must be included in every volunteer's walking list packet. For instance, (M) = male, (Rep) = Republican, (Gre) = Green Party, etc. All acronyms and codes must be used uniformly throughout the campaign.

Note: If the campaign selects five years of voter data to analyze, there may be twelve elections during that frame, including special elections (for school board members or library trustees) and primary and general elections. That particular spreadsheet field would list (0–12) under the field heading of "voter history" indicating in how many elections a resident had voted. The frequency of voting will place people in the categories the campaign selects for base, core, valence, and swing voters. Those categories will be electronically sorted by spreadsheet fields to determine how and when individual voters are contacted by the campaign (see Voting Blocs).

If there is a primary, the candidate may want to list only the voters affected by that election. If the candidate does not win the primary, there may be no need to list all registered voters for the general election. The general election voter data would include all registered voters from every party; the primary voter list would only list those eligible to vote in the primary. Nearly every state has its own laws governing who is eligible to vote in a primary.

Combining all enrolled voters for the primary and general elections into one list could be confusing to a neophyte volunteer. However, with an inclusive list of all voters, the canvassing volunteers can determine which houses are vacant or have occupants who are not registered. If a residence is not listed on the combined walking list, the residents are not registered to vote. The volunteer should inquire if the occupant(s) would like to enroll or note that household as a target for future campaign or party registration drives.

Tip: In some states, voters must register a certain number of days before the election to be eligible to vote.

The BOE, political party, and even the post office may have voter or residency lists available for campaign use. Government agencies and private contractors usually charge for a list of voters or residents. The county or state BOE should have voter data available on compact disc, by e-mail attachment, as a download, or, as a last resort, in hard copy. The relevant information should be printed and provided by the campaign in each volunteer's packet for the area being canvassed (see Volunteer Coordinator/Recruiter).

Endorsement by a major party may offer the campaign access to that party's databases, if they exist, or access to lists from past candidates. The Republican Party has a database called Voter Vault that is very useful in targeting voter contacts (Pelosi 2007, 52). Candidates for the Democratic Party may be able to access its Voter Activation Network (VAN), NGP VAN, Catalist, or the party's current database.

City or county political committees often obtain voter walking lists or database downloads for endorsed candidates. As the US Postal Service becomes less and less of a resource, cutting-edge technology for data mining of voter information is the next big step for political campaigns. New and enhanced software products can only augment but never supplant personal contact between the voter and candidate.

The party chair should guide political candidates and entities under their umbrellas to adopt a uniform spreadsheet format. It is advantageous for all candidates of the same party during an election cycle to share walking lists and updates on absentee ballots, polling data, and voter-registration initiatives.

Some former candidates, who no longer wish to revisit candidacy, may have lists they are willing to share. Voter and fundraising lists must be periodically updated as they can rapidly become obsolete (see Door-to-Door Canvassing).

b) Registration drives

Voter-registration drives must be organized well in advance of any cutoff date that prevents people from voting in the upcoming election. Depending on the political climate and local culture, it may be advantageous for each candidate of a political party to coordinate efforts in several areas, such as absentee ballots and voter registration (Grey 1999, 15; see Door-to-Door Canvassing and Sage Counsel).

A door-to-door voter-registration and absentee-ballot drive is usually performed in conjunction with an effort to obtain the maximum number of nominating petition signatures. Needless to say, it is useful for the campaign to know which residents are (and are not) registered to vote. Fine tune and update existing voter histories while the canvassing volunteers are obtaining nominating petition signatures (Grey 1999, 33).

The proper manipulation of lists can sometimes produce startling results. US census, city directory, USPS, and assessors' lists can be merged, purged of duplicates, and then compared against the BOE's voter-registration list (updated based on door-to-door canvassing). This will produce a list of people who reside within the voting district who are not yet registered to vote.

Place newly enrolled voters, of the candidate's party, on a separate list for special attention during the GOTV effort. New voters have a tendency to vote in their first election. The GOTV initiative should include a phone call, snail mail, or e-mail correspondence reminding newly registered voters to vote, where to vote, who to vote for, and inquiring whether they need an absentee ballot or transportation to the polls on Election Day.

c) Government and other lists

City, town, and county property tax assessors' residence lists are public documents and will state a property's market value as well as other vital statistics relevant to the campaign, such as property tax exemptions. A freedom of information request (FOIA) may have to be filed for some lists, even though they are gathered and maintained by public departments. It may also be in the campaign's best interest to acquire a list of the county's elected officials; county, and state employees residing within the election district; and county or city budgets.

> *Tip:* The property tax assessment list might include property tax exemptions for veterans, senior citizens, or homeowners with qualifying income levels. When these lists are merged with other lists—such as those from veteran organizations, senior citizen groups, and the BOE—the statistician might notice that certain residents may not be taking full advantage of their lawful property tax exemptions.

Note: Sorting or extrapolating data lists by gender, age, organizational membership, and party affiliation are important for the targeting of specific populations. It is also important to adopt new technology as it evolves.

The following is a sampling of organizations that may be active in the candidate's election district. There are hundreds more that are not listed. Be creative. Remember, some PACs, business organizations, ethnic, senior, and veterans groups may offer monetary donations and volunteers to endorsed candidates. Screen organizations carefully as not every endorsement may be beneficial (see Endorsements).

Business: economic development corporation (EDC), chamber of commerce, builders' association, real estate license holders, bankers clubs, investment clubs, professional clubs

Community: historical and preservation societies, parents of Boy/Girl Scouts-Cubs/Brownies; theater, museum, travel, and horticulture groups

Education: teachers, school administrators, library supporters and trustees, school board and parent teacher associations (PTA) members, college professors, public library card holders and supporters, museum donors, community theater and orchestra donors.

Environmental: property assessors; Nature Conservancy, Green Party, 4-H Club, and Sierra Club members

General lists: political parties, municipal employees, professional licensing (engineers, nurses, doctors, lawyers, real estate agents, and veterinarians), US Census, or any list that is public or included in the city directory

Housing: seniors, Section 8, condominium members, homeowners' associations, and assessors' lists (may include senior citizens' and veterans' tax exemptions)

Health care: medical centers, doctors, nurses, hospital employees, rescue squads, licensed EMTs, hospital guild members

Law and order: police (local, county, state), firefighters (city and volunteer), judges, lawyers (county and state bar associations), NRA members, rod and gun club members, pistol permit holders, corrections officers, security guards, community and neighborhood watches, mothers and students against drunk driving (MADD/SADD)

Political organizations: Young Republicans, Young Democrats, League of Women Voters, EMILY's List, NOW, PACs (political action committees must be registered with the BOE), political parties and their support groups

Religious: YMCA, Salvation Army, Knights of Columbus, members of any organized religious group

Seniors: senior citizen centers, AARP members, property tax exemption status (assessor's list), seniors' travel clubs, social organizations, and elderly housing domiciles; place a senior in charge of this group

Social and civic groups: Kiwanis, Rotary Club, Lions, Elks, Jaycees, Civitan International

Sports: Little League, Pop Warner football, tennis and swim clubs, country clubs, golf, skiing, polo, tri-athlete clubs, horse owner associations, yacht clubs and marinas, car and motorcycle clubs, hiking and mountaineering clubs, canoe and kayak groups, and bird-watching clubs.

Unions: teachers, postal employees, UAW, AFL/CIO, Teamsters, trade unions, e.g., plumbers, carpenters, masons, and electricians

Veterans: Veterans of Foreign Wars (VFW), American Legion, Disabled American Veterans (DAV), Military Order of the Purple Heart (MOPH), Marine Corps League (MCL), Paralyzed Veterans of America (PVA), American Veterans (AmVets). There are at least a dozen major veterans' groups, and each one has a mailing list. Try to place a veteran in charge of this area.

Many of the above organizations may offer not only their membership rosters to the candidate but also their volunteer and donor lists.

> *Tip:* Nearly every organization listed above has a website on the Internet. Search engines are very adept at locating service organizations and groups. *Political Tool Kit* rarely mentions specific websites because their mortality rate is high, obsolete before press time; two exceptions are www.yellowpages.com and www.city-data.com.

III. Fundraising lists:
It is important for the candidate's team to know the value of computerized lists and understand how to create door-to-door canvassing, polling, enrolled voter, and fundraising lists from scratch, and how to update and optimize a party's existing lists for voter and fundraising purposes (Simpson 1972, 102).

Several different fundraising techniques are discussed in the chapter concerning the fundraising chair's job assignments. The tool kit section of this book outlines the specifics involved in organizing a fundraising event. It also explains how to gather names for fundraising and invitation lists. Detailed lists allow a greater selection and finer sort for the precise targeting of populations. In addition, once lists are obtained they can be merged and sorted for specific purposes (McNamara 2008, 46).

For instance, as mentioned above, membership rosters containing raw data can be merged and sorted to create lists of donors and enrolled voters. Voters and contributors can be transformed into two completely different lists. People who contribute to the campaign do not have to be registered to vote or may even live outside of the election district.

IV. Demographic and statistical lists:
These lists are utilized to capture people who may volunteer, vote, and donate to the candidate. These raw-data lists must be compiled and worked into the productive lists to be used in the previous three sections (see Statistician/Researcher).

The optimal utilization of support groups is an important factor in compiling quality lists. Nearly every voter has affiliation with some type of support group.

Conclusion

An elected official must represent every constituent equally. However, candidates running for elected office have limited resources and must focus their entire campaigns around the residents of an election district who vote. Creating accurate computerized lists of residents who vote will determine the election results.

Such lists will allow the campaign to deliver issue-related messages to specific groups. Door-to-door canvassing; newspaper, TV, and radio advertising; US mail and e-mail can all be used to deliver the candidate's message, but the core to a successful election is the proper utilization of accurate computerized lists of voting residents in the election district.

Accurate lists will also allow the candidate to establish a relationship with voters and identify a common ground, the invisible thread. If the campaign is aware of the voter's association with a special-interest group—such as veterans, senior citizens, property owners, or country or yacht club members—the candidate can expand that common thread of trust into votes (see Internet Precinct and Door-to-Door Canvassing/The Invisible Thread).

The accuracy of lists must be continuously honed through door-to-door canvassing, event sign-in sheets, US mail ancillary imprints, residency software programs, the campaign's website, and every other legal means to target voters in a language and with issues and methods to which they can relate (Faucheux 2002, 140, 199).

Voting trends transition very rapidly, as do election laws and methods of contacting voters. Thirty-two of the fifty states currently allow early voting. In those states GOTV efforts will build slowly until reaching optimal exposure the day before the election. Campaigns that peak too early or late will lose voters on Election Day. In essence, alternative voting methods and early-voting practices have altered a campaign's approach to the final GOTV initiative, but not the tools utilized to capture votes (Elliott and Kuhnhenn 2012).

FUNDRAISING EVENTS

▼

Events Where Food Is Served

The weekly team meeting must address the items listed below.

Internal

- Budget for fundraiser.
- Calculate cost of sit-down dinner, buffet, or cocktail party.
- Decide on menu selections: options and cost.
- Determine if beverages are included in ticket price.
  - o Open bar or cash bar?
  - o Complimentary, campaign-furnished wine, beer, and soda?
  - o Is auxiliary bar needed? Patio bar or room for overflow?
- Decide whether to incorporate a wine-tasting table featuring local wineries or a beer-tasting table featuring breweries.
- Entertainment: fit the music to the patrons.
- Make sure there is ample parking.
- Discuss the minimum and maximum number of guests allowed.
- Find out what percentage of patrons the restaurant owner will allow to pay at the door.
- Develop contingency plans for inclement weather.
- Avoid schedule conflicts with anything else (internal and external to election district).
- Utilize internal mailing lists for attendee solicitation (see Computer Lists).
- Create an RSVP phone tree using key "star power" players.
- Find a guest speaker with "star power" and a backup speaker.
- Set a check-in table at the door:
  - o Alphabetize name tags and lists of the people who have paid.
  - o Have candidate's palm cards, lawn signs, and campaign literature available.
  - o Organize check-in to a high degree; have plenty of volunteers.
  - o Encourage early-bird sign-in by offering a predinner drink or socialization hour.

    o   Prepare for unidentified guests in corporate-sponsored ticket blocks.
    o   Plan for a secure cashbox to professionally house cash and check donations.

External

Invitations should include:

+ Event sponsor, if any: Senator so & so invites you to attend . . .
+ Day, date, and time: Friday, August 21, 2009, 6:00 p.m., drinks, 7:00–9:00 p.m., dinner
+ Place of dinner: physical address (for GPS mapping) and phone number(s)
+ Menu options: chicken, fish, beef, vegetarian; buffet; or hors d'oeuvres
+ Bar and drink options: open bar, cash bar, or complimentary wine, beer, soda
+ _____ number of guests attending event
+ RSVP by *date* and to *address, phone, e-mail* (listing all three is best)
+ Is donation amount set or graduated?
      o   Requested contribution: $150 + matching funds sponsor, if included—do not exceed contribution limits (see Fundraising Chair/Matching Funds)
      o   We are unable to attend but send a contribution of _____
+ Dress: formal, business, casual (indicate grade of casual)

Cuisine

Ensure the style of food, music, and ambiance is commensurate with the targeted attendees and reflects the campaign's theme.

Press coverage

Issue a press release (before and after the event) about the guest speaker and candidate.

If the RSVPs from the invitation mailing are returned in time for the fundraiser, there may not be a need for a costly newspaper advertisement. Sometimes publications will list events at no cost if it is considered a community service. A follow-up phone tree is vital in securing early ticket sales. Website inclusion and an e-mail solicitation for the event is a must.

Overhead: ticket price determination

+ Restaurant and bar cost, plus waitstaff tips
+ Design and printing of invitations
+ Postage for invitations and envelopes for RSVPs
+ Table arrangements, such as flowers
+ Party favors
+ Entertainment (orchestra, band, singer, guitar soloist, pianist, DJ, etc.)
+ Small gifts for volunteers (a drink ticket or complimentary dinner)
+ Postevent thank-you notes with volunteer card sent to all attendees
      o   Postage and printing for thank-you notes

Dinner Strategy

A great deal of thought and care goes into the planning and execution of a dinner or buffet designed to raise funds for a political candidate. Volunteers must be solicited to ensure that the event goes smoothly, and invitations must be printed in a timely manner, mailed, and tracked. A venue and time must be selected during the open-forum session at a weekly meeting.

The timing for the event cannot conflict with other social functions in or near the election district. Consult with the scheduler and look on the event calendar to avoid any possible cross-planning of events. Determine the cuisine and the price of the tickets.

Sit-down dinners and buffets are very pricey. Overhead calculations will determine the minimum number of donating attendees the campaign needs to break even. For such a dinner to be successful, star power will be required in the form of a prominent name as guest speaker. Local country clubs or yacht clubs may offer a quality ambiance at a reasonable price, especially during the off-season.

The financial affluence associated with the projected guest list will determine what the market can bear regarding the ticketing price. Be careful not to list a donation that is over the legal limit. In certain states, there is a cash limit or donation limit that requires the donor to be listed individually in the campaign's financial disclosures.

> *Tip:* For instance, if the legal limit for a ticket donation is $100 in the state where the fundraiser is located, a ticket price of $95 may allow the treasurer to list all ticket sales under an aggregate, "unitemized" amount instead of individually listing each donor. Some states also have limits on cash donations, which will influence walk-in cash ticket sales.

A sliding scale may be utilized for the ticketing structure. For example, if the gross overhead with one hundred attendees is $85 (i.e., $8,500), set the minimum ticket price at $100 per donor, with $150 silver, $250 gold, $500 platinum, $2,500 maximum, or (_____ other). On the other hand, a lower flat fee, say $150–$250, may also be used. Explore the possibility of a matching funds request if donations (tickets) are a fixed amount (see Fundraising Chair/Matching funds).

Besides the publicity associated with having a celebrity guest speaker, it is worth attracting a certain tier of donors as well. This group should receive mementos of their evening, such as a photograph taken with the featured guest speaker or a high-level politician. It is always good to have an event sponsor prominently listed at the top of the invitation, such as a US representative or senator, state senator, or mayor.

To be certain that "desirable" names are in attendance, issue free tickets to select individuals. Big names at prominent campaign functions nearly always receive complimentary tickets. Select members of the press corps may also be comped.

It is important to have some friends and family standing by with complimentary tickets just in case the minimum seating number at the restaurant is not reached. This tactic offers a practical solution to some potential last-minute inconveniences. A fundraiser should be well-attended and should never have a large number of unoccupied seats. In this context, a complimentary dinner could be offered to a volunteer or staff member as a reward for outstanding performance while also creating an atmosphere of optimal attendance at events.

Seating Coordination

There may also be an opportunity to call people who have paid for their tickets in advance and entice them to upgrade in return for a photo shoot with the guest speaker. Seating is largely determined by ticket price. High-end donors will be seated closer to the dais or guest speaker. Signs marked "reserved" should be placed on these tables to distinguish them for this reason. Have a volunteer or monitor ensure that the tables' signs are neither moved nor removed from their designated locations.

Seating is important. Personality conflicts or political vendettas may be irritated by haphazard seating arrangements, so please be careful. Conversely, some may increase their donations to be seated at certain tables.

Whether it is an upscale dinner gathering or a cocktail party, certain name and address lists may have to be consolidated to create a unique invitation list: country club, yacht club, doctors, lawyers (county or state bar association), business owners or chambers of commerce members, and all political appointees at county and state level. For a high-end fundraiser, it may also be advantageous to include the assessor's list as a way of selecting homeowners whose houses are valued over a specific price, say $750,000 or $1 million. Offer first selection to homeowners who are members of the candidate's political party, and to those determined to be the swing voting bloc.

After the invitation list has been compiled, sort alphabetically by last name and again by street address to remove all duplicate entries. A professional husband and wife may have different last names but still reside at the same address (see Computer Lists).

Depending upon the type of event and clientele, there will always be a few walk-ins who appear at the last minute and want to pay at the door. Be aware that upscale restaurants are extremely reluctant to allow for an unspecified number of guests at a sit-down dinner. They are usually not very flexible. Discuss this point in detail and arrive at an understanding with the restaurant owner or events manager during the planning stages of the event.

The candidate can usually intercede and ask for a few extras, if needed. The requirement for specific attendance numbers will be more flexible if there is a buffet-style dinner.

Always remember that this is a political event, and there will be a lot of competition among restaurants whose owners are in the candidate's political party. If the candidate is a Republican and the event is held at a prominent Democrat's restaurant, or vice versa, there had better be a really good reason for it. Many of the above items should be brainstorming topics at weekly executive committee meetings.

Another suggestion is to ask an organization that has already endorsed the candidate to sponsor a fundraising event or sign a fundraising letter that will be sent to their membership (see Endorsements). The cost of sponsoring a fundraising event or a letter of solicitation for a candidate may be considered an in-kind donation; check with the BOE. Work closely with the sponsoring organization. Always keep the campaign treasurer in the loop.

The *minimum time* for planning a fundraiser is usually two months. It takes one month advance notice for attendees and contributors, two weeks for the invitations to be designed, printed and mailed; two weeks for the invitees to RSVP. Traditionally, there is a one-in-ten return on invitations. Planning time is commensurate with the style of fundraiser. A small cocktail party may require only two weeks' advance notice.

Note: More time may be needed with high-profile attendees, as their schedules may be booked months in advance.

Phone Tree

When organizing the fundraising events, remember that people who are sent invitations should receive at least one follow-up phone call as a reminder (Woo 1980, 25). This personal phone contact will greatly enhance the attendance rate. A phone tree can be initiated by utilizing several proven methods. The most effective way is to enlist a dozen or more key volunteers to form a phone tree. The spouses of elected officials or business leaders are a great resource for phone-tree volunteers.

The key phone-tree participants will peruse the invitation list and select people they know to call, and ask those people to call others familiar to them. Calls should be made about a week to ten days after the invitations are mailed, and again if people have not responded. Phone trees often increase attendance rates far beyond the normal 10-percent ratio. This unpretentious style of social persuasion is practically an art form unto itself.

Picnics and Barbecues

Many organizations, such as the Kiwanis, Knights of Columbus, Rotary Club, American Legion, Elks, Veterans of Foreign Wars, and chambers of commerce, are not only experts at organizing picnics and barbecues, they usually have the facilities to rent.

Civic picnic areas often feature covered pavilion-style structures (pole buildings) in case of inclement weather. The host organization's liability insurance coverage may also be included in the lease. Insurance covering such areas should be articulated and documented in the contractual agreements for the space rental. Campaigns should also inquire about their liability in certain areas (see Sage Counsel).

Many civic organizations also furnish people to cook and do waitstaff chores, if requested. Tip those who help, and make sure to mention the candidate's name. Place them on a mailing list to remind them to vote for your candidate. Send them thank-you notes if deemed appropriate (Pelosi 2007, 143).

The candidate and campaign staff members must attend functions, give brief speeches, and greet attendees. Campaign volunteers often have a tendency to gravitate into specific areas. Send one or two campaign volunteers to each table to mingle with the voters. Extend an effort to make the voters feel included, not excluded; this is an integral part of the campaign.

   Tip: Outdoor events are great fundraisers. Feed people, and they will come.

SECTION 5

Meetings: The Glue That Binds the Team Together

BEFORE THE FIRST MEETING

▼

Building the Campaign Team

Candidates define their candidacy as an extension of "self"—who they are as people and on which path they wish to lead constituents. At this preliminary meeting, the candidate and their fledgling campaign teams embark on the journey from conceptualization to concrete action.

The candidate must recruit and assign the positions of campaign manager and treasurer before this meeting, as well as anyone who has expressed interest in the campaign's executive committee. Every meeting participant should read *Political Tool Kit* and all job assignments thoroughly. The main focus of this meeting will be to identify the people who will fill the key functional manager positions below and determine which positions may be consolidated. The positions below are executive committee members who will attend weekly meetings:

- Candidate
- Campaign Manager/Chair
  - Sage Counsel
  - Statistician/Researcher
- Financial Officer/Treasurer
- Communications Director
- Scheduling Officer
- Advertising Coordinator
- Volunteer Coordinator/recruiter
  - Vote Coordinator
- Fundraising Chair
- Office Manager
  - Secretary/Scribe
- Unit Managers: a large campaign has several assigned to various geopolitical districts

The candidate will discuss their vision, strategic direction, and focal issues for the upcoming election with those in attendance. This brainstorming session will be noted and continued at the first meeting with the new executive committee. The newly organized campaign team will identify the candidate's attributes, project short- and long-term goals, and determine the "invisible thread" of common interest that links the candidate to voters. Determine which subjects will be on the point of the spear of leadership by answering the following questions:

- What current issues are foremost with voters?
- Where has government failed in the election district? What is the remedy?
- How will the candidate address and cure specific problems?
- Where has each party in the election district succeeded and failed? Why?
- What four talking points can be used as central campaign issues?

The candidate's message to the voters must be

- Clear, concise, and substantive (in common, everyday language)
- Honest and related to current voter issues
- Focused on accentuating the differences between candidates and this election's uniqueness
- Targeted toward the most important populations in the election district
- Repeat the candidate's campaign message for future governance again, and again, and again (O'Day 2003, 22; see Foundation: Getting Started)

The upbeat positive atmosphere created in the first three campaign meetings will be the momentum generated throughout the entire campaign. The candidate will transfer their values to the team (Hendricks 1996, 19). Now (potential) political vision will move to (kinetic) action, and overall objectives will be communicated to functional managers with defined sequential tasks. The vision of a few becomes the involvement of the many (Melum and Collett 1995, 95).

It is now that the candidate's political vision comes alive.

FIRST MEETING: EXECUTIVE COMMITTEE

▼

The first organizational meeting establishes the team's internal character by setting the tone and motivational level and defining the strategic direction of the candidate's campaign initiative. This is the only executive committee meeting facilitated by the candidate. In all subsequent meetings, the campaign manager presides; preferably they will all take place at the same location and time (Grey 1999, 106).

The candidate calls the meeting to order and organizes the topics. There should be approximately eight to twelve people in attendance: they are the inner circle of the executive committee (McNamara 2008, 21). They are 100-percent loyal to the candidate, without question (Woo 1980, 23).

Note: Around 7:00 p.m. on a weeknight may be the best time for executive committee meetings. They should be held at the same location, time, and day of the week, unless otherwise agreed upon by members. If managers cannot attend a meeting, they must send a representative.

If a campaign HQ cannot be arranged, the CM should obtain a local attorney's office as a meeting site. If none is available, a local business such as an insurance office with a conference table and adequate phones should be used.

A restaurant or bar may not be a wise choice for a meeting place. Any public place will be subject to intrusion, and conversations may be overheard by those who are not campaign members (unless a private conference room is available). Meetings at a location where alcohol is served may open the campaign to allegations of impropriety or worse, especially if alcoholic beverages are served to team members who operate motor vehicles (Shaw 2000, 212).

The executive committee members are
+ Candidate

- Campaign Manager/Chair: campaign organization, emcee at events, candidate advocacy
- Financial Officer/Treasurer: all financial transactions and disclosure statements
- Secretary/Scribe: takes minutes (not a voting committee member)
- Vice Chair: supernumerary, assigned as needed

Some of the assignments below may remain open until the second or third meeting. A list of possible names to fill the vacancies must be discussed at the first meeting. Then, the candidate and campaign manager will both reach out to those selected to fill key positions in the campaign. If positions are to be consolidated, now is the time to consider it. The following positions can also be considered part of the executive committee, unless otherwise agreed upon.

- Communications Director: media, Internet, speeches, pictures of the candidate, letters to the editor, media inquiries and interviews, phone banks, computers, lists, speeches, and debates
- Volunteer Coordinator/Recruiter: petitions and door-to-door canvassing
  o   Vote Coordinator: registration, absentee ballots
- Advertising Coordinator: TV, radio, print advertising, palm cards, lawn signs, billboards, photography, graphic designer, and campaign mailings.
- Fundraising Chair: plans events and dinners—raises funds through various enterprises
- Scheduling Officer: calendar of events, coffees, meet and greets, picnics and events
- Sage Counsel: attorney for legal advice (petition and campaign legal issues)
- Statistician/Researcher: collects election data, demographics, and voter histories
- Office Manager: oversees campaign headquarters

The candidate should give those in attendance a brief speech concerning the tasks to be accomplished as well as their vision for reaching a successful resolution on Election Day. The speech should touch on their strong points and what they want to do for the electorate. The core inner circle of the campaign is comprised of the most talented and loyal people obtainable. The candidate must stress the need to run a positive campaign with a shared team vision that is vital to an Election-Day victory. The candidate then steps aside and says:

> Soon, John Doe, the campaign manager, will take charge of this and all subsequent meetings. I realize many of us know each other, but there are aspects of our lives that must be brought to bear during this campaign. I have chosen you for your expertise and loyalty. You are the best of the best. I would like people to introduce themselves, detail their life experiences, and explain how those experiences will benefit the campaign. Please include membership in any community organization, vocation, hobbies, education, or relevant experience during your two- or three-minute biographies. Please start from my right and continue counter-clockwise.

Note: Only activate the round-robin style of introduction when most of the executive committee's managerial positions are filled and the people are in attendance.

This method of introduction is utilized for several reasons. Even though many on the team may have known each other for years, it will be surprising how much each team member brings to the table. A brief uninterrupted personal introduction will help to establish an individual social bond between team members—one of respect, honor, and trust. The secretary should enter key attributes and strengths from each person's biography into the minutes of the meeting.

Note: The CM's duty will be to guide managers and help to build a winning campaign through the strengths of others.

At the end of each meeting, all committee members should walk away energized, with a clear vision of what is expected of them as individuals and how vital their mission is to the election (Andreas and Faulkner 1996, 98). After the third meeting, limiting meetings to one hour will enhance productivity, attendance, and participation.

Note: Most of the people on the campaign team will be volunteers. The campaign manager and candidate must always remind them of how important their efforts are to the election. Value them.

A biographical information questionnaire should be distributed to and filled out by every team member. It must include name; e-mail address; cell, home, and work telephone numbers; a list of all organizational memberships; current and past offices held; and hobbies. The statistician will enter this data onto a spreadsheet, and distribute it by e-mail that week to every team member. Only name, address, e-mail, and phone numbers should be distributed, not their organizational affiliations or other personal data. It is also important to evaluate questionnaires to obtain information such as rosters from organizations where staff and managers are members.

Statistical files, texts, and messages should be sent in a readable format common to all attendees. However, software uniformity and e-mail communication is vital for the executive committee and every volunteer. The weekly EC meeting agenda must be sent to all concerned at least one or two days before every meeting.

If the candidate is seeking a state or national office—i.e., if geographical distances are large—the CM may wish to introduce a phone communications network for meetings. A communications technology such as SKYPE may be explored for campaign use. SKYPE is currently a free download and has a real-time webcam and multiple participant conferencing capabilities.

SECOND MEETING: CAMPAIGN MANAGER

▼

The second campaign meeting is when the organizational power is turned over to the campaign manager. This not only frees the candidate from daily housekeeping and organizational chores but also disassociates him or her from day-to-day campaign drudgery and minor internal disputes.

However, the candidate is nearly always in attendance at weekly executive committee meetings. The one exception is if the meeting conflicts with an external fundraiser or other event the candidate must attend.

Note: Sometimes campaign managers want to be in complete control of the campaign, often treating the candidate as an automaton who only visits meetings and does what they are instructed to do. However, no matter how much control the CM is allowed by the candidate, there should be no doubt in anyone's mind that the candidate is the initiator of the global campaign vision. The CM may articulate objectives and goals, but the candidate must always be aware of policy and overall campaign direction. The only way for candidates to effectively accomplish this goal is to attend weekly executive committee meetings.

Campaign meetings will keep the managers informed as to the campaign's progress. In turn, the managers will keep the volunteers and staff informed. Everyone must be aware that the candidate is working hard. The campaign workers will slow to a crawl if there is the slightest implication that the candidate is not totally on board and committed to their own election. The candidate must always work the hardest.

Both the candidate and the campaign manager must know who is circulating nominating petitions and coordinate times to walk with them door-to-door in the candidate's election districts. Geographical areas of high-canvassing density often have a larger voter turnout.

The CM has the option of introducing one-shot mentoring, visiting experts, or consultants for mini-training seminars and updates in specialty areas such as nominating petition canvassing, election laws, palm card and lawn sign distribution, fundraising, phone banks, and other topics as needed.

Some items to be addressed:

+ Establish training program for nominating petition circulators via the sage counsel.
+ Identify training needs with specific numbers of volunteers and functional managers.
+ Have each functional manager submit a projected budget to the CM.
+ Decide on the candidate's palm card and lawn sign design; choose vendors.
+ Create a voter registration and absentee-ballot program.
+ Evaluate the candidate's photo layout; choose the best pictures for palm cards and advertising (Faucheux 2002, 171).
+ Identify major issues the candidate must address through talking points.
+ Inform everyone which bank the campaign uses to do business, the PO box number, and mailing address. This will be the treasurer's first report.
+ Inquire what the treasurer's maximum expenditure is without authorization. Usually this amount is $50-$100 per transaction (consult BOE and sage counsel on election laws).
+ Research available office space for a campaign headquarters.
+ Determine a template design for thank-you notes and campaign letterhead.
+ E-mail an organizational roster to each executive committee member.

Note: Introduce the type of calendar to be used by the campaign to schedule events (see Scheduling Officer).

Refer to the Foundation: Getting Started section and to each functional manager's job description for additional topics regarding meetings. Be proactive.

WEEKLY EXECUTIVE COMMITTEE MEETING

▼

Once the campaign team members are on-board and assigned duties by the CM, it is important to establish a timeline to merge training, tasks, and team goals. The only two times everyone on the campaign team will be deployed are during the door-to-door canvassing with the nominating petition cycle and the GOTV phase in the last days of the campaign. Most other campaign tasks are sequential.

The first three campaign meetings (before the first, first, and second) are "special" meetings. The third weekly executive committee meeting will establish a format for how subsequent meetings are to be conducted and all quorum-based meetings recorded by the secretary/scribe. See the following example:

Executive committee meeting
Date: **Time:**   **Location:**

Attendees: The secretary will not take a roll call, but will note who is in attendance. Lagging attendance may be an indicator of deeper problems within the campaign or with an individual; both types must be addressed by the CM.

Call to order.

Secretary/Scribe's report: Minutes of last meeting.

Treasurer's report, if desired.

Introduce specialists or guest: Invited experts in a particular field.

Meeting agenda:
Old business: items still pending (bullet-point important issues).

New business:
+ Scheduling officer presents calendar of events.
+ Discuss any barriers to success or anticipated problems.
+ Discuss training.
+ Assign weekly tasks.

Report from functional managers: plans for fundraisers, volunteer recruitment, absentee-ballot and voter-registration drives, etc.

Visiting expert's report on the campaign's effort in specific areas, such as nominating petitions, legal campaign issues, training, door-to-door canvassing, etc.

Unfinished business to be addressed.

Closure, on an upbeat positive note.

Note: The agenda should be sent to all attendees two to three days prior to the meeting.

ne plus ultra

S E C T I O N 6

Appendices A–K

☞ A: Volunteer Postcard and Volunteer Lists
☞ B: Master Spreadsheet, Voters
☞ C: Master Spreadsheet, Volunteers
☞ D: Candidacy Announcement
☞ E: Outline for Palm Card
☞ F: Sample Palm Card
☞ G: Budget Table
☞ H: State Board of Election Addresses and Felony Voter Lists
☞ I: Demographic Sampler from 2007
☞ J: Targeted Mailing on Water Quality
☞ K: Sample Testimonial/Letter of Support

APPENDIX A:
VOLUNTEER POSTCARD AND VOLUNTEER LISTS

▼

Name _____

Address _____

City/Zip_____

Phone _____ E-mail _____

Volunteer for (sign name):_____

- ☐ Phone bank
- ☐ Lawn sign
- ☐ Fundraiser
- ☐ Any requirement

- ☐ Door-to-door
- ☐ Petitions
- ☐ Host a party
- ☐ Lend name to publication

- ☐ Poll watcher
- ☐ Driver
- ☐
- ☐ Send a letter to the editor

Name _____

Address _____

City/Zip_____

Phone _____ E-mail _____

Volunteer for (sign name):_____

- ☐ Phone bank
- ☐ Lawn sign
- ☐ Fundraiser
- ☐ Any requirement

- ☐ Door-to-door
- ☐ Petitions
- ☐ Host a party
- ☐ Lend name to publication

- ☐ Poll watcher
- ☐ Driver
- ☐
- ☐ Send a letter to the editor

Name _____

Address _____

City/Zip_____

Phone _____ E-mail _____

Volunteer for (sign name):_____

- ☐ Phone bank
- ☐ Lawn sign
- ☐ Fundraiser
- ☐ Any requirement

- ☐ Door-to-door
- ☐ Petitions
- ☐ Host a party
- ☐ Lend name to publication

- ☐ Poll watcher
- ☐ Driver
- ☐ Send a letter to the editor

APPENDIX B:
MASTER SPREADSHEET, VOTERS

▼

voter category master list										Party	v freq	DTD	Voluntr		
Name (last)	Name (first)	street #	Street name	city	state	zip code	phone	E-mail							
Doe	John	291	Know Way	Whoville	NY	55555	555-555-4444	DoeXXX@gmails.com	2	R	5	4			
Doe	Jane	200	Staya Way	Whoville	NY	55555	555-555-1234	DoeXYZ@gmails.com	4	D	6	0	Y		
Roosevelt	Teddy	1600	Pennsylvania	Wash	DC	21001	555-555-1255	teddy000@gmails.com	6	B	10	3	N		
										C					
										G					
			APPENDIX B							L					
										I					
										W					
										S					
										O					

APPENDIX C:
MASTER SPREADSHEET, VOLUNTEERS

▼

Volunteer Master List

Name (Last)	Name (First)	St. #	Street Name	City	State	Zip Code	Phone	E-mail	Phone B	DTD	Poll W	Lawn S	Petition	Driver	Event F	Host P	Name Pub.
			APPENDIX C														

APPENDIX D:
CANDIDACY ANNOUNCEMENT

▼

February 14, 2004
Committee to Elect John Doe as Hot Dog Ville Supervisor, Ward 4
[*Place political party endorsements here*]

Press Release

RE: John Doe to Run for Hot Dog Ville Board of Supervisors

The Committee to Elect John Doe is pleased to announce that John has decided to seek the office of Hot Dog Ville Supervisor representing Ward 4.

Mr. Doe is a lifelong resident of the fourth ward and has roots dating back to the 1980s, when his family started to work at the Hot Dog Ville Basket Weaving Company. He is a graduate of Hot Dog Ville High School and earned a bachelor of science degree in skylarking and a master's degree with a focus on animal husbandry from New Hot Dog State University. Mr. Doe is an army veteran from the Banana Wars and is retired from the US Goldbrick Company.

Mr. Doe's political experience includes currently serving on the Hot Dog Ville County Republican Committee, having served a four-year term as secretary of the Hot Dog Ville Democratic Committee. He was the Frankfurter County Chairman for Senator Bertha Butt's original New York State Assembly campaign in 2005 and was the treasurer for Frankfurter County District Attorney Kitty Kat's campaign in 2003.

Commenting on his decision to run, Mr. Doe said, "Over the many years I have lived in Hot Dog Ville, specifically the fourth ward, the complexion of our city has changed dramatically from what I knew and loved as a child. I've watched surrounding communities, like Burger Ville, New Relish, and Ole Vadalia, experience positive and exciting growth while Hot Dog Ville has struggled. Our community once had many things to offer, including safe neighborhoods, great access to health care, superior cultural events, and high-performing schools. Through creative planning, sound decision making, and prudent negotiating with our neighbors, I am convinced Hot Dog Ville can regain the prominence we once enjoyed. I am excited about the possibility of further serving the community and optimistic about our future."

John and his wife, Jane Mustard-Doe, have twelve children between the ages of 14 and 20 and live on Bunn Street. Jane has worked for the local What Ville School District for sixteen years and is an elementary school psychologist.

Mr. Doe will be releasing more details on his positions regarding the major issues facing Hot Dog Ville as the campaign proceeds. He can be reached at (555) 555-5555.

From: The Committee to Elect John Doe as Hot Dog Ville Supervisor.

APPENDIX E:
OUTLINE FOR PALM CARD

▼

Palm Card Criteria
(handbill, door hanger)

Front of card:
+ picture of the candidate (full front, shoulders to top of head) on right or left side of card
+ candidate's slogan under the picture (leadership by example, experience counts, etc.)
+ last name of candidate on top in large letters
+ first name of candidate on side in smaller letters
+ name of elected office being sought
+ bullet (three to four words each) with circle or star, etc.
+ talking points (government efficiency, reduce taxes, greater services, etc.), ideology (party or personal), outstanding attributes (party committee member for fifteen years, relates well to current elected officials, raised ten children, master's degree, etc.)—eye-catching but not busy, one to four words each
+ campaign's website address (www.JohnDoeforMayor.com)
+ attributes: election district residency (if long-term), education, experience, military service, employment (e.g., VP, First National Bank)

Reverse of card:
+ candidate's picture (optional) with family: spouse and children; mother, father, siblings, etc.
+ last name of candidate in large letters at top
+ first name of candidate in smaller letters, usually on the side
+ party endorsements (Republican, Democrat, Liberal, Conservative, Independence, etc.)
+ the election district in which the candidate is running

- bullets with four to eight items, in one to four words each: greatest concerns and challenges facing residents that the candidate will address
- Election Day date, e.g., Tuesday, November 6
- list, in larger letters, one of the greatest concerns expressed by residents that the candidate intends to address, such as a recent increase in gang violence

For emphasis, the palm card should have areas in italics, bulleted, boxed, and/or in bold lettering, e.g.:

END GANG VIOLENCE

The entire card must be able to be read by a voter within fifteen to thirty seconds. Some candidates may wish to consider a bilingual message for their palm cards.

APPENDIX F:
SAMPLE PALM CARD

▼

RON PARSONS

Family Values

★ **Endorsed Bull Moose Party Candidate** ★

HOME TOWN USA CITY MANAGER

Reduce Property Taxes

Election Day: **November 8th**

Appendix F

• Modernize City Charter
• Share Municipal Services
• Downtown Development
• Smaller Government
• Rebuild Infrastructure
• Re-energize Shared Vision

RON PARSONS

★ *Grass-roots Support*
★ *Cost Efficient Government*
★ *Maturity, Honor, Integrity*
★ *Full-time Responsibility*
★ *Communication with Elected Officials*

Lifelong City Resident ~ Master's Degree in Business
Combat wounded U.S. Marine
Retired Federal Employee ~ Political Experience

Leadership by Example

APPENDIX G:
BUDGET TABLE

▼

Category	Line Item	March	April	May	June	July	August	Sept.	Oct.	Nov.
Advertising										
	palm cards									
	lawn signs									
	bumper stickers									
	literature									
	mailings									
	newspaper									
	printing									
	television									
	radio									
	graphic designer									
	photographer									
Headquarters										
Transportation										
Total Expenses										
Total Income										
Balance										
Cash on Hand										

APPENDIX H:
STATE BOARD OF ELECTION ADDRESSES AND FELONY VOTER LISTS

▼

ALABAMA

Janice McDonald, Elections Director

Office of Secretary of State

PO Box 5616

Montgomery, AL 36103

(334) 242-7559 FAX (334) 242-2444

janice.mcdonald@sos.alabama.gov

http://www.sos.state.al.us/election/index.cfm

ALASKA

Gail Fenumiai, Director, Division of Elections

PO Box 110017

Juneau, AK 99811-0017

(907) 465-4611 FAX (907) 465-3203

gail.fenumiai@alaska.gov

http://www.elections.alaska.gov

AMERICAN SAMOA

Soliai T. Fuimaono, Chief Election Officer

P.O. Box 3970

Pago Pago AS 96799

011-684-633-2522 FAX 011-684-633-7116

Asgelect@samoatelco.com

http://www.americansamoaelectionoffice.org

ARIZONA
Amy Bjelland, Election Director
Arizona Secretary of State's Office
1700 W. Washington, 7th Floor
Phoenix, AZ 85007
(602) 542-6167 FAX (602) 542-6172
abjelland@azsos.gov
http://www.azsos.gov/

ARKANSAS
Bob Hammons, Interim Director of Elections
Office of the Arkansas Secretary of State
State Capitol, Room 062
Little Rock, AR 72201
(501) 683-3733 FAX (501) 683-3732
bobhammons@sos.arkansas.gov
http://www.sosweb.state.ar.us/elections.html
http://www.arkansas.gov/sbec

CALIFORNIA
Jana Lean, Chief of Elections
1500 11th St., Elections Division 5th Floor
Sacramento, CA 95814
janalean@sos.ca.gov
(916) 65-5144 FAX (916) 653-5634
http://www.ss.ca.gov/

COLORADO
Judd Choate, Director of Elections
Colorado Secretary of State's Office
1700 Broadway, Suite 270
Denver, CO 80290
(303) 894-2200 FAX (303) 869-4861
Judd.Choate@sos.state.co.us
http://www.sos.state.co.us/pubs/elections

CONNECTICUT
Peggy Reeves, Director of Elections
30 Trinity Street
Hartford, CT 06106

(860) 509-6123 FAX (860) 509-6127
peggy.reeves@ct.gov
http://www.sots.state.ct.us/ElectionsDivision/Electionindex.html

DELAWARE

Elaine Manlove, State Election Commissioner
111 S. West Street, Suite 10
Dover, DE 19904
(302) 739-4277 FAX (302) 739- 6794
elaine.manlove@state.de.us
http://www.state.de.us/election/

DISTRICT OF COLUMBIA

Cliff Tatum, Executive Director
Board of Elections & Ethics
441 Fourth St., NW, Suite 250N
Washington, DC 20001
(202) 727-1911 FAX (202) 347-2648
ctatum@dcboee.org
http://www.dcboee.org

FLORIDA

Maria Matthews, Director of Elections
Gary J. Holland, Esq., Division of Elections
Division of Elections, Dept. of State
R.A. Gray Building, Room 316
500 S. Bronough Street
Tallahassee, FL 32399-0250
(850) 245-6200 FAX (850) 245-6217
Maria.Matthews@DOS.MyFlorida.com
Gary.Holland@DOS.MyFlorida.com
http://election.dos.state.fl.us

GEORGIA

Linda Ford, Director of Elections
Georgia Secretary of State, Brian P. Kemp
2 Martin Luther King Jr. Drive SE
Suite 1104 West Tower
Atlanta, GA 30334
(404) 656-2871 FAX (404) 651-9531

gaelections@sos.ga.gov
Anh Le, Ass't Elections Director/ Deputy General Counsel
cale@sos.ga.gov
http://www.sos.state.ga.us/elections/

GUAM
Gerald A. Taitano
Election Commission
PO Box BG
Agana, GU 96910
(671) 477-9791 Fax: (671) 477-1895
httP://www.guamelection.org/

HAWAII
Scott Nago, Chief Election Officer
Office of Elections
802 Lehua Avenue
Pearl City, HI 96782
(808) 453-8683 FAX (808) 453-6006
elections@hawaii.gov
http://www.hawaii.gov/elections

IDAHO
Tim Hurst, Chief Deputy
Idaho Secretary of State
304 North 8th, Suite 149
P.O. Box 83720
Boise, Idaho 83720
phone: 208-334-2852 fax: 208-334-2282
thurst@sos.idaho.gov
http://www.sos.idaho.gov/elect/eleindex.htm

ILLINOIS
Rupert Borgsmiller, Executive Director
State Board of Elections
2329 C. MacArthur Boulevard
Springfield, IL 62704-4503
(217) 782-4141 FAX (217) 524-5574
rborgsmiller@elections.il.gov
Becky Glazier, Executive Assistant to the Director

State Board of Elections
1020 S. Spring St
Springfield, IL 62704
(217) 782-4141 FAX (217) 782-5959
bglazier@elections.il.gov
http://www.elections.il.gov

INDIANA
Brad King, Co-Director
Indiana Election Division
302 W. Washington, Rm E204
Indianapolis, IN 46204
(317) 232-3939 FAX (317) 233-6793
bking@iec.in.gov
Trent Deckard, Co-Director
Indiana Election Division
302 W. Washington, RM E204
Indianapolis, IN 46204
(317) 232-3939 FAX (317)233-6793
tdeckard@iec.in.gov

IOWA
Sarah Reisetter, Director of Elections
Lucas Building
321 E. 12th St.
Des Moines, Iowa 50319
(515)242-5071
sarah.reisetter@sos.state.ia.us
Website: www.sos.state.ia.us

KANSAS
Brad Bryant, Deputy Assistant for Elections
120 SW 10th Ave.
First Floor, Memorial Hall
Topeka, Kansas 66612-1594
(785) 296-4561 FAX (785) 291-3051
BradB@kssos.org
http://www.sos.ks.gov

KENTUCKY
Maryellen Allen, Executive Director
State Board of Elections
140 Walnut St.,
Frankfort, KY 40601
(502) 573-7100 FAX (502) 573-4369
maryellen.allen@ky.gov
www.elect.ky.gov

LOUISIANA
Angie Rogers, Commissioner of Elections
LA Secretary of State's Office
8549 United Plaza Blvd.
P.O. Box 94125
Baton Rouge, LA 70802-9125
(225) 922-0900 FAX (225) 922-0945
Angie.Rogers@sos.louisiana.gov
www.GeauxVote.com

MAINE
Julie L. Flynn, Deputy Secretary of State
101 State House Station
Augusta, ME 04333-0101
(207) 624-7734 FAX (207) 287-5428
Julie.Flynn@maine.gov

MARYLAND
Linda Lamone, Administrator of Elections
State Board of Elections
P.O. Box 6486
Annapolis, Maryland 21401-0486
(410) 269-2840 FAX (410) 974-2019
llamone@elections.state.md.us
http://www.elections.state.md.us/

MASSACHUSETTS
Michelle Tassinari, Director of Elections, Legal Counsel
Election Division
One Ashburton Place, Room 1705
Boston, MA 02108

(617) 727-2828 FAX (617) 742-3238
Michelle.Tassinari@sec.state.ma.us
http://www.state.ma.us/ele/eleidx.htm

MICHIGAN
Christopher M. Thomas, Director
Bureau of Elections
Richard H. Austin Building, 1st Floor
430 W. Allegan Street
Lansing, MI 48918
(517) 373-2540 FAX (517) 241-2784
ChristopherT@Michigan.gov
http://www.michigan.gov/sos/0,1606,7-127-1633---,00.html

MINNESOTA
Gary Poser, Director of Elections
174 State Office Building
100 Rev. Dr. Martin Luther King Jr. Blvd.
St. Paul, MN 55155
(651) 556-0612 FAX (651) 296-9073
Gary.poser@state.mn.us
http://www.sos.state.mn.us

MISSISSIPPI
W. Heath Hillman
Assistant Secretary of State for Elections
Office of Mississippi Secretary of State
401 Mississippi Street (39201)
PO Box 136
Jackson, MS 39205-0136
(601) 359-6360 FAX (601) 359-1499
heath.hilman@sos.ms.gov
http://www.sos.ms.gov

Kim Turner, Attorney
Elections Division
Mississippi Secretary of State's Office
401 Mississippi St.
Jackson, MS 39205

(601) 359-5137 FAX (601) 359-1499
Kim.Turner@sos.ms.gov
http://www.sos.ms.gov

MISSOURI
Kay Dinolfo, Director of Elections
Missouri Secretary of State's Office
PO Box 1767
Jefferson City, MO 65102
(573) 751-2301 FAX (573) 526-3242
kay.dinolfo@sos.mo.gov

Waylene Hiles
Interim Deputy Secretary of State for Elections
Secretary of State Robin Carnahan's Office
P. O. Box 1767
Jefferson City, MO 65102
573-751-1869
573-526-3242 (fax)
Waylene.hiles@sos.mo.gov

MONTANA
Lisa Kimmet, Deputy for Elections
PO Box 202801
Helena, MT 59620-2801
(406) 444-5376 FAX (406) 444-2023
lkimmet@mt.gov
http://sos.mt.gov

NEBRASKA
Neal Erickson, Deputy Secretary of State
State Capitol, Room 345
Lincoln, NE 68509
(402) 471-4127 FAX (402) 471-7834
Neal.Erickson@Nebraska.gov
www.sos.state.ne.us

NEVADA
Scott Gilles, Deputy Secretary of State
Secretary of State

101 North Carson St., Suite 3
Carson City, NV 89701
(775) 684-5793 FAX (775) 684-5718
http://sos.state.nv.us

NEW HAMPSHIRE
Anthony Stevens
Assistant Secretary of State
State House, Room 204
Concord, NH 03301-4989
(603) 271-8238 FAX (603) 271-7933
astevens@sos.state.nh.us
http://www.sos.nh.gov/electionsnew.htm

NEW JERSEY
Robert F. Giles, Director
NJ Division of Elections
225 West State Street, 3rd Floor
PO Box 304
Trenton, NJ 08625-0304
Tel: (609) 292-3760 Fax: (609) 777-1280
TTD/TYY: 1-800-292-0039
Robert.Giles@sos.state.nj.us
njelections@sos.state.nj.us
URL: http://www.njelections.org

NEW MEXICO
Bobbi Shearer, Director
Bureau of Elections
New Mexico Secretary of State's Office
325 Don Gaspar, Suite 300
Santa Fe, NM 87503
(505) 827-3643 FAX (505) 827-8081
Bobbi.Shearer@state.nm.us
www.sos.state.nm.us

NEW YORK
Todd Valentine, Co-Director
State Board of Elections
40 Steuben Street

Albany, NY 12207
(518) 474-8100 (518) 486-4068
tvalentine@elections.ny.gov
http://www.elections.ny.gov

Robert A. Brehm, Co-Director
State Board of Elections
40 Steuben Street
Albany, NY 12207
(518) 474-8100 (518) 486-4068
rbrehm@elections.ny.gov
http://www.elections.ny.gov

NORTH CAROLINA
Gary Bartlett, Executive Director
State Board of Elections
PO Box 27255
Raleigh, North Carolina 27611-7255
(919) 733-7173 FAX (919) 715-0135
gary.bartlett@ncsbe.gov
http://www.sboe.state.nc.us/

NORTH DAKOTA
Jim Silrum
Deputy Secretary of State
600 E Boulevard Ave Dept 108
Bismarck, ND 58505-0500
(701) 328-3660 FAX (701)-328-1690
jsilrum@nd.gov
http://www.nd.gov/sos/

OHIO
Matt Damschroder, Deputy Assistant SOS & Director of
Elections
180 E. Broad St., 15th Floor
Columbus, OH 43215
(614) 466-2585 FAX (614) 752-4360
mdamschroder@ohiosecretaryofstate.gov

OKLAHOMA

Paul Ziriax, Secretary
State Election Board
Room 6, State Capitol
Oklahoma City, OK 73105
(405) 522-6615 FAX (405) 521-6457
pziriax@elections.ok.gov
http://elections.ok.gov

OREGON

Stephen Trout, Director of Elections
Office of the Secretary of State
255 Capitol Street NE, Suite 501
Salem, OR 97310
(503) 986-1518 FAX (503) 373-7414
steve.trout@state.or.us
http://www.sos.state.or.us/elections/elechp.htm

PENNSYLVANIA

Jonathan Marks, Commissioner
Bureau of Commissions, Elections and Legislation
Pennsylvania Department of State
210 North Office Building | Harrisburg, PA 17120
Phone: 717.787.5280 Fax: 717.705.0721
jmarks@pa.gov
www.dos.state.pa.us

PUERTO RICO

Hon. Héctor J. Conty-Pérez
Puerto Rico State Election Commission
P.O. Box 195552
San Juan, PR 00919-5552
(787) 777-8675 FAX (787) 296-0173
hconty@cee.gobierno.pr
http://www.ceepur.org

RHODE ISLAND

Robert Kando, Executive Director
State Board of Elections
50 Branch Avenue

Providence, RI 02904
(401) 222-2345 FAX (401) 222-3135
http://www.elections.state.ri.us

SOUTH CAROLINA
Marci Andino, Executive Director
State Election Commission
Post Office Box 5987
Columbia, SC 29250
(803) 734-9060 FAX (803) 734-9366
marci@elections.sc.gov
http://www.scvotes.org

SOUTH DAKOTA
Brandon Johnson, Election Supervisor
Office of the South Dakota Secretary of State
500 East Capitol Avenue
Pierre, SD 57501
(605) 773-3537 FAX (605) 773-6580
Brandon.Johnson @state.sd.us
http://www.sdsos.gov

TENNESSEE
Mark Goins, Coordinator of Elections
Tennessee Secretary of State's Office
312 Rosa L. Parks Avenue
9th Floor - William R.Snodgrass - TN Tower
Nashville, TN 37243
(615) 741-7956 FAX (615) 741-1278
Mark.Goins@tn.gov
http://state.tn.us/sos/election/index.htm

TEXAS
Keith Ingram
Director of Elections
Post Office Box 12060
Austin, TX 78711-2060
(512) 463-5650 FAX (512) 475-2811
kingram@sos.state.tx.us
http://www.sos.state.tx.us/elections/index.shtml

UTAH
Mark Thomas, Office Administrator
Office of the Lieutenant Governor
Utah State Capitol Suite 220
P.O. Box 142325
Salt Lake City, UT 84114-2325
(801) 538-1041 FAX (801) 538-1133
mjthomas@utah.gov
http://lg.utah.gov

VERMONT
Kathy Scheele
Director of Elections and Campaign Finance
Office of Secretary of State
26 Terrace Street, Drawer 09
Montpelier, Vermont 05609-1101
(802) 828-2363 FAX (802) 828-5171
kscheele@sec.state.vt.us
http://www.sec.state.vt.us

VIRGIN ISLANDS
Supervisor of Elections
Election System of the Virgin Islands
Post Office Box 1499, Kingshill
St. Croix, VI 00851-1499
(340) 773-1021 FAX (340) 773-4523
abramsonjohn1@hotmail.com
electionsys@unitedstates.vi
http://www.vivote.gov

VIRGINIA
Donald Palmer
Secretary, State Board of Elections
Commonwealth of Virginia
Washington Building
1100 Bank Street, First Floor
Richmond, VA 23219
(804) 864-8903 FAX (804) 371-0194
Don.Palmer@sbe.virginia.gov
http://www.sbe.state.va.us

WASHINGTON STATE
Lori Augino, Director of Elections
Office of Secretary of State, Elections Division
Legislative Building, P.O. Box 40220
Olympia, WA 98504-0220
(360) 902-4156 FAX (360) 664-4619
lori.augino@sos.wa.gov
http://www.vote.wa.gov

WEST VIRGINIA
Layna Valentine Brown, Manager of Elections
1900 Kanawha Boulevard E.
State Capitol Room 157-K
Charleston, WV 25305-0770
(304) 558-6000 FAX (304) 558-0900
lbrown@wv.sos.com
http://www.wvsos.com

WISCONSIN
Kevin J. Kennedy, Director of General Counsel
Wisconsin Government Accountability Board
212 East Washington Ave., 3rd Floor
P.O. Box 7984
Madison, WI 53707-7984
(608) 261-8683 FAX (608) 267-0500
Kevin.Kennedy@wi.gov
http://gab.wi.gov

Michael Hass, Director of General Counsel
Wisconsin Government Accountability Board
212 East Washington Ave., 3rd Floor
P.O. Box 7984
Madison, WI 53707-7984
(608) 267-0715 FAX (608) 267-0500
Michael.Hass@wi.gov
http://gab.wi.gov

WYOMING
Peggy Nighswonger, Director of Elections
Wyoming Secretary of State's Office

200 W. 24th Street
Cheyenne, WY 82002-0020
(307) 777-3573 FAX (307) 777-7640
Peggy.Nighswonger@wyo.us
http://soswy.state.wy.us/Elections/Elections.aspx

http://www.nased.org/roster

Elections Department E-mail Addresses
for Election Laws Concerning Felony Conviction Voting

Alabama	Voter.cancellations@vote.alabama.gov
Alaska	elections@alaska.gov
American Samoa	Asgelect@samoatelco.com
Arizona	elections@azsos.gov
Arkansas	voterservices@sos.arkansas.gov
Colorado	State.electionsdivision@sos.state.co.us
Connecticut	LEAD@ct.gov
Delaware	COE_RESEARCH@state.de.us
Florida	bvrshelp@dos.state.fl.us
Georgia	gafelonlist@sos.ga.gov
Idaho	elections@sos.idaho.gov
Illinois	webmaster@elections.il.gov
Indiana	elections@iec.in.gov
Iowa	Sos@sos.state.ia.us
Kansas	election@kssos.org
Kentucky	Sbe.webmaster@ky.gov
Louisiana	elections@sos.lousiana.gov
Maine	Cec.elections@maine.gov
Maryland	info@elections.state.md.us
Massachusetts	elections@sec.state.ma.us
Michigan	disclosure@michigan.gov
Minnesota	Elections.dept@state.mn.us
Mississippi	Federal.convictions@sos.ms.gov
Missouri	elections@sos.mo.gov
Montana	soselections@mt.gov

Nevada	nvelect@sos.nv.gov
New Hampshire	NHVotes@sos.nh.gov
New Jersey	njelections@sos.state.nj.us
New York	info@elections.state.ny.us
North Carolina	Elections.sboe@ncsbe.gov
North Dakota	soselect@nd.gov
Ohio	elections@sos.state.oh.us
Oklahoma	info@elections.ok.gov
Oregon	elections.sos@state.or.us
Pennsylvania	voterreg@state.pa.us
Rhode Island	www.elections.ri.gov
South Carolina	elections@elections.sc.gov
South Dakota	elections@state.sd.us
Tennessee	Shelly.adams@tn.gov
Texas	elections@sos.state.tx.us
Utah	elections@utah.gov
Vermont	State law currently allows felons to vote
Virginia	verisoperation@sbe.virginia.gov
Washington State	VRSupport@sos.wa.gov
West Virginia	elections@wvsos.com
Wisconsin	gabhelpdesk@wi.gov
Wyoming	elections@state.wy.us

APPENDIX I:
DEMOGRAPHIC SAMPLER

▼

This is a demographics sample from Warren County, New York.

WARREN COUNTY INFORMATION (data is from 2007)

Discover Warren County (from Warren County EDC) http://www.edcwc.org/
The Glens Falls Metropolitan Statistical Area (MSA) covers both Warren and Washington Counties, New York. Demographics are as reported in the 2000 Census unless otherwise noted. The Farmers Insurance Group of Companies, in its annual study, named the Glens Falls MSA fifth in the nation as the most secure place to live among small metros. The criteria measured were crime, extreme weather, natural disaster, and employment statistics.
—Farmers Insurance Group website, 2007

Time Zone
+ Eastern Standard or Eastern Daylight Savings

Climate
+ Temperate:USDA Zones 3 & 4 Average Temperature: January 19.8 degrees F. Lows can reach -30 degrees F. July: 70.9 degrees F. Highs in the 90s are not uncommon Average Precipitation: Rain: 39.27 inches. Snow: 68.3 inches. Average first snow in November. Average last snow in March.

Geography
+ Elevation: Highest: 3,580 ft. (Gore Mtn.) above sea level. Lowest: 357 ft. above sea level. Adirondack Park: 6 million acres Terrain: South—Flat to rolling hills. North—Mountainous broken by lakes, ponds, rivers and streams Flora: 85% forested (21% hardwoods)

Land area
+ 869.3 sq. mi.

Water area
+ 62.4 sq. mi. The largest lakes are George, Schroon, Glen, Brant, and Trout. Primary rivers are the Hudson, Schroon, and Sacandaga.

County population
+ 2008 estimate: 66,400. Growth since 2000: 4.4% 2013 projected: 68,305

Races in Warren County
+ White Non-Hispanic: 96.8%
+ Hispanic: 1.0%
+ Two or more races: 0.9%
+ African American: 0.6%
+ American Indian: 0.6%
+ (Total can be greater than 100% because Hispanics could be counted in other races)
+ Number of foreign born residents: 1,541 (65% naturalized citizens)

Median age
+ 39.0 years
+ Males: 48.5%
+ Females: 51.5%

Elementary, secondary and private schools (list all)
+ Glens Falls Warren County public schools spend $10,229 per student. The average US expenditure is $6,058. There are about 16 students per teacher in Warren County (Sperling, 2008). The New York State estimated cost per pupil is $18,768. (NYS Commission on Property Tax Relief, 2009).

Colleges and universities that serve the political area (list all)

Education
+ Current college students: 2,944 People 25 years of age or older with a high school diploma or higher: 84.6% People 25 years of age or older with a bachelor's degree or higher: 23.2%

Households
+ Average household size: 2.41
+ Per capita household income (2007): $24,006

- Median household income (2007): $41,184

Median house sale price (2008, Albany Times Union):
- City of Glens Falls—$159,418
- Town of Queensbury—$255,719
- Village of Lake George—$593,177
- Warren County—$185,000

Median rent for a 2-bedroom apartment (2007): $737/month
Total Sales (2007): $1,976,685,000
2007 Statewide 56 County Ranking:
Taxes Per Capita: #3 Warren County $1,255

2007 Statewide 56 County Ranking: Social Services Per Capita
- #35 Warren County $449 Source: Office of the NYS Comptroller, excluding the New York Metropolitan area.

2007 Capital Region Ranking: Total Expenditure Per Capita
- #1 Warren County—$2,166. Information provided by the Public Policy Institute, the research affiliate of the Business Council of New York State, and the Empire Center for New York State Policy.

Industries providing employment:
- Education, health, and social services: 23.0%
- Retail trade: 13.3%
- Manufacturing: 11.9%
- Arts, entertainment, recreation, accommodation, and food services: 11.8%

Type of workers
- Private wage or salary: 74%
- Government: 17%
- Self-employed, not incorporated: 9%
- Unpaid family work: 0%

Employment
- Average weekly wage (June 2007): $645 (US DOL Bureau of Labor Statistics)
- Unemployment rate September 2009 (NYS DOL): 7.2%
- Mean travel time to work: 21.4 minutes

NYS DOL Analysis—September 2009:
- From September 2008 to September 2009, the number of private-sector jobs in the Albany-Schenectady-Troy area fell 10,500, or 3.0%, to 334,600. Job gains were limited to educational and health services (+400). Losses were greatest in natural resources, mining and construction (-2,600), business services (-1,900), trade, transportation and utilities (-1,700) and manufacturing (-1,300).

Transportation (address, phone numbers, and person to contact)
Air: list airports and airlines servicing them.
Rail: list railway services and train stations
Waterways: all access by water for business and pleasure
Bus: bus line companies servicing area with bus depot locations
Car/truck: major routes and access to area by state and federal highway system

Agriculture
- Average size of farms:
- Average value of agricultural products sold per farm:
- The value of nursery, greenhouse, floriculture, and sod as a percentage of the total market value of agricultural products sold:
- The value of livestock, poultry, and their products as a percentage of the total market value of agricultural products sold:

For additional information, please contact the EDC Warren County at (518) 761-6007 or at www.edcwc.org.

Top Employers in the Adirondack Region (chamber website)

1) GLENS FALLS HOSPITAL
   David Kruczlnicki, President & CEO
   100 Park Street Glens Falls, NY 12801
   Tele: (518) 926-1000
   No. of Employees: 2,810
   Product/Service: Health Care

2) C. R. BARD, INC.
   Jason Gaede, Plant Manager
   289 Bay Road Queensbury, NY 12804
   Tele: (518) 793-2531
   No. of Employees: 941
   Product/Service: Medical Devices

3) FINCH PAPER LLC
Joseph Raccuia, President
One Glen Street Glens Falls, NY 12801
Tele: (518) 793-2541
No. of Employees: 880
Product/Service: Pulp & Paper
There are 26 corporations listed (as in 1–3 above), sorted by number of employees.

Important Resources for Adirondack Businesses (from the chamber website)

Municipalities
+ City of Glens Falls, Mayor John "Jack" Diamond, mayor@cityofglensfalls.com, www.cityofglensfalls.com
+ Town of Queensbury, Supervisor Daniel Stec, danstec@queensbury.net, www.queensbury.net
+ Town of Fort Edward, Supervisor Mitchell Suprenant Jr., ftedsupervisor@roadrunner.com, www.fortedwardnewyork.net
+ Village of Hudson Falls, Ellen Brayman, clerk/treasurer, hfvillage@albany.twcbc.com
+ Lake George, www.lakegeorgechamber.org
+ North Creek/Gore Mountain Region, www.goremtnregion.org
+ The Cambridge Valley, www.cambridgenychamber.com
+ The Towns and Villages of the Battenkill Valley, www.visitbattenkillvalley.com
+ Granville Area, www.granvillechamber.com
+ Greater Greenwich, www.greenwichchamber.org
+ Salem, www.salemnychamber.com
+ South Glens Falls/Town of Moreau, www.sgfchamber.com
+ Ticonderoga, www.ticonderogany.com

County Governments
+ Warren County, www.warrencounty.org
+ Washington County, www.washingtoncounty.org
+ Saratoga County, www.saratoga.org
+ Essex County, www.essex.ny.us
+ Hamilton County, www.hamiltoncounty.com

State of New York
+ Governor David Paterson, www.161.11.121.121/govmail
+ Attorney General Andrew Cuomo, Project Sunlight Website, www.sunlightny.com
+ State Comptroller Thomas DiNapoli, Open Book website, www.openbooknewyork.com

- State of New York, www.state.ny.us
- Majority Leader Dean G. Skelos, skelos@senate.state.ny.us
- NYS Senator Elizabeth O'C. Little, 45th Senate District, www.senatorlittle.com/45/Contact.aspx
- NYS Senator High T. Farley, 44th Senate District, farley@senate.state.ny.us
- NYS Senator Roy McDonald, 43rd Senate District, www.nyssenate43.com/43/Contact.aspx
- NYS Assembly Speaker Sheldon Silver, speaker@assembly.state.ny.us
- Assemblywoman Teresa R. Sayward, 113th Assembly District, saywart@assembly.state.ny.us
- Assemblyman Tony Jordan, 112th Assembly District, jordanJ@assembly.state.ny.us
- New York State Assembly, www.assembly.state.ny.us
- New York State Dept. of Labor, www.labor.state.ny.us
- New York State Office of Parks, Recreation and Historic Preservation, www.nysparks.state.ny.us
- NY Loves Small Business, www.nylovessmallbiz.com
- I Love New York, http://www.iloveny.com/Home.aspx
- NYS Canal Corp., www.canals.state.ny.us
- NYS Department of Environmental Conservation, www.dec.ny.gov
- Adirondack Park Agency, www.apa.state.ny.us
- Lake Champlain-Lake George Regional Planning Board, www.lclgrpb.org

Federal Government
- President Barack Obama, www.whitehouse.gov/CONTACT/
- Vice President Joe Biden, vice.president@whitehouse.gov
- US Senator Charles E. Schumer, www.schumer.senate.gov/new_website/contact.cfm
- US Senator Kirsten E. Gillibrand, www.gillibrand.senate.gov.contact/
- Congressman Chris Gibson, Chris.Gibson@mail.house.gov
- US House of Representatives, http://www.house.gov/
- US Senate, http://senate.gov/

Business Information
- EDC Warren County, www.warrencounty.org
- Washington County Local Development Corp., www.wcldc.org
- Counties of Warren & Washington IDA, www.warren-washingtonida.com
- Saratoga County Economic Development Corp., www.saratogaedc.com
- Saratoga Convention & Tourism Bureau, www.discoversaratoga.org
- Essex County Industrial Development Agency, www.essexcountyida.com
- Hamilton County Department of Planning, Tourism & Community Development, www.hamiltoncounty.com

- Empire State Development Corp., www.empire.state.ny.us
- NYS Small Business, www.nylovessmallbiz.com
- Business Council of New York State, www.bcnys.org
- US Small Business Administration, www.sba.gov or www.business.gov
- Chamber Alliance of New York State, www.canys.org
- New York's Tech Valley Website, http://www.techvalley.org/
- Service Core of Retired Executives (SCORE), www.scorealbany.org

APPENDIX J:
TARGETED MAILING ON
WATER QUALITY

▼

June 9, 2020

Mr. & Mrs. Waterfront Property Owner
Assembly Point Road
Clovin Bay, NY 55500

Dear Property Owner:

On Election Day, Tuesday, November 6, I will ask the voters of northern New York's 99th Congressional District for the honor and privilege of representing them in the House of Representatives.

Having lived in the Adirondack Region my entire life, I share your respect and admiration for the resources from which most of us derive our incomes, hobbies, and recreation. Our lakeside municipalities survive by acquiring grants and low-interest loans for drinking water and wastewater treatment facilities as well as storm-water management.

The many lakes in northern New York are crucial to the business and tourist economy for our entire region. As a property owner, you hold a vested interest in the continued health and vitality of the lakes. Lake George, Lake Champlain, the St. Lawrence River, along with numerous other small ponds and streams, are drinking-water sources for many year-round residents, business owners, and visitors. The recreational opportunities the watershed provides play a significant role in our region's tourism industry as well as our own quality of life.

Invasive species, such as Eurasian milfoil and zebra mussels, threaten recreation opportunities, property values, and the health and safety of lake enthusiasts. Preventing these and other nuisance species from invading and spreading in our water requires our constant vigilance.

Simply put, water, our water, is a valuable resource that deserves continued attention for future generations to enjoy as we do. It is imperative that we advocate for new community-based programs to express our financial need to the federal government and the state of New York for the preservation of water quality.

The 99th Congressional District is vast, and I am asking for your assistance in my efforts to reach all voters to convey my message. If you have already contributed to my campaign, I truly thank you. Should you be in a position to assist financially or wish to volunteer, I'd appreciate the help.

Sincerely,

Johnny Doe
www.friendsofjohnnydoe.com

APPENDIX K:
SAMPLE TESTIMONIAL/LETTER OF SUPPORT

▼

287

BIBLIOGRAPHY

▼

Andreas, Steve, and Charles Faulkner. 1996. *NLP: The New Technology of Achievement.* New York: HarperCollins.

Bai, Matt. 2007. *The Argument: Billionaires, Bloggers, and the Battle to Remake Democratic Politics.* New York: Penguin Press.

Beaudry, Ann, and Bob Schaeffer. 1986. *Winning Local and State Elections.* New York: Free Press.

Block, Peter. 1996. *Stewardship.* San Francisco: Berrett-Koehler.

Campbell, James. 2000. *The American Campaign.* College Station, TX: Texas A&M University Press.

Creech, Bill. 1995. *The Five Pillars of TQM.* New York: Penguin Books USA.

Dalton, Philip D. 2006. *Swing Voting.* Cresskill, NJ: Hampton Press.

Downs, Anthony. 1957. *An Economic Theory of Democracy.* New York: Harper & Row Publishers.

Drew, Elizabeth. 1999. *The Corruption of American Politics.* Secaucus, NJ: Carol Publishing Group.

Elliott, Phillip, and Jim Kuhnhenn. 2012. "Campaigns Target Early-voting States." *Glens Falls Post Star,* September 5.

England, Robert. 1992. *So You Want to Run for Political Office.* Glens Falls, NY: Coneco Litho Graphics.

Faucheaux, Ronald A. 2003. *The Debate Book*. Arlington, VA: Campaigns and Elections Publishing Company LLC.

_____. 2002. *Running for Office*. Lanham, MD: M. Evans.

Faucheux, Ronald A., and Paul S. Herrnson. 2001. *The Good Fight*. Washington, DC: Campaigns and Elections.

Gingrich, Newt, and Dick Armey. 1994. *Contract with America*. New York: Times Books/ Random House.

Grey, Lawrence. 1999. *How to Win a Local Election*. New York: M. Evans and Company.

Green, Donald P., and Alan S. Gerber. 2004. *Get Out the Vote*. Washington, DC: Brookings Institution Press.

Grinder, John, and Richard Bandler. 1976. *The Structure of Magic*. Palo Alto, CA: Science and Behavior Books.

Habermas, Jurgen. 1989. *The Structural Transformation of the Public Sphere*. Cambridge, MA: MIT Press.

Harding, James. 2008. *Alpha Dogs*. New York: Farrar, Straus and Giroux.

Hendricks, William Dr. 1996. *Coaching, Mentoring, and Managing*. Franklin Lakes, NJ: Career Press.

Hoffman, Jon T., and Beth L. Crumley. 2002. *USMC Complete History*. Quantico, VA: Hugh Lauter Levin Associates.

Hunt, Jim, and Bob Risch. 2011. *Warrior: Frank Sturgis*. New York, NY: Tom Doherty Associates, LLC.

Iyengar, Shanto. 1990. "Framing Responsibility for Political Issues: The Case of Poverty. Political Behavior." *Cognition and Political Action* 12, no. (March):19–40. www.jstor.org/stable/586283.

Jacobs, Lawrence R., and Robert Y. Shapiro. 1995. "Presidential Manipulation of Polls and Public Opinion: The Nixon Administration and the Pollsters." *Political Science Quarterly* 110 (Winter 1995–96 [http://epn.org/psnixo.html]). http://ejournalofpoliticalscience.org/psnixo.html.

Jamieson, Kathleen Hall. 2000. *Everything You Think You Know About Politics*. New York: Basic Books.

Jones, Patrick. 2002. *Running a Successful Library Card Campaign*. New York: Neal-Schuman Publishers, Inc.

Joslyn, Richard. 1984. *Mass Media and Elections*. New York: Random House.

Kessler, Ronald. 2009. *In the President's Secret Service*. New York: Crown Publishers.

Key, V. O. Jr. 1966. *The Responsible Electorate: Rationality in Presidential Voting*. Cambridge, MA: Harvard University Press.

Lazarsfeld, Paul F., Bernard Berelson, and Hazel Gaudet. 1968. *The People's Choice*. New York: Columbia University Press.

Marsh, S., J. W. Moran, S. Nakui, and G. Hofferr. 1991. *Quality Functional Deployment*. Mathuen, MA: GOAL/QPC.

McNamara, Michael. 2008. *The Political Campaign Desk Reference*. Denver, CO: Outskirts Press.

Melum, Mara Minerva, and Casey Collett. 1995. *Breakthrough Leadership*. Chicago: American Hospital Publishing.

Morris, Dick. 1999. *VOTE.com*. Los Angeles: Renaissance Books.

O'Day, J. Brian. 2003. *Political Campaign Planning Manual*. Moscow, Russia: National Democratic Institute for International Affairs (NDI).

O'Toole, Fintan. 2005. *White Savage*. New York: Farrar, Straus and Giroux.

Payne, Ruby. 2001. *A Framework for Understanding Poverty*. Highlands, TX: aha Process.

Payne, Ruby K., Phillip E. DeVol, and Terie Dreussi Smith. 2009. *Bridges Out of Poverty*. Highlands, TX: aha Process.

Payne, Ruby, and Don L. Krabill. 2002. *Hidden Rules of Class At Work*. Highlands, TX: aha Process.

Pelosi, Christine. 2007. *Campaign Boot Camp*. Sausalito, CA: PoliPointPress.

Rodriguez, Rosemary E., Donetta L. Davidson, and Gracia M. Hillman. 2008. U.S. Election Assistance Commission. *Alternative Voting Methods*. www.**eac**.gov/assets/1/workflow_staging/ Page/54.PDF.

Senge, Peter M. 1990. *The Fifth Discipline*. New York: Currency, Doubleday.

Senge, Peter M., Art Kleiner, Richard Ross, Charlotte Roberts, and Brian Smith. 1994. *The Fifth Discipline: Fieldbook*. New York: Currency, Doubleday.

Shadegg, Stephen C. 1964. *How to Win Elections*. New York: Taplinger.

Shaw, Catherine. 2000. *The Campaign Manager: Running and Winning Local Elections*. Boulder, CO: Westview Press.

Shea, Gordon F. 1997. *Mentoring*. Menlo Park, CA: Crisp Publications.

Simpson, Dick. 1972. *Winning Elections*. Chicago: Swallow Press.

Tague, Nancy R. 1995. *The Quality Toolbox*. Milwaukee, WI: ASQC Quality Press.

Thomas, Robert J. 1999. *How to Run for Local Office*. Westland, MI: R&T Enterprises.

Underwood, Paula. 1991. *Who Speaks for Wolf: A Native American Learning Story*. San Anselmo, CA: A Tribe of Two Press.

Wallenberg, Martin P. 1991. *The Rise of Candidate-Centered Politics*. Cambridge, MA: Harvard University Press.

Woo, Lilian C. 1980. *The Campaign Organizer's Manual*. Durham, NC: Carolina Academic Press.

INDEX